A Concise Companion to
English Renaissance Literature

Blackwell Concise Companions to Literature and Culture
General Editor: David Bradshaw, University of Oxford

This series offers accessible, innovative approaches to major areas of literary study. Each volume provides an indispensable companion for anyone wishing to gain an authoritative understanding of a given period or movement's intellectual character and contexts.

Published

Forthcoming

University of Hertfordshire

College Lane, Hatfield, Herts. AL10 9AB

Learning and Information Services

For renewal of Standard and One Week Loans,
please visit the web site **http://www.voyager.herts.ac.uk**

This item must be returned or the loan renewed by the due date.
The University reserves the right to recall items from loan at any time.
A fine will be charged for the late return of items.

A Concise Companion to
English Renaissance Literature

Edited by Donna B. Hamilton

Blackwell
Publishing

BLACKWELL PUBLISHING
350 Main Street, Malden, MA 02148-5020, USA
9600 Garsington Road, Oxford OX4 2DQ, UK
550 Swanston Street, Carlton, Victoria 3053, Australia

First published 2006 by Blackwell Publishing Ltd

1   2006

Library of Congress Cataloging-in-Publication Data

A concise companion to English Renaissance literature / edited by Donna B. Hamilton.
    p. cm.—(Blackwell concise companions to literature and culture)
    Includes bibliographical references and index.
    ISBN-13: 978-1-4051-1357-1 (hardcover : alk. paper)
    ISBN-10: 1-4051-1357-X (hardcover : alk. paper)
    ISBN-13: 978-1-4051-1358-8 (pbk. : alk. paper)
    ISBN-10: 1-4051-1358-8 (pbk. : alk. paper)
    1. English literature—Early modern, 1500–1700—History and criticism
—Handbooks, manuals, etc. 2. England—Civilization—16th century
—Handbooks, manuals, etc. 3. England—Civilization—17th century
—Handbooks, manuals, etc. 4. Renaissance—England—Handbooks, manuals, etc.
I. Hamilton, Donna B. II. Series.
PR411.C68 2006
820.9′003—dc22

2005032599

A catalogue record for this title is available from the British Library.

Set in 10/13pt Meridien
by SPI Publisher Services, Pondicherry, India
Printed and bound in Singapore
by Markono Print Media Pte Ltd

The publisher's policy is to use permanent paper from mills that operate a sustainable forestry policy, and which has been manufactured from pulp processed using acid-free and elementary chlorine-free practices. Furthermore, the publisher ensures that the text paper and cover board used have met acceptable environmental accreditation standards.

For further information on
Blackwell Publishing, visit our website:
www.blackwellpublishing.com

Contents

Contents

Notes on Contributors

Ralph Bauer is associate professor of English at the University of Maryland. His research interest is the colonial literatures of the Americas. His articles have appeared in collections and journals such as *American Literature, Early American Literature,* and *Colonial Latin American Review.* His books include *The Cultural Geography of Colonial American Literatures: Empire, Travel, Modernity* (2003) and *An Inca Account of the Conquest of Peru* (2005), as well as edited collections of essays and literary anthologies.

S. P. Cerasano is the Edgar W. B. Fairchild professor of literature at Colgate University and the editor of *Medieval and Renaissance Drama in England.* The author of books and essays on theatre history, she has most recently written about literary and theatrical commercialism in *A Routledge Literary Sourcebook on William Shakespeare's "Merchant of Venice"* (2004). She is currently working on a book about Philip Henslowe, the owner of the Rose playhouse.

Richard Dutton is humanities distinguished professor of English at the Ohio State University, joining the faculty there in 2003. Prior to that, he taught for almost 30 years at Lancaster University in England. His books include *Mastering the Revels: The Regulation and Censorship of English Renaissance Drama* (1991), *Licensing, Censorship and Authorship in Early Modern England: Buggeswords* (2000), *Ben Jonson: To the First Folio* (1983), and *Ben Jonson: Authority: Criticism* (1996). He has edited *"Women Beware Women" and Other Plays by Thomas Middleton* (1999) and Jonson's *Epicene* (2003) for the Revels Plays, of which he is a general editor; he is currently editing Volpone and working on *A Handbook on Early Modern English Theatre.*

Andrew Hadfield is professor of English at the University of Sussex. His most recent books include *Shakespeare and Renaissance Politics* (2003) and *Shakespeare and Republicanism* (2005). He has also co-edited, with Raymond Gillespie, *The Oxford History of the Irish Book. Vol. III: The Irish Book in English 1550–1800* (2005). He is a fellow of the English Association.

Donna B. Hamilton is professor of English at the University of Maryland. In addition to essays, her publications include *Virgil and The Tempest: The Politics of Imitation* (1990), *Shakespeare and the Politics of Protestant England* (1992), and *Anthony Munday and the Catholics, 1560–1633* (2005).

Paul E. J. Hammer teaches in the School of History at the University of St Andrews and is the author of *The Polarisation of Elizabethan Politics: The Political Career of Robert Devereux, 2nd Earl of Essex, 1585–1597* (1999), *Elizabeth's Wars: War, Government and Society in Tudor England, 1544–1604* (2003), and numerous other publications. He is currently completing a book on the earl of Essex and the late Elizabethan crisis of 1598–1603.

Carole Levin is Willa Cather professor of history at the University of Nebraska. Her books include *The Heart and Stomach of a King: Elizabeth I and the Politics of Sex and Power* (1994) and *The Reign of Elizabeth I* (2002), as well as a number of co-edited collections, most recently *High and Mighty Queens of Early Modern England* (2003) and *Elizabeth I: Always Her Own Free Woman* (2003). She was the historical consultant on the Newberry Library exhibit "Elizabeth I: Ruler and Legend."

Peter Mack is professor of English and comparative literature at the University of Warwick. His books include *Renaissance Argument: Valla and Agricola in the Traditions of Rhetoric and Dialectic* (1993), *Renaissance Rhetoric* (1994), and *Elizabethan Rhetoric: Theory and Practice* (2002). He was editor of *Rhetorica* 1998–2002. He is currently working on a book comparing Shakespeare's and Montaigne's use of their rhetorical and ethical inheritance.

Cynthia Marshall was professor of English at Rhodes College. In addition to articles, her publications include *Last Things and Last Plays: Shakespearean Eschatology* (1991), *The Shattering of the Self: Violence, Subjectivity and Early Modern Texts* (2002), and as editor *Shakespeare in Production: As You Like It* (2004).

Lena Cowen Orlin is professor of English at the University of Maryland Baltimore County and executive director of the Shakespeare Association of America. She is the author of *Private Matters and Public Culture in Post-Reformation England* (1994), editor of *Material London, ca. 1600* (2000), and co-editor (with Stanley Wells) of *Shakespeare: An Oxford Guide* (2003). Her current book projects are "Locating Privacy in Tudor England" and "The Textual Life of Things in Early Modern England."

Alan Stewart is professor of English and comparative literature at Columbia University. He is the author of *Close Readers: Humanism and Sodomy in Early Modern England* (1997), *Hostage to Fortune: The Troubled Life of Francis Bacon* (with Lisa Jardine, 1998), *Philip Sidney: A Double Life* (2000), and *The Cradle King: A Life of James VI and I* (2003).

Heather Wolfe is curator of manuscripts at the Folger Shakespeare Library, Washington, DC. She is the editor of *Elizabeth Cary, Lady Falkland: Life and Letters* (2001) and a forthcoming collection of essays on Elizabeth Cary. She has published essays on early modern reading and writing technologies and on the manuscript culture of English Benedictine nuns. She edited the exhibition catalogue *The Pen's Excellencie* (2002), and co-wrote *Letterwriting in Renaissance England* (2005) with Alan Stewart.

Introduction

Donna B. Hamilton

This *Concise Companion* approaches Renaissance literature not from the perspective of authors, texts, or chronology, but by way of categories and contexts understood to have informed this literature from the later decades of the reign of Elizabeth I to the end of the reign of James I, or 1575–1625. Each chapter provides a self-contained introduction to a topic, as well as an entry point into a subfield for the reader who wishes to pursue more particular research and study. Chapters on economics, religion, and education deal most directly with the ideological underpinnings of Renaissance culture. Chapters on manuscripts and on patronage and licensing consider the mechanisms by means of which ideas circulated in the public sphere. The chapters on treason and rebellion and on private life and domesticity compare the one-sidedness of treatises written to dictate behavior to the many actions that flaunted those rules. Consideration of exploration, royal marriage, and those the English regarded as "outsiders" takes us to matters of English national identity, to the economic and religious significance of travel, and to the political and ideological implications of defining England in isolation from or as a part of nations in Continental Europe. Finally, two chapters on the human subject – one from the perspective of cosmology and the body and one from the perspective of life-writing – turn our attention in yet a different way to the individual as a part of a cultural system.

Our study of the English Renaissance begins from the perspective of business and economics not only because the topic is foundational but because it gives easy entry to the period. We all know something about money and business, at least as those topics affect our own lives. Then as now, the production of art – music, painting, entertainment, and literature, including play-writing – had an economic basis. During the reign of Elizabeth, one of the great innovations in business was the

1

large public playhouse, the first of which, built in London in 1576, was called the Theatre. The business model for a playhouse that could hold 2,000–3,000 paying customers mimicked that of other entertainments, such as bear baiting, which people attended at a set time and for which they paid money. By 1594, two playing companies dominated the theatre scene, the Lord Admiral's Men and the newly created Lord Chamberlain's Men. Philip Henslowe, who together with his son-in-law Edward Alleyn built the Rose theatre, mostly hired writers for plays to be acted by the Lord Admiral's Men. Shakespeare belonged to the Chamberlain's Men. These companies competed with each other for their market share of the public's attention.

In her chapter "Economics," Susan Cerasano defines the economic situation in Renaissance England by focusing on the economics of the theatre business. Using as a baseline the monopolies granted to individual guilds, Cerasano defines the late sixteenth-century theatre business as characterized by a set of "innovative business models" that depended to a large extent on what she calls "dynastic capitalism," a system comprised of family business and dependent on family connections – such as those shared by Henslowe and Alleyn. In developing that definition, she sees that such a self-contained structure with close-knit relational rules was also "guild-like." These definitional terms help us understand both the business aspect of the theatre and the theatre's complex relationship to other institutional practices. Her attention to plays by William Shakespeare, Ben Jonson, and Thomas Middleton leaves no doubt that for the playwright timeliness in topics often included economic issues.

The topic of religion in Renaissance England is as well known as it is elusive, as Donna Hamilton emphasizes in her chapter on religion. The basic narrative that underlies all discussions must be that of Henry VIII's break with Rome in 1534, combined with the process by which Protestant beliefs and practices replaced over time their Roman Catholic counterparts. The high stakes involved in this shift can hardly be overstated.

In breaking from Rome, Henry VIII eliminated the political control of English institutions that had been the pope's prerogative. The English monarch was now head of church and state. Throughout the rest of the sixteenth and well into the seventeenth century, matters of royal or dynastic marriage, treason and rebellion, war with European countries, competition in trade, and the treatment of English citizens abroad and of English Catholics in England remained bound up with the implications of taking actions that might return

England to papal control, a destiny most people decried but others sought. Clinging to the political and religious autonomy they had gained in the separation from Rome, the English struggled to come to terms with competition and threat from Spain but also with a recurring desire to cultivate Spain as an important ally. In matters of religious belief and practice, England's break with Rome meant first a long struggle in England to work out what the English church would be. It was not until the late 1580s that Protestantism clearly dominated as the religion of England. Throughout the 1570s, strong Catholic communities existed throughout England, even as the tactics to enforce uniformity in religion gradually became more effective. The execution of Mary Queen of Scots in 1587 and the defeat of the Spanish Armada in 1588 completed the task of making England a Protestant nation, even as Catholics continued their less public religious existence. To read Renaissance literature with understanding requires that one be attuned to the religious register. Protestant characterizations of Catholic traditions as superstitious hocus-pocus, their disparaging of Catholic emphasis on meritorious deeds, and their mocking Catholic belief in purgatory document ongoing religious debate. Protestants understood their differences from Catholics as necessary reform; Catholics saw them as innovations that were destroying the unity of Christendom. Despite some sharp differences between Catholics and Protestants, there remained much in common. Many individuals converted back and forth between Protestant and Catholic beliefs. Any notion of an essentialized Protestant or Catholic identity does injustice to the variation within communities, the indecisiveness of individuals, and the hybridity in all kinds of religious experience in a nation where a single generation had seen the standards of strict uniformity change at least once and sometimes three times from Edward VI to Mary to Elizabeth.

Matters of royal marriage and succession felt strongly the implications of religious controversy, especially when the marriage involved a foreign power of a different religion than England. The long-drawn-out negotiations for a marriage between Queen Elizabeth and the duke of Anjou, a French Catholic, carried a double threat. England might succumb to Catholic influence, and, as Paul Hammer emphasizes in this volume, Elizabeth might succumb to French domination, an especially fearsome prospect should she die in childbirth. For this momentous controversy, both Sir Philip Sidney and Edmund Spenser made their publishing – in manuscript and print – debuts, with some damage to their careers as a result. Hammer's review of the pressure

brought to bear on Elizabeth by her rival Mary Queen of Scots introduces a second rivalry rooted in issues of succession and religion. Many
English Catholics longed for events that would put Mary on the
throne; others acted subversively and treasonably to try to make that
happen. Any idealized view of Elizabeth clouds the political force of
those plots and masks the continuing significance of Catholic opposition to the royal supremacy. One element of this significance lay in
the claims to the English throne that were made by Philip II of Spain.
Further, having finally executed Mary, Elizabeth and her nation had
then to face the prospect of eventually welcoming Mary's son James VI
of Scotland to England as their own James I. With the accession of
James, England once again had a royal family. Understanding fully the
international implications of royal marriage, James eventually succeeded in marrying his daughter Elizabeth to a Protestant and his son
Charles to a Catholic. Both negotiations caused political upheaval at
home and abroad. The disastrous reign of Elizabeth's husband, the
Elector Frederick of Bohemia, led shortly to a Spanish invasion of the
Palatinate and the Thirty Years War. After an involved courtship with
the Spanish Infanta, Charles finally married Henrietta Maria, a marriage alliance that did not bring peace between the two nations.

Alongside economics, religion, and the international implications of
marriage and succession, patronage stands as the central social system
of the period. Suitors looked for advancement by offering service to a
patron, and the reward the patron gave in return advanced his own
standing with his superior, a reciprocity that encouraged a repeat
performance of the entire cycle. Writers could attract patrons because
their skills were highly regarded by the ruling class.

Richard Dutton introduces us to the many-sided aspects of patronage by reviewing the patronage relationships of Ben Jonson, who
celebrated his patrons in poems printed in *Epigrams* and *The Forest,*
and also sought and received commissions to write occasional shows
and entertainments, Lord Mayor shows, and masques for the court.
Also a playwright, Jonson withdrew from writing plays after King
James I granted him a pension, thereby again proving his capacity to
avoid the world of business and make a living instead by way of the
patronage system.

More telling about the relationship between patronage and the
theatre is what we know of the office of Master of the Revels, which
held the power to license plays. This power was somewhat moderated
by the simultaneous requirement that playing companies had to have
patrons who beginning in 1594 were members of the Privy Council.

Nevertheless, the licensing power meant that the Master of the Revels could allow plays to be performed, could censor plays, and could give a company exclusive rights to perform a play. Dutton provides important examples of all actions.

In a seminal discussion, Dutton examines the intricacies of the licensing and patronage systems by way of the uproar caused by the publication of *The First Part of the Life and Reign of King Henry IV*, printed first in February, 1599. Months later, when Essex objected to the dedication, it was removed. Still later, after a second printing, the entire print run was burned. Eventually, Essex's involvement with Hayward's books was used as evidence for charging him with treason. Thus, concludes Dutton, licensing and patronage systems were for the most part "*inclusive* processes, calculated to keep writers, dramatists, publishers, and players within the circle of authority, rather than to exclude them from it."

The study of rhetoric, which constituted early modern training in reading and writing, helps us deal with that conclusion. As Peter Mack urges, in acquiring knowledge of the skills on which Elizabethans depended for "communicative competence," a skill set based in a curriculum comprised of Greek and Roman writers, we gain greater access to the implications of their writing. Study of sentence structure, of figurative language, and of pertinent examples from the writings of Greek and Roman writers constituted the central elements of grammar-school and university rhetorical training. Such training enabled the virtuoso writing of Sidney and Shakespeare, as Mack demonstrates. That training also set the standards for the controversial literature of the period, as well as for the more indirect forms of argument that populate history writing and prose narrative.

Mack's densely packed chapter furnishes both an introduction for the student uninitiated in rhetoric and concise reminders for those with more familiarity. Stylistic tools direct us to the implications of content and to the community of readers that are the object of address. Writers knew what their rhetorical options were, and that those options included choice of genre. Rhetorical options also affected and were affected by the means of publication.

In the Renaissance, there were basically two means of publication: print and manuscript. Publication in the form of a printed book or pamphlet meant entering a system governed by licensing regulations, and affected nearly always by the economics and sometimes by the ideological leanings of publishers, printers, and bookshop owners. Watershed dates for the publication of material on various topics are worth bearing in mind. Sometimes the initial date is especially import-ant, such as that of *Tottel's Miscellany* in 1557, or *The Shepheardes Calender* in 1579. Sometimes the repeated publication over many years may seem more significant, the situation for *The Paradise of Daintie Devices*, printed in 1576, 1578, 1580, 1585, 1590, 1596, 1600, and 1606. Some-times key historical events affect our understanding of why a text or group of texts made an appearance at a certain time. The negotiations for the marriage of Queen Elizabeth to the duke of Anjou (1579–82) and the execution of Edmund Campion in 1581 merit study together for their effect on writing and printing. In instances where works were revised prior to reprinting, it often matters a great deal which edition one cites. One would rarely cite the first edition of John Foxe's *Actes and Monuments*, printed in 1563, because it was vastly changed already by 1570. However, if one is citing Foxe in relation to a work, let us say, in the 1590s, then the edition one probably should use is the one in 1583, the last edition Foxe himself had a hand in prior to his death.

An important alternative to print, manuscript publication defined itself in relation to the standard practices developed for printed works. Prior to the point where print had reached dominance, manuscript publication had been the central, if not the only, means to circulate writing. With the prevalence of print, manuscript transmission took on new significance. Confining the circulation of one's work to a manu-script usually meant that one was writing more privately to a selected audience. As Heather Wolfe emphasizes, the agendas for such writing ranged across domestic, legal, and business transactions. And while such writing could have seriously private significance, use of manu-script transmission for subversive political and religious texts displays yet another strength of manuscript publication. While the significance of some famous examples – *Leicester's Commonwealth* or *The Game at Chesse* – is readily accessible, in other cases the intimacy of the social context for the production, revision, and rearranging of works in manu-script eludes us. By the same token, in instances where works originally in manuscript made their way into print, the conventions of printing and the very act of making something more public removed the manu-script from the conventions of privacy that might have given us access to a work's significance. Understanding some of the opportunities as well as the challenges that lie in the study of print and manuscript must remain a central part of our work in English Renaissance literature.

Certain genres have seemed more resistant to ideological classifica-tion or cultural attribution, especially poetic miscellanies, history writing, prose narratives, chivalric and pastoral romances, and travel writing. Length contributes to their seeming impenetrability. In this volume, Ralph Bauer's discussion of travel literature gives this category of works a new accessibility.

Working across a body of works spanning the period 1580–1620, Bauer draws a dividing line between works printed before and after 1613. As Bauer notes, while travel writing from the medieval period onward focused primarily on an inner spiritual progress, beginning in 1580 such writing began to grapple more specifically with the external world. Competition for geographical knowledge and trade routes motivated the production of manuals on how to travel. Expeditions began to include personnel with a wider range of skills, including the skill to sketch and paint what travelers had seen. Maps and lists of natural resources soon populated the reports. To reach these conclusions, Bauer surveys the works of Richard Hakluyt, Francis Bacon, Jerome Turler, Thomas Palmer, Sir Walter Raleigh, and Thomas Harriot. Across all of them, Bauer finds narratives that held up the European standard for discovery while reconstructing the task as one meant for Protestant dominance.

As Bauer argues, a major shift in definition of the travel and commerce project came with the writing of Samuel Purchas. In a series of works announced as post-Hakluyt – *Hakluytus Posthumus* – Purchas redefined the project ideologically as consonant with a growing corporate and transoceanic imperial state. Instead of praising the accomplishments of individuals, Purchas understood the project as an initiative of the monarchy and of strong central government. This ideological repositioning built on a growing understanding of imperial ideology as dependent on a notion of British identity, that is, of Britain as a composite kingdom comprised of three kingdoms – England, Scotland, and Ireland – functioning as one. Though fledgling and barely surviving, the Jamestown settlement in 1607 was one step in the process of England's evolving interests in discovery and commerce. The most lasting settlement in Plymouth in 1620 was another.

Writings about private domestic life pose still other challenges. In her survey of relevant texts, Lena Orlin considers the range: guidebooks to courtship, marriage, child rearing, and servant supervision; instructions from the church; diaries and letters – in all of which texts there is a striking absence of challenges to the basic structure and expectations of the household. Conflict and opposition have no representation.

However, as in other instances from the period, if one shifts to other genres the information and perspective change, in some cases erasing the opacity, in others exchanging one form of veiling for another.

Church-court records in particular record charges of adultery, fornication, and beatings. These documents expose the conflict, discord, and aberrant behavior that instruction manuals and homilies forbade. But even these records are not always what they seem, according to Orlin. Because the church courts deployed sexualized language for many topics, one cannot always tell whether the issue was in fact the sexual matter that the language expresses literally. This peculiarity dims the light that court records seem to shed on private matters, while at the same time clarifying that a sexualized discourse, to whatever it refers at any moment, nevertheless registers anxiety about the culture's ability to maintain monolithic control over private matters. According to Orlin, some of the most graphic representations of disorder in the domestic sphere exist in stageplays, where spouse killing, adultery, and other forms of disobedience abound.

Matters of obedience and disobedience as represented for the private sphere had a corollary in the public sphere, where disobedience could be labeled treason or rebellion and punished by execution, issues discussed by Andrew Hadfield. Issues of treason and rebellion were regularly related to matters of religion. In a period in which uniformity in religion was mandated in the context of great religious controversy, open expression of opposition could be understood or defined as treason. In 1536, opposition to Henry VIII's break with Rome resulted in the uprising known as the Pilgrimage of Grace, in which an army of approximately 30,000 gathered in the north to protest the enforced change in religion, with several hundred subsequently executed in punishment. In 1570, the Catholic nobility in the north of England led what we know as the Northern Rebellion or the Rebellion of the Northern Earls. Later the Ridolfi Plot, one of several plots against Queen Elizabeth's life, resulted in the execution in 1572 of Thomas Howard, fourth duke of Norfolk. Another attempt on Elizabeth's life, the Babington Plot of 1586, led directly to the execution of Mary Queen of Scots in 1587.

Questions about succession raised issues regarding the source of a monarch's power and so the conditions under which a monarch might succeed to the throne or be removed from it. Everyone understood that an English monarch ruled by divine right and was God's substitute on earth. But that idea was conjoined with and interrelated to other ideas. A number of political thinkers argued that the king held his power also from the people. In the stronger versions of this republican notion there was advocacy for an elected monarch and for the ability of the people to depose a ruler. Obviously, one implication of such ideas could be the possibility that rebellion was not treason. Hence, such notions were offered and quashed, offered and quashed.

The full range of these ideas makes its way into the poetry and plays of Shakespeare, confirming that the ideas had currency for him and members of his audience. These were not topics for the reclusive legal scholar, but matters that affected the daily lives of the English people, who had to gauge how their spiritual, domestic, economic, and social lives might be determined or affected by how they chose to express their citizenship.

In her discussion of marginalized "others" in England, Carole Levin considers how identities that made some of the English uncomfortable are recorded in various literary works, tracts, and treatises. Discussions elsewhere in this volume of the power of religious controversies are enriched by Levin's noting the expressions of anti-Spanish and anti-French feelings. An example of how Shakespeare's Joan of Arc attempts to find a safe association for herself points to a contemporary self-consciousness around these issues. In discussions of Africans and Jews, Levin takes up the otherness of race and religion that was inscribed in Renaissance culture by law and custom, including Elizabeth's attempt to expel all of African descent in 1601 and her unflagging efforts to make all "others" conform outwardly to the nation's official religion. In a surprise closing, Levin points to evidence of a tradition that the inability to enjoy music was regarded as a characteristic of those of a race or religion regarded as inferior.

The systems of thought and practice that defined the spheres of language and action during 1575–1625 included ideas about cosmology and the body, the topic of Cynthia Marshall's chapter. Within this topic, there is the same range of clarity and complexity as in others. The conservative view of the human place in the cosmos credited divine control over the heavens with influencing human existence, individually and generally. Such understanding provided the basis for expressing all political, social, familiar, and individual affairs in hierarchical terms. The result, says Marshall, was a template for regarding relationships and identities as "essential and fixed, not as historically and culturally derived." This system incorporated most aspects of the natural world, fending off full acceptance either of Copernicus' ideas about a heliocentric model of the solar system, offered in 1543, or of Kepler's description of the laws of planetary motion in 1619. John Donne and others speculated that these theories called others into question. But for the most part there continued ongoing belief in planetary influence on human affairs, as well as in the need to achieve balance of the four humors corresponding to the natural elements of earth, water, air, and fire. Blood-letting and purging were standard treatments for a range of ailments. When we come across this language in the literature of the English Renaissance, our challenge always is to understand not only the theory behind it but the implications of its particular use. When does our identifying it instruct us in a worldview radically different from our own, and when does it refer to a situation of another sort for which humoral language provides expression?

In a chapter that implicitly crosses virtually all topics in this volume, Alan Stewart considers the significance of the genre of life-writing during the English Renaissance. The centrality of the genre is neatly illustrated by Sir Thomas North's translation of Plutarch's *Lives of the Noble Grecians and Romanes*, and by the fact that Edward Hall, Raphael Holinshed, John Stow, William Camden, and others organized their writing of English history according to the period of each monarch. Within the hagiographical genre of saints' lives, the goal was to use the example of an individual to teach how to live a holy life, not always the goal of the history writers, who recorded mixed views of emperors and monarchs. The use of life-writing to fashion an exemplary life was especially useful for self-fashioning. In his *Life of Sidney*, Fulke Greville represented the nobility of Sidney by interpolating from Plutarch's *Life of Alexander* the story about providing water for a soldier, but making Alexander's action into an action by Sidney. The fact that Greville incorporated his account of Sidney's life into a preface for a book of his own, not Sidney's, poems suggests that self-representation was a key motivator in the construction even of the account of Sidney. Stewart's discussion of Francis Bacon, an author about whom Stewart has written previously, takes his account in yet another direction. At the end of his life, having been discredited by impeachment, Bacon represented the private, individual significance of his downfall by comparing his situation to that of some of the greatest Greeks and Romans – Demosthenes, Seneca, and Cicero – all of whom had been redefined by the justice systems as criminals. In claiming that he merits comparison with these predecessors, he identifies himself both with their fate and with their greatness, while passing brutal judgment on those who had engineered his downfall. Here and elsewhere, Stewart's examples challenge any satisfaction we may have with how we have understood one or another biographical (or other) account by a Renaissance writer.

Chapter 1

Economics

S. P. Cerasano

On January 3, 1589, actor Richard Jones signed a deed of sale surrendering his share of "playing apparel, playbooks, instruments, and other commodities" to another, more eminent actor named Edward Alleyn with whom Jones had performed for at least six years, probably since both were members of the Earl of Worcester's Company in 1583. In return for his share Jones was to be paid £37 10s., a substantial sum equal to roughly three times the annual income for a schoolmaster of the same period (Greg 1907: 31–2). From what little historians know of the next few years it appears that Jones had decided to leave Alleyn's company in order to travel on the Continent with a touring company; but by 1595 he had returned to London, and he was again performing alongside Alleyn as one of the Lord Admiral's Men. So for a second time Jones purchased a share in the company. Despite the fact that these financial arrangements might, at first, appear unusual to us, Jones and Alleyn were clearly comfortable with such transactions. By the late 1580s it was customary for actors to venture their own money in order to share the risk of operating an entertainment business. The players understood that they were investing not only in the aesthetic business of play production, but also in the financial necessities associated with making a living as professional players.

As the Jones–Alleyn transaction, and so many documents of the Elizabethan theatre, make clear, the mixture of players, property, and profit was central to the organization of professional theatre. By Shakespeare's day acting companies had relied on their own financial resources for generations, even though this had not always been the case. A hundred years earlier the court interluders who were patronized by Henry VII, and subsequently by his son Henry VIII, collected an annual fee (on a per-player basis) along with occasional rewards from the monarch; and between these sources of income the players were guaranteed a basic wage. Under this arrangement, whatever earnings could be brought in through performance constituted income over and above what the players were guaranteed. However, by the early years of Elizabeth I's reign the situation had altered completely. In the 1560s playing companies began to depend primarily upon their performances (often conducted in provincial locales) in order to make a living; the queen no longer provided an annual fee, although some companies enjoyed occasional rewards for performances at court. Thus, in large part the players were required to fund themselves, an arrangement that transformed acting into an even more precarious profession than it had been previously. To complicate matters, not all of the players' earnings were returned to them in the form of salaries. The profits had to defray the costs of purchasing playbooks, costumes, and props, not to mention the expenses incurred by travel.

This economic model persisted well into the last quarter of the sixteenth century when the Queen's Men (established 1583) still made their living on the road, having only the queen's livery to show for their association with the monarch. Patrons – whether royal or aristocratic – offered their blessing in the form of a patent, a gesture that allowed actors to assume the status of servants; but ultimately patrons did not provide a salary. In some measure this hands-off approach was a useful arrangement since it allowed the players more artistic freedom than a more dependent relationship with their patrons might have permitted. Yet it did not provide a regular income, a key element influencing the preservation and development of any profession. Under an arrangement such as that which governed the Queen's Men, actors gained access to a large market in the provinces; but they had to make their living outside of London's more convenient theatrical marketplaces.

However, a few companies were more fortunate than this; and the business model that they evolved prevailed into the seventeenth century. By the 1590s what set Alleyn and Jones apart from those players who made a living on tour is that they enjoyed the advantages of performing in a permanent playing space (the Rose playhouse, located on Bankside, just across the river from the city of London). Furthermore, the company could depend upon the backing of a financier (Philip Henslowe) to assist them in meeting their ongoing expenses. Both of these factors guaranteed the Admiral's Men an important level of professional security; but more than any other development it was the construction of the early public playhouses (the Red Lion in 1567, the Theatre in 1576, the Curtain in 1577, and the Rose in 1587) that transformed, in a fundamental way, the financial basis of stage-playing. Nevertheless, as favorable as these conditions were, they did not occur randomly; nor did investors undertake such projects for altruistic reasons. Rather, the construction of the playhouses and the financing of actors were encouraged by other economic trends during the second half of the sixteenth century. The gradual professionalizing of theatre, as a business, converged with the growing climate of capitalist expansion that predominated at the time.

The Economic Conditions: Europe and England

Because the profession of playing was inextricably bound up with financial arrangements, the story of theatrical economics is rooted more generally in the economic history of the early modern period; and, in turn, the economic conditions that shaped the early modern period were influenced by several previous centuries that alternately experienced devastation and growth. In general, economic historians describe the thirteenth century as an unusual time, an era that exemplified the culmination of several centuries of relative stability and consistent increases, both in terms of a swelling population and in terms of expanding trade and commerce. These elements heightened the productivity that normally accompanies such growth; and although various social crises, such as war and pestilence, occasionally disrupted this upswing, the thirteenth century marked an auspicious period that preceded more catastrophic times. Douglass C. North and Robert Paul Thomas characterize the thirteenth century as a period of "economic awakening": "Urban places expanded. Trade and commerce flourished locally, regionally and internationally. In short, this was a dynamic era" (North and Thomas 1973: 46).

By the beginning of the fourteenth century things had begun to change, and the effects of these changes peaked in the middle of the century when the Black Death (1347–51) not only decimated the population in many parts of Western Europe, but destroyed the underpinnings of the economy as well (North and Thomas 1973: 46, 73). Although precise estimates of the actual decline in population disagree with one another, it is generally accepted that the Great Plague – in combination with other elements, and less severe plague periods that followed in the second half of the fourteenth century – reduced the European population by 20–5 percent. The economic results were very mixed: while the labor market and the markets for goods shrank, simultaneously wages rose and rents fell (North and Thomas 1973: 71–3, 88). During the second half of the fifteenth century a combination of population growth and commercial expertise, shored up by the stability of secure nation states (that had replaced the former city states), fostered expansion and economic vitality. "The market expanded, efficiency required the substitution of money payments for labor dues in a new contractual arrangement. In the process serfdom died, labor became free to seek its best rewards, land received rent, and the basic feudal-manorial relationship withered and died" (North and Thomas 1973: 92).

By the end of the sixteenth century these trends were firmly embedded in both Europe, as a whole, and England, in particular. The European economy featured new growth in population, an absence of plague (at least, in comparison with what had occurred earlier), and an accompanying increase in trade. In some sense, of course, there was not one organized, overarching European economy, but many smaller "economies." Some of these were regionally based industries, while others tended to be exported for sale outside of local and national borders in a kind of quasi-"international" market (although this lacked the kind of sophisticated organization that such terminology might suggest). The cloth trade, which had sustained the European economy for several centuries, remained the seminal industry (despite the fact that heavy woolens were eventually replaced by lighter woolens), while other emerging industries, such as the silk trade and later on various metal trades, emerged to take their place alongside the woolen industry. With the development of trading routes to the east, a market for spices, china, and other luxury goods opened up new possibilities for commerce.

These trends were replicated in the economic history of England, despite the fact that the country suffered major setbacks in the centuries up to 1500, which included the Hundred Years War, the War of the Roses, and the ravages of the Black Death. Nonetheless, by 1550 foreign trade was flourishing, and the wool industry, still strong, remained the staple of the English economy (Bowden 1962). In the wake of these auspicious developments London gradually became a city where sophisticated economic transactions could take place. In June, 1566, Sir Thomas Gresham laid the cornerstone for the first Exchange at Threadneedle and Cornhill streets, which was modeled after the Bourse in Antwerp. The building – which contained shop space and meeting rooms, halls, and gardens – would, according to Gresham, offer "cloistered walkways to shelter our merchants from the elements while they conduct their business, 'an inside ... will be halls and rooms aplenty for their pleasure ... [The shops will be spaces in which] your wives and ladies may buy their fill of exotic trinkets from beyond the seas ... or take sweets of an afternoon.'' The Exchange, which eventually acquired the status of being "Britain's Bourse,'' was such an overwhelming success that Queen Elizabeth paid it a personal visit in 1571, whereupon she gave the building its official name, the Royal Exchange of England ("to be henceforth so designated and called, and not otherwise!''). It stood, in great splendor, at its full height of three stories, with a steep-pitched roof, statues of the queen adorning the parapets, and a tower whose bell rang out twice daily, calling the merchants to business, until it burned down in the Great Fire of 1666, whereupon another exchange was constructed on the same site (Gresham 1995: 241–2, 289).

All this is not to say that the economy of sixteenth-century England was wholly without problems; but even in the face of declining real wages, substantial inflation, food shortages, and periodic setbacks due to plague or war, the economic landscape was marked by a spirit of innovation, amidst which the capitalist adventurer and the investor-shareholder seemed to gain substantial ground. D. C. Coleman, noting that there is considerable controversy over the condition of life for the "ordinary person" of the late Tudor period, commented: "The gainers were to be found in all ranks of life but more especially amongst the enterprising yeomen and landowning gentry, amongst traders, merchants, and lawyers'' (1977: 26–9).

Concepts of Capitalism

One of the hallmarks of the changing economy during the sixteenth century was what historians have referred to, generally speaking, as a "new capitalism." However, when they invoke this term they are not referring to the kind of widespread industrialization and free market capitalism that characterizes the modern western world. Rather, they are suggesting that there was vigorous activity amongst speculative entrepreneurs, and perhaps even that the numbers of such investors increased (Grassby 1999: 1–17). For many theorists early versions of capitalism have also been associated with the cult of individualism, which looms large in discussions of the early modern mentalité. None-theless, as useful as these theoretical constructs might be, it is important to bear in mind that early manifestations of the capitalist enterprise were radically different from contemporary concepts. To begin with, there was no organized economic "system," either on the Continent or within England. Further, the sense of open, self-regulating trade that defines contemporary theoretical ideas of capitalism was wholly missing. Trades were regulated through the granting of monopolies to individual guilds; and the guild system was so extensive – incorporating 75 percent or more of adult males over the age of 28 in London – that it not only provided professional training, but also maintained control over the quality of the goods produced by its members and regulated competition. Thus, through their well-established internal court system individual guilds were in a position to perform a policing function for their trade (Archer 1991: 114–31). In these circumstances trade was not conducted within individualized standards. Instead goods were produced according to specific professional expectations. Tradesmen's business practices were established by the tradition and custom of guilds.

Two concepts were central to the inner workings of early capitalism: the first was "innovation," in all of its aspects, from the creation of new products to new markets to new commercial structures; and the second was what modern economists frequently refer to as "dynastic capitalism," which, in simpler language, refers to the degree to which family-owned businesses controlled trade, sometimes for generation after generation. Increasingly during the decades between 1550 and 1600 the impulses to mercantilism and the evolution of a mercantile culture – which had been evident since the late Middle Ages – were stimulated by the emergence of new kinds of businesses, as well as by the fact that increasing numbers of people began to speculate in businesses. The great trading companies, such as the Muscovy Company (chartered in 1555 to explore trading opportunities with Muscovia and Russeland, both located in modern Russia, and Cathay, now part of China), also provided new kinds of organized structures for investment. Consequently, it was a combination of innovative business models and the increasing prevalence of dynastic capitalism that served as the motor of economic growth. In his book-length study of this phenomenon Richard Grassby concludes: "The business family was in several respects the individual writ large ... In the early modern period the economy would have grown at a much slower pace without corporations and lone adventurers, but it would not have functioned at all without family networks" (Grassby 2001: 416–17).

In this, theatrical businesses were no exception. The Theatre (constructed in 1576) was, in actuality, the property of the Brayne–Burbage family (although the widow Brayne claimed that she was never adequately compensated for her deceased husband's investment in the playhouse). The partnership between a wealthy dyer named Philip Henslowe and his son-in-law, the actor Edward Alleyn, eventually came to include the Rose (1587), Fortune (1600), and Hope (1613) playhouses. In addition, two successful theatrical companies (the Lord Chamberlain's Men at the Theatre, and the Lord Admiral's Men at the Rose and Fortune) were tied to the playhouses in which they performed through family connections. Because the sense of "family" was much more broadly defined during the early modern period than it is now – encompassing members of one's extended family, as well as relations by marriage, by adoption, and often by professional affiliation, such as apprentices and business partners – dynastic capitalism exerted an influence on the theatre business that was unprecedented. In fact, a surprising number of players were married to sisters, daughters, and nieces of other players, both within and across company boundaries; and apprentices were taken on regularly by master players. As a result, the personal familiarity engendered by the overwhelming number of family connections, coupled with the closeness of the players that developed as they worked together professionally, allowed the companies to act as "guild-like" structures that regulated many aspects of the trade, from training their members, to supervising the quality of output, to controlling the ways in which theatrical finances were allocated. In these ways, the companies managed to function well without the necessity or intervention of a formal guild. In other ways, however, the players' trade was continually imperiled by their lack of formal status, as will be discussed in the next section.

Theatre as a New Business

Before the middle of the sixteenth century, the idea of turning playing into an established business was unheard of; but as the century wore on, investors were increasingly swept along by the tide of growing capitalistic impulses. Still, existing mercantile structures were unaccustomed to accommodating an "industry" such as theatre that did not have a material output; and it is doubtful that the term "industry," in the way that we use the word today, adequately conveys the sense of theatre as a business in Shakespeare's time. To begin with, because acting was not recognized as a trade it was a struggle for players to find a professional niche; and some historians would argue that, in fact, the players never found an established position within the socio-economic hierarchy during the period under discussion. (To a great degree players were more tolerated than accepted. They were thought of more as mere entertainers than as artisans cultivating art.)

To complicate matters, because the actors had no recognized guild to protect them they were vulnerable to various kinds of economic and socio-political pressures. As stated in the opening section of this chapter, players could not be guaranteed a specific wage for work, or count on a certain consistent level of income; nor could they reap the benefits of a well-established professional network, like other tradesmen, or count on a stable export market that went beyond the boundaries of England. And even when the companies performed in London at an established venue, such as the Rose or Globe playhouses, they could not count on the theatre being open consistently. Various events – from closure orders issued by the city fathers because of plague or social disruption, to Lenten practices or holiday customs – periodically interfered with the performance calendar. These could force the closure of the London playhouses, almost at a moment's notice, and the players had little recourse when this occurred. For this reason actors were exposed to commercial peril on a daily basis. Additionally, the early years of professional playing witnessed a continual struggle because "the theatre" as an institution was extremely modest in size by comparison with the many other groups of established tradesmen. In fact, the "theatre industry," even in its most robust years (between perhaps 1593 and 1620), consisted of only a handful of playing companies and playhouses.

Lastly, playing was considered a new "trade," which operated outside of the established norm because the mode of production and the nature of the "goods" that were produced were so different from the usual sorts of commodities that were manufactured by the tradesmen and artisans of the traditional guilds. Paying a fee to attend a performance of a play was spending money on transient goods, on something that was to be consumed and enjoyed for a few hours, but that then disappeared. By contrast, musicians – who had enjoyed a guild since the fourteenth century – could justify themselves according to their professional function. Peripatetic they might have been, but their work was tied to socially sanctioned public and private events, such as weddings, and music was an integral part of church services and state occasions. Furthermore, like dancing masters, musicians often made a living by teaching. They could therefore claim a place within society as tutors. Yet with the exception of the occasional court entertainments, or entertainments at the homes of noblemen, players could not claim equal "usefulness" or similar ties to social respectability. For all of these reasons, then, the theatre business, in its infancy, must have seemed an unusual "trade" for anyone to pursue. Nevertheless, some London entrepreneurs recognized the potential for financial gain in "selling entertainment." After all, the Bankside baiting arenas had, for years, charged admission to view blood sports, while archery matches, wrestling and dueling matches, and acrobatic displays had all been performed in various locales in return for money. On the basis of this premise, theatrical adventurers realized that they could maximize returns if they could charge admission to a performance offered at a particular time and in a specific location.

Not surprisingly, both the greatest expense and the greatest risk in this "new business" were undertaken by the investors who constructed the first purpose-built theatres. Owing to the large size of the playhouses, such construction was expensive. Owing to the playhouses' fairly restricted use, the investors were risking money to build structures that could be leased for entertainment but for little else. Without a playing company to lease the playhouse an entrepreneur could not be guaranteed any financial return; nor could he hope to sell the building to another owner, or to use it for another purpose. The early playhouses were not only experiments in architecture, they were experiments in finance; and the theatres were expensive both to construct and to maintain. In consequence, the majority of playhouse owners were not players themselves, but were members of other professions, professions that not only endowed their members with an acceptable social status (like "player," "theatrical financier" was not a profession), but also provided a necessary income and political connections within the city. The Rose playhouse was constructed by Philip Henslowe (a dyer), the Swan by Francis Langley (a goldsmith), and the Theatre by two men (a grocer and a joiner). The First Globe, constructed in 1599 by seven player-investors, was a rare exception to this trend (Chambers 1923: II, 417).

The expenses that financiers undertook in constructing a playhouse were formidable. In 1576, the owners of the Theatre hoped to spend £200 on their building, but it ended up costing them more than three times this amount (£700). In 1599 the first Globe cost £700. The Fortune was erected for £520 in 1600, and the owners of the Red Bull claimed that they had spent around £500 to construct their theatre in 1605. Still, these costs do not reflect the totality of the financial undertaking involved in playhouse ownership. There were annual expenses for ground rent (to lease the property on which the theatre stood), which varied (where this evidence is known) from £7 to £14. Also, there were expenses for maintaining both the playhouse and the property, which included periodic renovations (Henslowe spent over £100 on this at the Rose in 1592), sewer maintenance, and ground care. In addition to these expenses, theatrical properties generally included other structures that required maintenance. Most playhouse owners leased a small house near the theatre to a tapster or other person who sold food and drink on the premises.

In just a few years all of these expenses had escalated. By 1613, the second Globe cost twice (£1,400) what the first playhouse had cost to build fourteen years earlier. The second Fortune cost roughly £1,000 in 1622 and, at the latter end of the theatre-building phase, the Salisbury Court playhouse – a small, private theatre, offering much less capacity than a larger public playhouse, like the Globe – cost roughly £1,000, even though the owners were converting an existing structure (a barn) into a playhouse, rather than starting their construction from the ground up, which would have required an even greater expense. Predictably, perhaps, the investors who erected the early playhouses tended to be fairly young men who possessed a fair amount of ready cash, or who formed partnerships in order to raise the necessary funds. Of those playhouses that were erected and operated between 1567 (when the Red Lion Inn was renovated as a playhouse) and the late 1620s, when the theatre-building impulse began to fade due to increasing pressure from the puritanical opposition, roughly half were constructed by individual owners, while the other half were the creations of partnerships involving various numbers of investors.

Although most playhouse owners leased their buildings to a single playing company that paid rent to perform there, a few also invested in financing the other expenditures that were required for performance. These included the purchase of playbooks, costumes, and props, along with occasional travel expenses to and from the court, and, periodically, the revision of playbooks for performance. The company or theatre financier also paid a licensing fee of 7s. (equivalent to the cost of 84 loaves of bread, with bread costing 1d. per loaf) to the Master of the Revels, a court-appointed official, for each play that was performed. And other supernumeraries had to be paid, including the occasional "extra," or the gatherers who collected money at the playhouse doors. Thus, the indebtedness of players to playhouse

owners was often considerable. The Admiral's Men owed Philip Henslowe, who served as their financier, £300 when Henslowe tallied up
his accounts in July, 1600 (Foakes and Rickert 1961: 136).

Of the financiers who were successful in the theatre business,
perhaps the best known remains Philip Henslowe, whose "diary"
(1593–1603) provides historians with a detailed view of the economic
management of the Rose playhouse. From the beginning Henslowe
lived a life surrounded by the kind of social and economic privilege
that virtually guaranteed his success as an adventurer in the theatre
business. Henslowe, who became a citizen and dyer of London, was
raised in rural Sussex, where his family was well connected both to
the local aristocracy and to the crown. Henslowe's father served as the
Master of the Game in Ashdown Forest under Queen Elizabeth I, and
his uncle, Ralph Hogg, supervised iron mines in Sussex that served the
Royal Ordinance. It would be reasonable to hypothesize that Henslowe
migrated to London when he was around 17 years of age, at which
time he was apprenticed to a dyer in Southwark who also held the
position of bailiff to the earl of Arundel. Because of the thriving wool
trade, a dyer made a substantial living, enjoyed the membership of a
powerful, well-established guild, and had substantial economic and
political sway, both within London and throughout the country.
Whether Henslowe ever plied his trade or not is less significant than
his choice of trade, which placed him in a position of social and
financial prominence within the London business community.

Theatrical investors apparently made enough money to justify their
outlay, their income varied depending upon both large-scale
influences, such as socio-political events, and more mundane factors,
such as the day on which a particular play was performed, the time of
the year when the performance took place, the quality of the play on
offer, and less controllable factors such as the weather. Yet when conditions were favorable returns could be substantial. For instance, in a
seven-week period between February 19 and April 8, 1592, Henslowe
apparently earned almost £70 or roughly £10 per week. During this
segment of the theatrical calendar plays were being performed on a
daily basis (excluding Sundays, for all but one week), and some of the
plays – *Harey the vj*, *Jeronimo*, *Muly Molloco*, and *The Jew of Malta* – were
earning hefty receipts, particularly *Jeronimo*, which earned, at its worst,
26s. (or £1 6s.), and, at its best, well over £3 on a single performance.
(The lowest amount recorded in Henslowe's account book during the
years when receipts are regularly noted (February 19, 1592–May 27,
1596) was 5s. for a performance of *Huon of Bordeaux*, a play that was only

given three performances, while the greatest sum recorded for a single performance was £3 13s. 6d. collected at *The Tanner of Denmark*, a play that was only played once, on May 23, 1593.) On average, however, the successful plays in the repertory earned over £1 for each performance, and the most successful earned in the £2–£3 range (Foakes and Rickert 1961: 16–37).

Such profits might not seem sizable enough to justify an investor's outlay, but when they are placed in the context of other figures their magnitude becomes clearer. During the period between 1590 and 1627 a "middling sort of person" in the village of Stoneleigh, Warwickshire, might be worth around £50–£80 at his death, as inventories from a husbandman and a fuller indicate. A person deemed "poor" in the period between 1601 and 1613 might live in a house of two or three rooms, in the same region, and die with personal property worth as little as £8 (Alcock 1993: 94–5, 97, 144). By contrast, the more well-to-do villagers of Stoneleigh, such as John Benion, yeoman, left an estate evaluated at £199 in 1597 (Alcock 1993: 88–9).

John Manningham, a law student at the Middle Temple, kept a diary from 1602 to 1603 in which he noted a variety of monetary sums that might also be used for comparison; however, Manningham's records principally illuminate aspects relating to the upper echelon of society. From Manningham we learn that a "rich yeoman" was worth £550 and that Master John Sedley bought a house in Aylesford for £4,000 "with only fourteen acres of ground." Manningham notes that Queen Elizabeth's jewels were estimated to be worth £400,000 at her death, and that it cost around £3,000 to bring James VI of Scotland south into England for his coronation as James VI and I in 1603. On a more "scandalous" note, the earl of Essex was rumored to be keeping a mistress and her children at the cost of £1,700 per annum, and he apparently bought her a waistcoat worth £20 (Sorlien 1976: 50, 97, 218). According to Manningham's estimates, members of the aristocracy dealt in denominations of thousands of pounds (in earnings and expenditures) while the gentry dealt in hundreds of pounds for the same things. Considering all this, if the Rose playhouse operated fifty weeks of the year, and the companies' income was roughly £10–£15 per week, the plays would bring in £500–£750 per year. Investors like Henslowe would earn a portion of these profits, in addition to whatever rent would be paid by the players for the use of the house. Therefore, under these conditions, if the playhouse brought in even £100–£150 per annum for Henslowe, this was a substantial profit. Moreover, for Henslowe – as for many other theatrical investors – it denoted only a portion of his annual income, which was supplemented by other business investments. By comparison with the salary of the schoolmaster in Stratford-upon-Avon (£20 per annum, according to the 1553 town charter, and much more than the usual £12 per annum paid in most locales) the income from Henslowe's Rose was impressive (Chambers 1930: I, 10). In examining the range of dramatists' pay G. E. Bentley noted that William Haughton, one of the more successful dramatists who wrote plays for the Rose between 1597 and 1602, was paid roughly £24 per annum over a two-year period. Michael Drayton was paid around £32 by Henslowe over a ten-month period. George Chapman, who did not have a long-term association with the company, managed to earn over £28 for contributing to seven plays within a fourteen-month period (Bentley 1971: 102–3).

In this context a playwright like William Shakespeare – who both owned a share in the company profits and was wealthy enough to be a householder in the first Globe and the Blackfriars playhouses – enjoyed an income sufficient to purchase the second largest home in Stratford-upon-Avon. At his death he had the means to bequeath £150 to his daughter Judith (plus various additional sums should she have children living within three years of his death), £100 to his niece Elizabeth Hall, £50 to his sister-in-law Joan Hart, a dwelling called New Place (in which he lived at the end of his life) to his daughter Susanna Hall, along with various other sums to friends, nephews, fellow players, and the poor of Stratford-upon-Avon. The famous "second best bed" (which has been the subject of much debate) went to his wife, Anne, who, though older by eight years, outlived him by seven. Some historians conjecture that since, according to the Custom of London, a wife automatically inherited a third of her husband's estate, Anne Shakespeare would have come into a sizable (though unspecified) amount. Others note that the Custom of London was not necessarily observed in Warwickshire, hypothesizing instead that Anne was well on in years, and probably living with her daughter and son-in-law, John Hall, who saw to her needs. If the latter is the case, then Shakespeare's wife needed no additional income or property, a narrative that makes the playwright seem much less neglectful than some interpretations of his will would lead readers to believe (Honigmann and Brock 1993: 14, 105–9; Schoenbaum 1977: 300–5).

Because theatre was a speculative business and had not been established in London for very long before Shakespeare joined the Lord Chamberlain's Men in the 1590s, there were certain risks and liabilities that both theatre owners and playing companies had to face. Some of these were so common as to become almost routine, while others were unpredictable. Plague closures (fairly common during the warmer months of the year) were quite predictable, while the losses of dramatists and players (through retirement, illness, or even death) were not. Nonetheless, human factors played a key role in running a business that depended upon marketing talent. The death of Christopher Marlowe in 1593 altered forever the future of the Admiral's Men; the retirement of Shakespeare (many years later) changed the composition of the King's Men, as did the death of Richard Burbage, one of their senior players, in 1619. Other liabilities that bore financial implications for theatre investors related to their roles as landlords. The wear and tear on a playhouse building was costly, gardens and grounds had to be maintained, and there was a limitation on the size of an audience that could squeeze into a playhouse. Given the fact that government legislation limited the number of London theatres, there was no opportunity for investors to expand their market within the city, where the monetary returns were most sizable. Although plays were performed with some regularity in provincial locations the theatre business was essentially London-centric. The capital city – with its impressive playhouses and its ever-increasing population, a population swelled by merchants and foreign visitors of all kinds – provided the natural setting for entrepreneurs eager for profit. In this regard the theatre business was no different from other businesses.

These liabilities notwithstanding, several companies and investors were successful over a period of years; and those who did prosper seem to have done so admirably. But what factors made them unusual in this regard? Traditionally, literary critics have ascribed this to the quality of the dramatists that were writing for the major companies, while theatre historians have argued that the quality of the players was a key element in the success of the leading companies. However, while the quality of both plays and players doubtless contributed to the early success of some companies (and even to the literary posterity of some dramatists), it is significant that the best companies and theatre owners employed a set of smart business techniques that allowed them to maximize their profits. And although specifics are not known for every company of the period, certain elements seem to have been the case for all.

The greatest expenses of mounting a production consisted of purchasing the playbook, procuring costumes, and paying the fee required by the Master of the Revels so that the play could be performed. If travel was involved, or scenic curtains were called for, or unusual props were required, these involved additional expense.

The most fiscally wise companies invested most of their money in playbooks, costumes, licensing fees, and other expenses (in that order). In order to keep spectators coming into the playhouses regularly the companies tended to purchase many plays and to rotate them through the repertory quickly. (Of these, only a few became the kind of blockbusters that were performed year after year.) Next, the companies kept costuming costs to a minimum by purchasing a new suit of clothing for the actor in each play, while recycling used costumes from the tiring-house wardrobe in order to dress the other actors in a production (Cerasano 1994). This, in itself, helped to maximize the profit margin.

One concrete example will serve to illustrate these principles at work. In 1597 the Admiral's Men paid £4 for the playbook of *Phaeton*, £3 4s. for costumes, and 7s. to purchase a license so that the play could be performed in public. Altogether, these basics amounted to £7 11s. Two other props that were listed in the inventory of the tiring house in 1598 also cost money, although the precise sums are unknown ("Phaeton's limbs" and "a gold crown for Phaeton"). When the play was re-produced, three years later, for the court, the company laid out an additional £3. Occasionally the company put out a hefty sum for what is typically described as "mending a play" (which seems to mean adjusting the text in order to get it right, or to better accommodate the players or even the venue in which it would be performed; several plays were "mended" for court performance). Other extravagant outlays periodically went to costuming if the actors wanted to create a spectacular production. One instance in which unusually high expenses were undertaken occurred in the staging of *Cardinal Wolsey* at the Rose in 1601. Although the dramatists who wrote parts 1 and 2 of the play seem to have received the customary payment (£6 per play) for doing so, a year after the play was composed Henry Chettle (one of the playwrights who wrote the original book) was paid an additional £1 "for the mending of the first part" of the play. When the play was mounted during the previous year just over £37 was laid out for costuming, an exorbitant amount of money, even for a two-part play for which the costumes would presumably be used in both parts of the production (Foakes and Rickert 1961).

Along with the shrewd management of company finances, the owners of the Bankside playhouses (the Rose, Globe, Swan, and Hope) were aided by the fact that an entertainment network had built up in the area, one so unusual that foreign travelers came from the Continent drawn, in part, by the public playhouses. In this way, non-theatrical entertainments, which drew crowds to the bear-baiting arenas and archery matches, also attracted crowds to the playhouses. Consequently, even though the admissions fees at the public play-houses remained fairly steady throughout the period (1d. to stand in the pit, with more expensive fees (2d.) to sit in the galleries or to see a new play), and while the playhouses did not increase drastically either in number or in size, the dramatists and the companies for which they wrote managed to make a steady profit because they were able to keep their repertories fluid and their spectators interested in returning. But, ultimately, the plays were "the thing" that attracted spectators to the playhouses. This notwithstanding, the marked interdependence of various sectors of the theatre business is a striking indication of how greatly commercial practices were shaping art. The actors who were paid to bring the plays to life purchased their texts from dramatists and borrowed from their investors and paid rent to theatre owners. Amongst them, they created an economic narrative that ultimately depended upon a complex set of interactions.

New Businesses and Traditional Moralities

With the rise of sophisticated commercial structures, organizations, and enterprises, the spirit of "commodification" infused the society at large. In the words of one Jacobean balladeer, "profit and promotion / The world do over-rule"; or, in other words, "money makes the world go round" (Rollins 1920: 196). Nonetheless, this was a trend that was considered problematical by some thinkers, and that raised great concern amongst more than a few writers of the period. Francis Bacon, whose reputation rests largely upon his collection of fifty-eight essays, used three of these ("Of Expense," "Of Riches," and "Of Usury") to address, head-on, some issues concerning the potential ills of money and commerce, while he used two others ("Of Fortune" and "Of Negotiating") to worry around the edges of related issues. "Riches," Bacon deduced, are the "Baggage of Vertue ... For as the Baggage is to an Army, so is the Riches to Vertue. It cannot be spared, nor left behinde, but it hindreth the March; Yea, and the care of it, sometimes, loseth or disturbeth the Victory" (Kiernan 1985: 109). For Bacon, as for some philosophers and theologians of his time, money was potentially corrupting. Therefore, Bacon cautioned, "Riches are for Spending; And Spending for honour and good Actions" and *"Ordinary Expence* ought to be limited by a Mans Estate; And governed with such regard, as it be within his Compasse; And not subject to Deceit And Abuse of Servants" (Kiernan 1985: 87).

However, such cautions (and implicit criticism) were not restricted to philosophical debate, for the tendencies to acquisitiveness and the pervasiveness of the marketplace were everywhere evident; and the public playhouses were seen as commercial spaces, a factor that opened them up to criticism and prompted an economic debate in many plays of the period. Dramatists such as William Shakespeare, Ben Jonson, and Thomas Middleton, amongst many others, wondered whether citizens had become so caught up in their businesses that human beings and commodities had become interchangeable. In Shakespeare's *Merchant of Venice* the flesh-bond plot at the center of the play (in which flesh is put up as collateral for a loan of three thousand ducats) illustrates the degree to which the language of shareholders and bonds, exchange and credit, comes together in both the commercial world of the playhouse and the financial world that was London. In this way, the caskets used in the marriage test to determine who Portia will marry would have reminded spectators of the wedding caskets that were exchanged upon marriage. The gold rings that are "traded" by Bassanio and Gratiano to the lawyer and his clerk (in return for saving the life of their friend Antonio) put in question the "value" of the marriage vows "exchanged" between the young men and their wives earlier in the play. Nor can an audience overlook the implications of the many other "exchanges" that riddle the love plot of *Merchant*. Through the casket test Portia – the wealthy heiress of Belmont – is given in "exchange" by her dead father to Bassanio, who refers to her as the "golden fleece" sought by many suitors. Shylock's daughter elopes with Lorenzo, stealing much of her father's money and jewels; and when her father discovers her missing, he responds: "O my ducats! O my daughter!" (2.8.15). *The Merchant of Venice* is replete with images related to commercial transactions. In the final act of the play, the commercial world that Shakespeare has created incorporates a complex web of financial obligation, debit, credit, and exchange, which mirrors the historical world of Shakespeare's playhouse. The actors who performed *The Merchant of Venice* were investors and shareholders in their own professional setting; they risked and ventured money in attempting to make a living by performing plays; they were the adventurers of a new kind of commercial setting, and the traders of art for money.

In *Volpone* Ben Jonson explores economic interests as well; however, the play engages with these issues and with the definition of human nature more broadly than *The Merchant of Venice* does. In his elaborate scheme to swindle others out of their money Volpone ("the fox") feeds on the greed of other characters (typecast as a vulture, a raven, and a crow) who, in turn, feed their own greed and desire by feigning love for the ailing old fox in the hope that they can inherit his fortune. In Jonson's theatrical world, avarice and the worship of gold are staged in bold contrast to the ideal "Golden Age," an image with which some commentators of Jonson's day described their own age. The gold at the centre of Volpone's universe brings out the worst in human beings. Instead of "golden" virtue, the quest for gold encourages Jonson's characters to degenerate into the beasts that their names represent. Both within Volpone's house – which is managed by a servant named Mosca ("a fly," a parasite) and staffed by a dwarf and a eunuch (other "unnatural" creatures) – and without it, on the Venetian streets that seem to be heaving with greed and corruption, Jonson constructs a society that is wholly consumed by its taste for gold and enchanted by scams that are intended to cheat others. In the opening scene of the play, after Volpone raises a gold coin above his head in a perverted parody of the celebration of communion, he tells Mosca: "Yet I glory / More in the cunning purchase of my wealth / Than in the glad possession" (1.1.30–2). For Jonson, the economic motive is being driven by other faults that represent the darker side of human nature.

In the last moments of the play, Volpone and Mosca are brought to trial. Here, the judge characterizes the duo ironically. They are those who "possess wealth as sick men possess fevers, / Which trulier may be said to possess them" (5.12.101–2). With this, Volpone is sent off to prison, and Mosca is packed off to the bailiff. However, the judge's rhetoric, critical though it is, repeats only the most clichéd sentiments. Any criticism of avaricious behavior is undercut by the sense that materialism has become a fact of life. Thus, however much the acquisitive spirit might be condemned, in Jonson's view human beings are ultimately slaves to avarice and desire. Throughout the play Volpone's clever scheme remains the comic focus, so that even while Volpone is being taken off to prison Jonson's audiences are left to wonder where the next scam is being launched. *Volpone*, like *The Merchant of Venice*, makes much of its Venetian setting, a reference that prompted visions of opulence and wealth, for which Venice had become renowned throughout Western Europe. And although

Jonson's audience well understood that the grandeur of Venice had disappeared by the end of the sixteenth century, the *myth* of Venice as an ideal "golden republic" was still very much alive. For some Englishmen, it remained a model for their own aspirations, particularly as they moved in the direction of greater economic prominence.

Thomas Middleton – writing a few years later than Shakespeare and Jonson – dismisses all foreign settings, locating *A Chaste Maid in Cheapside* in the old marketplace of London, which extended from the northwest corner of St Paul's churchyard eastward to the Poultry. In his comedy the family, although more traditional, on the surface, than Volpone's menagerie, becomes a business, and the entire world is one grand marketplace. Like Jonson's Venetians, Middleton's Londoners are motivated largely by their lust for money, although the main plot adds sex to the (by now, common) mix of money and corruption. At the opening of the play Yellowhammer (a goldsmith) tries to forge a marriage between his daughter Moll and Sir Walter Whorehound in order to improve the family's fortunes by acquiring both money and land. Moll is essentially "for sale" and there is a price on every character in the play. Like Jonson, Middleton exploits images of food and carnality in depicting the corrupt world of Cheapside, where the pun on "cheapness," as it relates both to inexpensive wares and to loose women, is meant to undercut the concept of romantic love. As perhaps might be expected given the tenor of other romantic comedies of the time, such as *Merchant of Venice* and *Volpone*, Middleton's comedy presents a final movement in which a funeral is turned into a marriage ceremony; and happily for the audience, love triumphs over base coinage. But concurrently, Middleton's realism also shows through. The rhetoric of the play is governed by commercial images in which the usual "bargaining" and "exchanging" are extended into new territory with the inclusion of images relating to gaming and double dealing.

Like Jonson, Middleton trafficked in biting satire; and Middleton's London setting brought his spectators into brutal contact with a place and a society that they knew intimately. In this way Middleton's city comedy reminded audiences that virtually any location in the city, whether on the streets or in the marketplaces, potentially functioned as a commercial setting. From the work of many playwrights and prose writers what seems clear is that by the end of the sixteenth century, society and economics had become so fused that commercial motives seem to overshadow every social interaction. Therefore for Jonson and Middleton most human relationships involved "playing with credit" in some way, even those that centered on artistic endeavor. As the economic history of the "Jacobethan" theatres remind us, fortune hunters were everywhere, even on the London stages.

References and Further Reading

Alcock, N. W. 1993. *People at Home: Living in a Warwickshire Village, 1500–1800*. Chichester: Phillimore, 1993.

Archer, Ian W. 1991. *The Pursuit of Stability: Social Relations in Elizabethan London*. Cambridge: Cambridge University Press.

Bentley, G. E. 1971. *The Profession of Dramatist in Shakespeare's Time, 1590–1642*. Princeton: Princeton University Press.

Bowden, Peter J. 1962. *The Wool Trade in Tudor and Stuart England*. London: Macmillan.

Bowden, Peter J. 1990. *Economic Change: Wages, Profits, and Rents, 1500–1750*. Cambridge: Cambridge University Press.

Bruster, Douglas. 1992. *Drama and the Market in the Age of Shakespeare*. Cambridge: Cambridge University Press.

Cerasano, S. P. 1985. "The 'Business' of Shareholding, the Fortune Playhouses, and Francis Grace's Will," *Medieval and Renaissance Drama in England* 2: 231–51.

Cerasano, S. P. 1994. " 'Borrowed Robes,' Costume Prices, and the Drawing of *Titus Andronicus*," *Shakespeare Studies* 22: 45–57.

Cerasano, S. P., ed. 2004. *A Routledge Literary Sourcebook on William Shakespeare's "The Merchant of Venice."* London: Routledge.

Chambers, E. K. 1923. *The Elizabethan Stage*, 4 vols. Oxford: Clarendon Press.

Chambers, E. K. 1930. *William Shakespeare: A Study of the Facts and Problems*, 2 vols. Oxford: Clarendon Press.

Coleman, D. C. 1977. *The Economy of England: 1450–1750*. Oxford: Oxford University Press.

Duncan-Jones, Katherine. 2002. *Ungentle Shakespeare: Scenes from his Life*. London: Thomson Learning.

Duplessis, Robert S. 1997. *Transitions to Capitalism in Early Modern Europe*. Cambridge: Cambridge University Press.

Fischer, Sandra. 1985. *Econolingua: A Glossary of Coins and Economic Language in Renaissance Drama*. Newark: University of Delaware Press.

Foakes, R. A. and R. T. Rickert, eds. 1961. *Henslowe's Diary*. Cambridge: Cambridge University Press.

Grassby, Richard. 1995. *The Business Community of Seventeenth-Century England*. Cambridge: Cambridge University Press.

Grassby, Richard. 1999. *The Idea of Capitalism before the Industrial Revolution*. Lanham, MD: Rowman and Littlefield.

Grassby, Richard. 2001. *Kinship and Capitalism: Marriage, Family, and Business in the English Speaking World, 1580–1740*. Cambridge: Cambridge University Press.

Greg, W. W. 1907. *The Henslowe Papers*. London: A. H. Bullen.

Gresham, Perry E. 1995. *The Sign of the Golden Grasshopper*. Ottawa, IL: Jameson Books.

Harris, Jonathan Gil. 2004. *Sick Economies: Drama, Mercantilism, and Disease in Shakespeare's Plays*. Philadelphia: University of Pennsylvania.

Honigmann, E. A. J. and Susan Brock, eds. 1993. *Playhouse Wills, 1558–1642*. Manchester: Manchester University Press.

Ingram, William. 1992. *The Business of Playing: The Beginnings of Adult Professional Theatre in Elizabethan London*. Ithaca, NY: Cornell University Press.

Kiernan, Michael, ed. 1985. *Sir Francis Bacon: The Essayes or Counsels, Civill and Morall*. Cambridge, MA: Harvard University Press.

Knutson, Roslyn Lander. 2001. *Playing Companies and Commerce in Shakespeare's Time*. Cambridge: Cambridge University Press.

Leinwand, Theodore B. 1999. *Theatre, Finance, and Society in Early Modern England*. Cambridge: Cambridge University Press.

Muldrew, Craig. 1998. *The Economy of Obligation*. London: Macmillan.

North, Douglass C. and Robert Paul Thomas. 1973. *The Rise of the Western World: A New Economic History*. Cambridge: Cambridge University Press.

Ramsey, Peter H. 1971. *The Price Revolution in Sixteenth Century England*. London: Methuen.

Rollins, Hyder, ed. 1920. *Old English Ballads, 1553–1625*. Cambridge: Cambridge University Press.

Schoenbaum, S. 1977. *William Shakespeare: A Compact Documentary Life*. Oxford: Oxford University Press.

Sorlien, Robert Parker, ed. 1976. *The Diary of John Manningham of the Middle Temple, 1602–1603*. Hanover, NH: University Press of New England.

Sullivan, Ceri. 2002. *The Rhetoric of Credit: Merchants in Early Modern Writing*. Cranbury, NJ: Associated University Presses.

Turner, Frederick. 1999. *Shakespeare's Twenty-First Century Economics: The Morality of Love and Money*. Oxford: Oxford University Press.

Wrightson, Keith. 2000. *Earthly Necessities: Economic Lives in Early Modern Britain*. New Haven: Yale University Press.

Chapter 2

Religion

Donna B. Hamilton

In recent years, the study of religion in sixteenth- and seventeenth-century England has turned new attention to the history and impact of Catholicism in post-Reformation England. The continuity of Catholicism within England and England's relationship to Catholic and Protestant European powers comprise the main branches of this study. Within those two large categories belong the study as well of English Catholic writing, the prosecution and persecution of English Catholics, and the negotiated identity of the English Catholic. Historians have led much of this work, but increasingly literary scholars have been working in tandem with them. While it is now apparent that omitting attention to the Catholic presence coincided implicitly with a working assumption that English Renaissance literature was by definition a Protestant literature, the historical and critical emphases that will replace that construct are not yet clear. At the very least, a revisionist account needs to take in hand the degree to which Catholics remained in dialogue with Protestants. That recognition both reintroduces the Catholic activity and clarifies the degree to which Protestant writing was not merely anti-Catholic in general, but often constituted a reply to a specific Catholic challenge. The introduction of Catholic matters into discussions that have been oblivious of any English Catholic presence also embellishes the list of historical events in relation to which one maps both literary and historical narratives. In outlining some areas where the introduction of Catholic topics, writers, and historical events alters the literary-historical narrative, this chapter also suggests how further work can continue to open up the field.

A convenient starting point is the early 1570s. Well known as a period of early Puritan agitating, the early 1570s were a time for sorting out what kind of post-Henrician church would dominate Elizabethan England, an effort that would continue into the seventeenth century but that would culminate for Elizabeth's reign by the early 1590s when the failure of Presbyterianism had become clear (Collinson 1967). In addition to this internecine Protestant conflict, the early 1570s were marked by a continuation of the Catholic resistance that had characterized the earlier years of Elizabeth's reign. Leaders of this resistance included Thomas Stapleton and John Harpsfield, both of whom had lost position in the church upon the accession of Queen Elizabeth and had become oppositionist polemicists on behalf of Catholicism. Thomas Stapleton, living in Louvain, produced an English translation of Bede's *Ecclesiastical History of England* together with the accompanying treatise *The Fortress of the Faith*, both in 1565. The ready Protestant response to this challenge came from John Foxe, who prepared a massive revision of *Actes and Monuments*, and in the dedication to Elizabeth referred to the objections to his 1563 edition that had been raised by Catholics across England and on the Continent. Adding to this 1570 edition the representation of the "Image of both churches," the series of woodcuts depicting "The proud primacie of Popes," and a lengthy section on the soldier and rebel Sir John Oldcastle in which he attacked the writing of John Harpsfield, Foxe also answered Stapleton's harking back to the early English church. Toward that end, he added the sections on the Saxons that continued John Bale's view of them as foreign oppressors. Exemplifying an ongoing Catholic and Protestant debate and dialogue, *Actes and Monuments* did not merely represent Protestant anti-Catholic views but answered the Catholic writers who were and would remain highly engaged in the defense of their religion (Hamilton 2003).

The year this edition appeared coincided with the Revolt of the Northern Earls, an event that was to acquire an iconic presence in the writing of both Catholics and Protestants well into the seventeenth century. The repeated reprinting of Thomas Norton's tract denouncing the Northern Rebellion, *To the Quenes Majesties Pore Deceived Subjects of the North Countrey, Drawen into Rebellion by the Earles of Northumberlanda and Westmerland*, in itself marks the significance of this event and makes all the more notable the printing of a collected edition of Norton's tracts, *All Such Treatises as have been Lately Published by Thomas Norton*, in 1570 (see Razzi, unpublished paper). This larger context identifies a moment when Norton achieved a level of authority and usefulness preliminary to his becoming one of the enforcers of the torture of Catholics in the 1580s. The direct topicality of Norton's writing in this period differs from that of Thomas North, whose career would be marked not by writing in his own voice but by translations. In the aftermath of the Northern Rebellion, North published in 1572

his translation of the *Moral Philosophie of Doni*, and dedicated it to
Robert Dudley, earl of Leicester, who had supported Thomas Howard,
duke of Norfolk, in his quest to wed Mary Queen of Scots. Given
Norfolk's execution in 1572 for this risky behavior, North's translation
of a work that represents the many perils of court intrigue might best
be read within the context of that event as well as in relationship to
earlier and later projects of North's, including his earlier translation of
Antonio de Guevara's *Diall of Princes*, dedicated to Mary Tudor, and his
translation from French of Plutarch's *Lives of the Noble Grecians and
Romanes*, printed in 1579. A work that has been of interest as source
material for Shakespeare's plays, North's Plutarch, like his earlier
Guevara, takes up the role of the emperor, a subject at the center of
debate on the relation of church and state throughout the sixteenth
and seventeenth centuries. If brought to bear on the body of North's
work, a conjoined Catholic–Protestant context offers the best possibility of our coming newly to terms with North's *Doni*, with his two larger
publishing projects, and thus with his positioning across the reigns of
two monarchs. Such work could also engage the ideological opportunities available to the translator, who is in a unique position of deni-
ability should his work offend and of favor should his work please.

Christopher Haigh once accounted for the neglect of sixteenth-
century English Catholics by attributing to A. G. Dickens a representation of the English Reformation that paralleled the rhetoric of John
Foxe (Haigh 1987: 3). But how much and what kind of presence in
England did Catholics have? Earlier historians argued that Catholicism lay dormant in England until the mid-1570s, when the Jesuits
arrived; later historians have argued for unbroken continuity (Bossy
1962; Haigh 1987). What we assume to have been the case greatly
affects the extent to which Catholicism can be regarded as having any
normal, regular, and apparent presence in the culture. If the Jesuits
did not themselves bring Catholicism, their return strengthened it and
Catholic resistance, especially in the form of recusancy, the refusal to
attend Protestant church services. As part of the effort to bring a halt
to Catholic worship, Visitation Orders written by Archbishop Grindal
and John Aylmer, bishop of London, inquired about incidences of
morris dancing, piping, and playing in the church and churchyards.
As part of the same effort of suppression, officials issued orders in
1572 and 1575 to shut down the Chester plays, and in 1579 the same
fate befell the Corpus Christi plays. In 1575 an Ecclesiastical Commission was inquiring into offenses against the Acts of Uniformity and
Supremacy, and in 1577, bishops received instructions to gather

information about the value of goods and lands held by recusants, toward the end of imposing fines and imprisonment for nonconformity (Clegg 1997: 120; Parmiter 1998–9). In November 1577, authorities executed the first priest, Cuthbert Mayne. In 1581, the fine for recusancy was set at £20 per month (Haigh 1993: 263).

Such actions placed a high premium on Catholic interests and sympathies. From 1579 to 1582, the queen's negotiations for marriage to the Catholic duke of Anjou became embroiled in arguments over the extent to which alliance with Catholic Europe would be to England's advantage or detriment, arguments that would continue through the reign of King James. Recent attention to the Catholic presence in England has added a new set of elements to the consideration of the Anjou negotiations, namely the return to England of Jesuits Edmund Campion and Robert Parsons in summer 1580. It was a closely watched event, and Campion made little effort to be unobtrusive. Rather he created a public stir by issuing direct challenges to the authorities in his *Decem Rationes* (*Ten Reasons*), a pamphlet that declared the primacy of the Catholic religion and that Campion had distributed for students in the pews of St Mary's church on the day of the Oxford commencement ceremonies. Arrested in July, 1581, Campion was tried, found guilty of treason, and executed along with other priests in December, 1581. As currently understood, Campion's activities and execution, in combination with the numerous events and publications that issued as a result of what has been called "the Campion affair" (Lake and Questier 2000), establish Campion as perhaps the single central addition to the new canon of events that literary, political, and ecclesiastical history of the period used to bypass but must now include. Even as the Northern Rebellion is central to a literary and historical narrative that includes Catholics, no recitation of key events and persons from this period can afford to omit Edmund Campion and the events surrounding his execution. Still, scholars will estimate the Campion impact differently. To Lake and Questier, the Campion affair illustrates an unusual moment when the public sphere was available to a cacophony of opinion, an openness even encouraged by the authorities whose interests it could advance (cf. McCoog 2001). However, with the execution of Campion and a succession of other priests, that public sphere closed in again. The executions silenced most overt resistance.

The complications of this suppression argue for close re-examination of virtually everything written during the 1560s, 1570s, and 1580s – all years that were long displaced from the attention of literary scholars by the halo effect of Protestant dominance in the 1590s. In fact, and rarely noted, the literary narrative that has dominated Renaissance studies begins in earnest only in 1579, with Sir Philip Sidney and Edmund Spenser, moves on to the Marprelate tracts, and then to the deeply studied 1590s. As is readily apparent, anyone who turns back to the poetry, prose narratives, and translations of the 1560s, 1570s, and 1580s will find scant secondary material, modern editions of primary texts in short supply, and extraordinary opportunities – low-hanging fruit – for original and important work. For the three decades prior to 1590, both what was written and printed and the clientage networks that supported that writing require re-examination.

When one is on the look-out for it, Catholic–Protestant exchange, and not just Protestant one-sidedness, turns up repeatedly. For example, for the years 1579–82, the longstanding place that the anti-theatrical tracts have held as documents important to early theatre history bears continued scrutiny. Written between 1579 and 1582, Stephen Gosson's attack on the arts in *The Schoole of Abuse* (1579); Thomas Lodge's *Reply to Gosson*, a work defending the arts (1579 or 1580); Anthony Munday's attack in *A Second and Third Blast of Retrait* (1580); and Gosson's *Plays Confuted*, a reply to Lodge that followed in 1582, fall squarely across the fraught Catholic–Protestant context we have been considering. (Sir Philip Sidney's manuscript *Defence of Poesy* was apparently written during 1582 – 3.) While surely the tracts' focus on the arts carried more than one agenda, including an interest in dissuading employees and apprentices from leaving work to go to a play, Gosson's initial attack also represents at least an indirect assault on Catholics, something Lodge apparently understood and at which he took offense (Hamilton2005: 18 – 20). During the 1570s, Lodge was a student at Trinity College, Oxford, where Catholic presence remained strong. After the execution of Robert Southwell in 1596, he lived publicly as a Catholic and was often cited for recusancy. Mimicking Gosson's mystifying style filled with classical examples, Lodge's *Reply to Gosson* also relies on the classics, but his defense not only of music but also of piping is one of the details that tilts his work in the direction of a Catholic defense. The fact that Lodge's tract was immediately suppressed indicates the limits in the public sphere for this writer on this topic. Printed after the execution of Campion and also after the Anjou negotiations had ended, Gosson's next tract, *Plays Confuted in Five Actions Proving that they are Not to be Suffred in a Christian Common Weale, by the Waye both the Cavils of Thomas Lodge, and the Play of Playe* (1582), shifts away from classical examples to a direct attack on Lodge, as well as on images, idolatry, wrong religion, Italian devices, and even "the corruption of the *Corpus Christi* Playes that

were set out by the Papistes.'' Not the formulaic and generalized Protestant response that it has seemed, Gosson's response was contingent
not only on Lodge's earlier reply to him but on the anti-Catholicism
required by the fall-out from Campion's execution. While the anti-
Catholicism of Gosson's second tract is evident to any reader, the
significance of that rhetoric is lost on the modern reader who assumes
that such rhetoric was formulaic to a strongly Protestant position rather
than a participant in a dynamic exchange.

More than that, by means of the terms of Campion's execution,
the government defined the categories within which English Catholics could live and work safely and thus within which individual
Catholics might construct their identity. Whereas Catholic priests and
others practicing Catholicism insisted that their interests were based
only in their religion, death on behalf of which would allow them to
die as martyrs, the government insisted that Catholics who refused
conformity and who refused to deny allegiance to the pope were
guilty of treason. For the Catholic headed for death, the defining
binaries were thus treason or religion. A related but different set of
defining terms, important to those who decided to try to stay alive,
were treason or loyalty, a set of opposing concepts that, like the event
of Campion's execution, have now become standard to the lexicon of
English Renaissance studies. While we might take it for granted that
subjects were to be loyal, for the English Catholic subjects loyalty
carried a different dimension. However else they had or had not
adjusted their behavior or beliefs, they had to show themselves to
be loyal to England and the monarch. Implicit in this requirement
was recognition by the authorities that Catholicism continued to exist
in England, and recognition by Catholics that for most of them, safety
in England depended on an adjustment at the very least of their
public personae (Holmes 1981; Walsham 1993; Gallagher 1991;
Shell 1999; Marotti 2000). Understanding the options for these adjustments opens up new possibilities for research, on prominent
writers who masked their Catholicism and on minor writers whose
work has seemed to have little relevance to the important themes and
issues of the period. This new understanding can also alter the va-
lency of numerous references to concepts of loyalty and treason in the
poetry, drama, and prose narratives of the period.

The most commonly repeated narrative that accounts for and
describes the developing literary system (Helgerson 1992, 1983;
Marotti 1995) during the late 1570s to late 1590s presents one example
of how recognition of these options may modify that narrative. We

have understood that during the 1579–82 period, not only Sidney but also Edmund Spenser made some moves to indicate his place within the Protestant cause. In *The Shepheardes Calender* (1579), a work constructed for an exclusive audience, the prefatory materials, woodcuts, allusions to Virgil, and range of subject matter present the poet as worthy to take his place among those who were self-consciously shaping England's Protestant national identity. While Spenser deployed pastoral conventions to promote classical and medieval traditions, he also made them newly contemporary. He criticizes Elizabeth's desire to marry Anjou, and in three ecclesiastical eclogues – May, July, and September – warns about the threatening presence of Jesuits in England, while lamenting the fate of Archbishop Grindal, now fallen out of favor with the queen for having insisted on more preaching than she cared to permit. Registering a standard anti-Catholic view, as well as some of the discord that existed among Protestants, Spenser is understood to have also associated himself and his poem with the religious politics of Robert Dudley, earl of Leicester, who, following the Northern Rebellion, had repositioned himself more clearly as. a Protestant leader.

Conjoined to a certain understanding of the developing literary system has been an investment as well in notions of Spenser's laureate status and of the existence of a Spenser circle – the group addressed in *The Shepheardes Calender* and writers who later associated with Spenser. Among them, Thomas Watson, given his lyric elegance and Petrarchan sophistication, has seemed a particularly appealing addition. However, scholars focused primarily on Spenser have usually passed over Watson's connections to Catholic circles. During several months in 1576 and 1577, Watson spent time at the English College at Douay, home to some of the most distinguished and influential exiled English Catholics, including William Allen, Thomas Stapleton, and Gregory Martin. Watson's dedications in the 1580s to Philip Howard, earl of Arundel, Edward de Vere, earl of Oxford, and Henry Percy (whose father, the eighth earl of Northumberland, had been in prison for plotting Elizabeth's death) suggest his connections within the Catholic clientage circle. In the early 1590s, the Catholic William Cornwallis hired Watson to be his son's tutor (Eccles 1934: 42).

Understandably, Watson's *Hekatompathia* occupies a standard place in discussions of the development of English poetry. An early sonnet sequence, *Hekatompathia* first existed in manuscript as a group of seventy-eight poems modeled on Petrarchan sonnets. In 1582, the work, now expanded to 100 tripartite sonnets and dedicated to the earl of Oxford, includes seventy-nine untitled sonnets, and a final twenty-one all with the same title, "My love is past." The urgency of the early 1580s religious-political situation may provide more pointed information about the exigency of this sequence than do traditions of verse.

The publication of *Hekatompathia* in 1582 places it after Oxford had defected from Catholicism in December–January 1581 and also after the December 1581 execution of Campion, that period that resulted in the publication of Gosson's *Plays Confuted*. But Watson's task, related to that of Gosson, was also quite different. Like Petrarch, who ultimately abandons his love for Laura in order to serve the Virgin Mary, the speaker in *Hekatompathia* also withdraws from his love, until he can finally say, "My love is past." While the reader is allowed to consider this love as love of woman, a more likely conclusion is that Watson is using this imitation of Petrarch to announce his renunciation of his preferred Catholic religion. As such, the sonnet sequence stands as a public declaration of political loyalty and at the same time as a display of the art that might qualify him for patronage within an established coterie of approved Protestant poets (Hamilton 2005: 34–5).

Theatres too had patrons and clients. With the publication of a major new study of the Queen's Men, we now have an authoritative account of the Protestant ideological mission of that company (McMillin and MacLean 1998: 18–36). A company organized by Sir Frances Walsingham with actors pulled from a combination of other companies, the Queen's Men came on the scene in 1583, just prior to the translation of John Whitgift to the position of archbishop of Canterbury in 1584. The Queen's Men's play *Friar Bacon and Friar Bungay* is obvious about its anti-Catholicism, even as the Catholic sympathies of Anthony Munday's *John a Kent and John a Cumber*, probably intended for Lord Strange's Men, are easy to access once we think of looking for them. But other plays and playwrights remain less accessible, in part because not all writers write about religion directly, but invert or transform the religious ideologies that hold philosophical or topical interest for author and audience.

Christopher Marlowe's *Dr Faustus* may be a play in that category. Performed for the first time in 1594 by Lord Admiral's Men, the year following Marlowe's death, *Dr Faustus* was written sometime between 1589 and 1592 (Kinney 1999: 158; Gill 1990: xv–xix). Its basic elements are indisputable: a protagonist who in his discontent signs his soul over to the devil in order to pursue his desires, and a morality framework in which Good and Evil angels compete for his soul. The play is variously read, as a morality play with the shocking ending in which Christian man does not repent and goes to hell, as a representation of the mind of an atheist who is challenging Christian categories, as an engagement with occult philosophy and disparagement of the learning available at the university (Gill 1990; Davidson 1996; Kinney 1999). There is yet another context that may have some relevance to the play: the trial and execution of priests and other condemned traitors. What allows this speculation is familiarity with the formulae used for executions as reported in pamphlets.

An early record of this type exists in *A Breefe and True Reporte, of the Execution of Certaine Traytours at Tiborne* (1582), where Anthony Munday reported on the execution of seven priests, four on May 28, 1582, and five on May 30, and narrated in succession for each execution the routine that was followed. First, Sheriff Richard Martin promised the priest that life could be had for the decision to become a loyal subject. Next, representatives of the church called upon the priests to repent. When the priests responded by declaring that they would die Catholics, they were taken off to be hanged. In order to understand more fully the politics of this sequence, we should note that on this occasion William Charke was the minister for the executions of William Filbie and Lucas Kirby, and John Field for the execution of Thomas Cottam. Charke and Field were ringleaders within the radical Presbyterian movement that continued to give the ecclesiastical authorities so much trouble as the 1580s wore on. However, even as the authorities did not require conformity from radical Puritans in Lancashire, a Catholic stronghold, so did they find additional use for Protestant radicals in London. These Protestants' church politics may have been problematic, but their vehemence against Catholics was always useful.

By 1588, when thirty-one Catholics were executed in the aftermath of the Spanish Armada, and fourteen more on August 28 and 30 (*Miscellanea* 32: 404–10), this formula for proceeding seems to have been even more thoroughly institutionalized. In the anonymous tract *A True Report of the Inditement, Arraignment, Conviction, Condemnation, and Execution of John Weldon, William Hartley, and Robert Sutton*, which reports executions again on October 5, 1588, the author narrates how in each instance the preacher (not named this time) tried to persuade the accused to repentance and religious conformity, and the sheriff repeated the charge of treason, clarifying that these deaths could not be construed as a martyrdom. Also in each case, the Catholic remains defiant, and declares he will not pray with them and will die a Catholic – at which point, each is executed.

Dr Faustus cannot be said to be a replay of these scenes. None of the material is strictly parallel between play and pamphlet. But in both, there is a defiant protagonist, whose determined deviance from orthodoxy is made the subject of correcting pleas, and who in ultimately refusing correction goes to his death. If the language and formulae for treason and execution did not furnish a primary model for *Dr Faustus*, reminiscence of that context suggests another way to understand the ambiguity of the play. Any number of tracts might embellish the point. In *The Censure of a Loyall Subject: Upon Certaine Noted Speach & Behaviours of those Fourteen Notable Traitors*, a tract on the fourteen Babington conspirators executed in 1586 for conspiring to put Mary Stuart on the throne, George Whetstone explained that the conspirators were mere reprobates: "Those whose hearts it pleaseth God to harden, have neither eies to looke into their owne danger," and further declared that "Destruction followeth presumption."

Whatever elements Marlowe imaginatively assembled in putting *Dr Faustus* together, he made Faustus tantalizing in his intellectual reach and boldness and simultaneously foolish and deluded. Unwilling or unable to recognize the power of those who can undo him, especially the power of Mephistopheles, he careens forward making himself look more and more vulnerable. Sharply orthodox in its representation of punishment for separating oneself from right belief, the play also suggests more circumspectly the absolute power that stands against anyone who challenges the system. As a group, the Good and Evil angels, the Old Man, and Mephistopheles, all of whom try to get Faustus to do what each of them desires, not only hearken back to the medieval morality play, but capture the contemporary church–state battle for subjects' allegiance, the stakes of which were at least comparable to those represented in Marlowe's Wittenberg.

But we would not want to limit our thinking about *Dr Faustus* to the challenge posed by the Catholic faithful. Continuing Protestant reform movements offered their own challenge to authority. The Puritan movement of the 1570s and 1580s had criticized the use of the surplice associated with the pope and with bishops, and eschewed kneeling and the use of the cross in baptism. The Presbyterian movement that Charke and Field had led attacked the establishment on other grounds, because their program advocated parity among ministers and autonomy for individual congregations, views that challenged the underpinnings of both episcopacy and monarchy. In London, John Field had established such a significant network of churches devoted to the presbytery that it became possible to see the movement as a church within a church, or, as Thomas Fuller characterized it, "presbytery in episcopacy" (Collinson 1967: 329). To break the stride of this movement, the newly appointed archbishop of Canterbury, John Whitgift, crafted a set of interrogatories to which ministers and parishioners might be asked to reply. Not unlike the system of questions put to suspected Catholics to expose their allegiances, these interrogatories queried whether the subject had subscribed to the Book of Common Prayer. What made the interrogatories particularly onerous was that anyone subjected to them was required first to take the oath *ex officio mero*, an oath that required that the subject swear to answer the questions truthfully before being told what the accusation was. Some of the most important trials of Protestants during this period centered on efforts to make such forced self-accusation or self-incrimination illegal, an effort that would not find success until 1641.

Among the large number of tracts and treatises produced in relation to the Presbyterian movement, the best-known are the Martin Marprelate tracts, printed in 1588 and 1589 on secret presses and distributed around London and at court. Their authorship remains unknown, and their brash satiric power continues to defy measure. What is certain is that they released into the popular culture as direct a challenge to episcopal hierarchy as England had witnessed, a challenge that had uneasy implications for the monarch and sat sharply askew from what was considered acceptable public discourse:

> You are those who maime, deform, vex, persecute, greeve, and wound the church. Which keepe the same in captivity and darknes, defend the blind leaders of the blind, slander, revile and deforme Christes holy government, that such broken and woodden members as you are may be still maintayned. (Marprelate 1589: D3^r)

Intense efforts to shut down the presses and identify the authors of these tracts ensued, even as the authorities hired writers to reply to Martin. The Marprelate tracts that refer to Anthony Munday raise now the issue of whether the authorities who hired Protestant extremists also hired Catholics and Catholic sympathizers. Certainly, John Lyly falls into the latter category and Anthony Munday into the former (Hamilton 2005: 36). Historians have also felt that Martin's strategy for attack triggered a degree of ire against the Presbyterians that hardened the intent to eliminate them, a point that has also been made in regard to Jesuit agitating on behalf of Catholicism in England. Ultimately, this movement would be broken by violence, events also comparable in intent to the execution of Campion and other priests. In 1591, in the midst of an effort to pass a parliamentary bill that would extend to nonconforming Protestants the harsh treatment condoned for Catholics, separatists Henry Barrow and John Greenwood were hanged. Several weeks later, one of the Presbyterian leaders, the suspected author of the Marprelate tracts, John Penry, was also executed. Marprelate's raucous characterizing of the bishops as the "plague and pestilence of our Church" would be answered in 1589 by Richard Bancroft, bishop of London, who, in his famous Paul's Cross sermon, countered with a statement that declared that the episcopacy possessed divine right status. In 1593, in *Dangerous Positions*, Bancroft identified the two most dangerous groups in England as the Jesuits and the Puritans.

As Annabel Patterson has shown, Renaissance history writing is also at issue for the study of early modern Catholicism. Her study of the additions written for the 1587 edition of Holinshed's *Chronicle of England, Scotland, and Ireland*, many of which were expurgated, confirm that "the trials of Edmund Campion and others accused of Jesuit conspiracy appear as *the* political events that define the period from 1570 through 1584" (Patterson 1994: 128). More important, Patterson finds in Holinshed not a one-sided view of Catholicism, but repeated evidence that the chroniclers intended to present various sides of the situation. Noting that Abraham Fleming reversed Munday's language in his report on Campion, so that now the report reads that Campion was executed "for religion not treason," and focusing on the ambivalence of Fleming's account of Sir John Oldcastle, Patterson argues that such reversals and ambivalence capture the diversity of opinion that was from the start a guiding principle for the *Chronicles*. In the same vein, she also refers us to the oddities in the account of the Babington conspirators, where Fleming's inclusion of Aesopian fables points as much to the cruelty perpetrated on the conspirators as to their threat to England (Patterson 1994: 130–53, 257–61).

In a related revisionist treatment of history writing, Patrick Collinson has argued that we must stop denying the Catholicism of John Stow, whose books inspected in 1569 by government officials suspicious of his popery contained "a fairly complete library of the up-to-date Catholic literature of the English Counter-Reformation" (Collinson 2001: 42). Despite some signs in Stow's work of religious conformity, Collinson insists that Stow's Catholicism, captured especially in his antiquarianism, be taken for granted.

Explicit in the theses of both Patterson and Collinson is the notion that then as now the historical account was disputed territory. Stow staked his claim to a version of history that differed from that of Richard Grafton, Foxe to a version that differed from Nicholas Harpsfield's, Holinshed and his team of writers to a version that differed from Edward Hall's. Knowledge of the argument that shaped the result is easily lost. Even as Foxe's narrative is better known than Harpsfield's, so is the Protestant antiquarian tradition a long-established aspect of scholarship on early modern ecclesiastical, monarchical, and republican traditions. Less attention has been given to the contrary antiquarian views represented in Thomas Stapleton's translation of Bede's *Ecclesiastical History* and *Fortress of the Faith*, in Richard Verstegan's *A Restitution of Decayed Intelligence* (1605), and even in Stow's *The Survey of London*. Publishing in London in 1605, Verstegan did not argue directly against the Protestant tradition as Stapleton had but, using a coded rhetorical style, represented Protestant history and policy as mere constructions, lacking authority and intended only to protect the new power structure. Erasing Catholic precedents, institutions, traditions, and practices, Foxe, Thomas Cooper, bishop of Winchester, William Cecil, and others had, in Verstegan's view, replaced authenticity with a self-interested revision that depended for its success not only on silencing contemporary Catholics, but on eliminating from the historical and cultural record the basis on which English society rested (Hamilton 1999). Without knowledge of Stapleton's early challenges and Verstegan's later challenge, the rhetorical tenor of the Protestant accounts disappears from view. Here as in other cases, the Catholic context is the missing link that is needed to clarify which of the details were under contestation, including Elizabeth's association with Constantine, an association that Catholics preferred to own.

The history writing of Anthony Munday provides another example. Author of political tracts, poems, and plays during the Elizabethan decades, under James I and Charles I, Munday also produced some histories: *A Chronicle of the Successe of Times* (1611) and, in 1618 and 1633, two revisions of Stow's *The Survey of London*. Always covered with a shroud of English loyalism, Munday's Catholic sympathies can be elusive. However, the most easily accessible and conclusive evidence of his Catholicism resides in his history writing, where, without announcing polemically his own position, Munday could nevertheless record details that reintroduce Catholic records. For example, in his second revision of Stow's *The Survey of London* (1633), Munday included a report on the catastrophe that had occurred on October 26,

1623, known as the Fatal Vesper, in which as many as ninety Catholics died when the building in Blackfriars where 300 Catholics were holding a clandestine church service collapsed. Of the several pamphlets from which Munday could have taken his account, he chose not to summarize but rather to reprint the one that has been identified as containing a Catholic perspective, *The Fatall Vesper, or a True and Punctuall Relation of that Lamentable and Fearefull Accident*, by the unidentified W. C., a pamphlet that was immediately called in (Freeman 1967; Hamilton 2005: 188–9). Here as elsewhere, omission from our scholarship of the context of Catholic intervention results in an unnecessarily incomplete history of Renaissance literature that continues, if only by default and unintentionally, the Protestant polemic that was Elizabeth's goal.

While it is possible to recover with a considerable degree of specificity the opposing views represented by early modern history writing, that opposition has seemed less easily applied to the study of drama and especially to the drama of Shakespeare and his contemporaries. Biographical information, patronage connections, and, as with Munday, the availability of writing in more than one genre all present opportunities for gaining insight into the ideological positions a poet for the theatre might be inclined to represent. Peter Lake's readings of Ben Jonson's drama before and after his 1610 conformity to Protestantism make a significant advance for plays that have seemed unrelated to religious-political issues (Lake 2002). In Lake's case, what enables his readings is familiarity with the Elizabethan Catholic critique of the policies of Queen Elizabeth and William Cecil, Lord Burghley. As Lake understands, that critique was repeated in numerous documents that became part of the established canon on this topic: John Leslie's *Treatise of Treasons* (1572), the anonymous *Leicester's Commonwealth* (1584), and Richard Verstegan's *An Advertisement Written to a Secretarie of my L. Treasurers of Ingland* (1592) and *A Declaration of the True Causes of the Great Troubles, Presupposed to be Intended against the Realme of England* (1592). Not a place to look for ideas that confirm a concept of monarchical republicanism, these documents depict Elizabeth's councilors as base fellows who rose to high places through vicious and self-interested treachery. While sometimes bemoaned as the unwitting lady steered about by evil men, Elizabeth emerges ultimately as the persecutor who promulgated tyranny. Read with knowledge of these texts, the tyranny Jonson represents in *Sejanus* becomes a recollection of what Catholics had endured during the reign of Elizabeth, a pattern King

James needed to eschew while also recognizing the legitimacy and loyalty of the English Catholics.

Robert Parsons's *A Conference about the Next Succession to the Crowne of Ingland* (1594) can prove similarly suggestive. Debunking Protestant claims regarding what constitutes a legitimate succession, Parsons lays out the grounds that had governed succession in England's past, arguing that deposition, election, by-passing the first born, and foreign birth have all been legitimated by English precedent and should continue their authority. Featuring Richard III as analogous to Henry VIII, Parsons invites other comparisons between earlier English history and more recent times. According to his account, Richard II was justly deposed for perverting the law and doing violence to subjects (Parsons 1594: sig. V4). Central to his argument is the lineage of John of Gaunt, first married to Lady Blanch of Portugal, and from whom descends Arbella Stuart, daughter of Charles Stuart, earl of Lennox, and Parsons's choice to succeed Elizabeth. As Richard Dutton has argued, the history of Gaunt, well known in the sixteenth century, deserves to be brought to bear on readings of *Richard II* and *1 Henry IV* (Dutton 1998). However one assesses Shakespeare's relationship to religious issues – and Parsons's book may or may not affect that assessment – the contemporary availability of that book provided at the time an interpretation of the history of the houses of York and Lancaster that contested the Tudors' own mythology. With or without religion, Shakespeare's relentless interrogation of the nature of monarchy and succession aligns in certain ways with Parsons's.

More information about theatrical patronage and licensing can also change the critical landscape. In addition to Dutton's chapter in this volume, there is Susan Cerasano's suggestive description elsewhere of the patronage network of Philip Henslowe and Edward Alleyn. Arguing that Henslowe's and Alleyn's connections mark them as "patrician and politically conservative" (Cerasano 2001: 82), Cerasano describes the elite family connections they had inherited, and which they proceeded to cultivate in the 1590s. Primarily situated among the "Sussex gentry and nobilty," Alleyn's connections "encompassed all branches of the Howard family, including the earls of Arundel" (p. 83). Although Cerasano never mentions religion or religious affiliation, and although some of the Howards were certainly Protestant, the Howard family also included during the reigns of Elizabeth and James powerful Catholics as well as members who were executed for treason. In the wake of the Northern Rebellion, Thomas Howard, duke of Norfolk, had been executed in 1572 for his connections to Mary Queen of Scots.

Having moved toward Catholicism by the late 1570s and thereafter openly defied conformity, Philip Howard, earl of Arundel, was tried in 1589 for treason and confined to the Tower until his death in 1595 (May 1999: 214–15). Taken along with the Catholic Henry Wriothesley, earl of Southampton, into James I's Privy Council, Henry Howard, earl of Northampton, conformed outwardly, but remained an influential crypto-Catholic (Peck 1982: 8–9, 51–5, 111–13). The Catholic William Byrd dedicated *Gradualia* to him in 1605 (Byrd 1976–89: V, xiii–iv, xxxi, xxxvi–vii; Monson 1997: 348–74).

According to Cerasano, the Sussex aristocracy – among which were the Sussex Howards, earls of Arundel – were central as well to Henslowe and Alleyn. In the early 1560s, Edward Alleyn, Sr, threatened with loss of the keepership of Bedlam, received support for his cause from Henry Fitzalan, twelfth earl of Arundel. Especially prominent during the reign of Mary Tudor, this Arundel (1512–80) had two daughters. Mary wed Thomas Howard, later fourth duke of Norfolk; Mary died in 1557, shortly after giving birth to Philip Howard. Arundel's other daughter, Jane Fitzalan, married the committed Catholic John Lumley, Baron Lumley, whose father had been executed for participating in the Pilgrimage of Grace. Lumley was implicated in the Ridolfi Plot of 1571 and in the negotiations for the marriage of Thomas Howard to Queen Mary. Gregory Martin dedicated a manuscript to Arundel before leaving for Douay, and William Byrd dedicated one of his books to Lumley (see *Dictionary of National Biography*).

Associated with the Sussex Howards were important gentry families, including the Lewkenors. Cerasano mentions that Sir Lewis Lewkenor, who served as Master of Ceremonies, would have known Henslowe and Alleyn. Because she does not talk about religion, she does not mention that Lewkenor had conformed only in 1594 and would be rumored to have reverted to Catholicism in the 1620s (Loomie 1978: 98–105). Lewkenor published several works in 1594 that represented his conformed loyalty, including *The Estate of English Fugitives under the King of Spaine and his Ministers* (1595), which records the hispanophile activities of William Stanley in Deventer. Classifying past English–Spanish connections, Lewkenor listed several "English gentlemen of good houses that have perished in the King of Spaines service," including "Henrie Carew, Edward Allen" (Lewkenor 1595: E4[r]). In 1594, Ferdinando Stanley, brother to William Stanley and patron of Lord Strange's Men, had died under presumably strange circumstances shortly after the rumors that the Catholics were interested in his supplanting Elizabeth. At about the same time, the break-up of a number of theatre companies, including both Lord Strange's Men and the Queen's Men, led next to what would be a longstanding dominance of two companies, the Chamberlain's Men and the Admiral's Men, the latter controlled by the Howards.

As suggested, Cerasano's detailed account of the Henslowe–Alleyn connections documents an alignment with the conservative establishment that had close ties to the crown. More than anything else, such connections acknowledged the past and ongoing power of the Howard family. If one wishes to gauge the extent to which religion was at issue in this exchange of favor, one needs to go meticulously year by year and person by person, so complex and changing are the religious and political fields. Taken whole, however, the Henslowe–Alleyn–Howard connections do offer another opportunity to build into the history of 1590s drama a more confident acknowledgment of the presence of English Catholics and their interests in local and national politics. Proposed readings that accommodate such interests, such as Lake's (2002) work on Jonson, can begin the process of restoring to the literary history of Renaissance England the understanding of a continued English Catholic presence and accommodation throughout the reign of Elizabeth and during the reign of James. That history needs eventually to acknowledge that there existed under both monarchs a broad range within which Catholics loyal to England could exist in safety and make their influence felt and known, and that, whatever one's religion, that was not always the identity that mattered most in economic or social endeavors. Moreover, there existed broad – though sometimes intermittent – understanding that Spain and other Catholic nations could be immensely valuable to England's safety and success.

Moments of religious-political crisis or moments when the opposition was given virtually free rein provide convenient points of entry for this work. During the reign of Elizabeth, the points of crisis include the Northern Rebellion, the Anjou marriage negotiations, the execution of Campion, the defeat of the Spanish Armada, and the early 1590s. During the reign of James, they include the Gunpowder Plot, the stir caused by his proposed Oath of Allegiance, and the marriage negotiations for Princess Elizabeth and Prince Charles. For the years to which they apply, these guidelines are useful for all writers, including Shakespeare. In the early 1590s, the relevant plays by Shakespeare include at least *Titus Andronicus* (now generally understood to be focused on persecutory tactics) and *The Comedy of Errors*, a play anchored in anxiety about the church's capacity for inclusion. *Sir Thomas More*, which also dates from this period, contains a passage by Shakespeare on the need to be loyal.

Shakespeare's Gunpowder Plot play is indisputably *Macbeth*, a play that was not printed until it appeared in the First Folio in 1623 and has been thought to exist there in an abridged form. Like *Dr Faustus*, the play focuses on a figure whose decision to violate orthodoxy results in his destruction. Also as in *Dr Faustus*, the representation of this choice is shrouded in ambiguity. Macbeth lives in the world he inhabits as one steeped in equivocation, from which mode of being he justifies his actions. Drawing on the work of Stanley Cavell, Kent Cartwright writes on the skepticism inherent in *Macbeth*, which is created in part by a sense of an exterior world that is as unknowable as any person's interior world (Cartwright 2002). Surely, the religious wars of post-Reformation England and Europe bred skepticism, as individuals and nations careened back and forth between opposing religious allegiances. But if *Macbeth* participates in that drama of indecision, it also acknowledges the requisite hiddenness of identities that have been deemed unorthodox. In Protestant England these included both the need to hide one's Catholicism and the tempest of feelings that such hiding caused in many, including the Gunpowder plotters. As in *Dr Faustus*, in *Macbeth* too the supernatural competes for the hero's allegiance. And like Faustus choosing Mephistopheles over the Good Angel, Macbeth takes from the witches' warnings a story that matches his own ambition. Amenable to many readings and however incomplete or changed from its original, *Macbeth* registers a contempt for regicide as well as a representation of the combination of circumstances that can produce such a choice.

Like *Macbeth*, the main plot of *Cymbeline* takes an unequivocal line on behalf of orthodoxy, this time an orthodoxy that matches James's advocacy of an Oath of Allegiance that would require Catholics to swear allegiance to him as a temporal ruler. Written close to the time that Jonson finally found it necessary to conform, *Cymbeline* takes the standard line that one must render to Caesar what is Caesar's, that is, honor the authority of temporal rule. In the subplot of the exiled Belarius, however, Shakespeare represents the outsidedness that previous political decisions have created. In the sequence where Belarius is finally persuaded to withdraw from his chosen marginality and return to public life, Shakespeare takes up just as directly the mistakenness of any who choose to eschew the center, the option for Catholics who would listen to the archpriest Blackwell and refuse allegiance to James. Shakespeare represents such withdrawal as suicide, the same position John Donne took in *Pseudo-Martyr* (1610) when he denied that such choices could be dignified as martyrdom. To the extent that this reading works for readers other than myself, there is nothing in the reading itself that identifies the religion of the author. There is, however, much in the play that indicates that Shakespeare was representing and aligning with the policy of King James at this time.

Even as a list gradually grows of authors and works that map Catholic issues in the English Renaissance, certain progress on English Catholic writing will not go forward unless it is taken up by scholars with working knowledge of Catholic Europe. The genre of chivalric romance offers a case in point. Many of the romances that circulated in England were translations of Spanish, Italian, and French works – all Catholic in their originating versions. As I have suggested elsewhere (Hamilton 2005: 78 – 9), for Munday to translate these works into English, making only minor revisions, was tantamount to smuggling in foreign books with Catholic ideologies and worldview. To understand the broader implications of such importation one needs to have an understanding of the significance of the romance in its own originating time and culture, the starting point for the significance it will have when transferred to a different culture. Most importantly, in the European romances written between 1530 and 1560, we can expect at least some representation of the European perspective on what was happening in England with regard to Henry's break with Rome, Mary Tudor's reign and marriage to Philip I, and Elizabeth's succession. In the Munday translations I have studied, these issues appear most certainly, with the European works providing a way to transfer to England a critique of England's religious and political deviance, as well as the ideology of the competing view. Much more work remains to be done both on the romances Munday translated and on those by other Catholic translators, including Richard Harington and his translation of *Orlando Furioso*. That work can then re-engage the chivalric investment of Sidney, Spenser, and Mary Wroth.

In David Norbrook's essay on the "Elizabethan World Picture," he argued that one might substitute "generalising readings of the renaissance mentality" that are philosophical with readings that are rhetorical. This substitution, he argued, has the result of displacing monolithic constructions with readings that take more account of rhetorical aspects of writing, and thus with a broader understanding that rhetoric encouraged "a general pressure toward wider debate and discussion of public issues" (1994: 141). Catholic and Protestant writing can benefit from a similar procedural and methodological move. Restoring awareness of the Catholic voices to our knowledge base does not displace Protestant writers, but rather provides a more complete record of what they too were about.

References and Further Reading

Bossy, John. 1962. "The Character of Elizabethan Catholicism," *Past and Present* 21: 41, 39 – 59.

Byrd, William. 1976 – 89. *Gradualia*, in Philip Brett, ed., *The Byrd Edition*, 16 vols. London: Stainer and Bell, V, xiii – xiv, xxxi, xxxvi – xxxvii.

Cartwright, Kent. 2002. "Scepticism and Theatre in *Macbeth*," *Shakespeare Survey* 55: 219 – 36.

Cerasano, S. P. 2001. "The Patronage Network of Philip Henslowe and Edward Alleyn," *Medieval and Renaissance Drama in England* 13: 82 – 92.

Clegg, Cyndia Susan. 1997. *Press Censorship in Elizabethan England*. Cambridge: Cambridge University Press.

Collinson, Patrick. 1967. *The Elizabethan Puritan Movement*. Berkeley: University of California Press.

Collinson, Patrick. 2001. "John Stow and Nostalgic Antiquarianism," in J. F. Merritt, ed., *Imagining Early Modern London: Perceptions and Portrayals of the City from Stow to Strype, 1598 – 1720*. Cambridge: Cambridge University Press, pp. 27 – 51.

Davidson, Nicholas. 1996. "Christopher Marlowe and Atheism," in Darryll Grantley and Peter Roberts, eds., *Christopher Marlowe and English Renaissance Culture*. Aldershot, Brookfield, Singapore, and Sidney: Ashgate, pp. 129 – 47.

Dutton, Richard. 1998. "Shakespeare and Lancaster," *Shakespeare Quarterly* 49. 1 – 21.

Eccles, Mark. 1934. *Christopher Marlowe in London*. Cambridge, MA: Harvard University Press.

Freeman, Arthur. 1967. "'The Fatal Vesper' and 'The Doleful Evensong': Claim-Jumping in 1623," *Library* (5th ser.), 22: 128 – 35.

Gallagher, Lowell. 1991. *Medusa's Gaze: Casuistry and Conscience in the Renaissance*. Stanford: Stanford University Press.

Gill, Roma, ed. 1990. *Dr. Faustus*, in *The Complete Works of Christopher Marlowe*, vol. 2. Oxford: Clarendon Press.

Haigh, Christopher. 1987. *The English Reformation Revised*. Cambridge: Cambridge University Press.

Haigh, Christopher. 1993. *English Reformations: Religion, Politics, and Society under the Tudors*. Oxford: Clarendon Press; New York: Oxford University Press.

Hamilton, Donna B. 1992. *Shakespeare and the Politics of Protestant England*. Hampstead: Harvester Wheatsheaf; Lexington: University of Kentucky.

Hamilton, Donna B. 1999. "Richard Verstegan's *A Restitution of Decayed Intelligence* (1605): A Catholic Antiquarian Replies to John Cooper, John Fox, and Jean Bodin," *Prose Studies* 22:1 – 38.

Hamilton, Donna B. 2003. "Catholic Use of Anglo-Saxon Precedents, 1565 – 1625: Thomas Stapleton, Nicholas Harpsfield, Robert Persons, Richard Verstegan, Richard Broughton and Others," *Recusant History* 26: 537 – 55.

Hamilton, Donna B. 2005. *Anthony Munday and the Catholics: 1560 – 1633.* Aldershot and Burlington: Ashgate.

Helgerson, Richard. 1983. *Self-Crowned Laureates: Spenser, Jonson, Milton, and the Literary System.* Berkeley: University of California Press.

Helgerson, Richard. 1992. *Forms of Nationhood: The Elizabethan Writing of England.* Chicago and London: University of Chicago Press.

Holmes, P. J., ed. 1981. *Elizabethan Casuistry.* London: Catholic Record Society.

Kinney, Arthur, ed. 1999. *The Tragicall History of Dr. Faustus*, in *Renaissance Drama.* Oxford and Malden: Blackwell.

Lake, Peter. 2002. "Ben Jonson and the Politics of Roman (Catholic) Virtue." Lecture at the University of Maryland, November 21.

Lake, Peter and Michael Questier. 2000. "Puritans, Papists, and the 'Public Sphere' in Early Modern England: The Edmund Campion Affair in Context," *Journal of Modern History* 72: 587 – 627.

Lewkenor, Lewis. 1595. *The Estate of English Fugitives under the King of Spaine and his Ministers.* London.

Loomie, Albert J. 1978. *Spain and the Jacobean Catholics. Volume II: 1613 – 1624.* Thetford: Catholic Record Society.

McCoog, Thomas M., S. J. 2001. "The English Jesuit Mission and the French Match, 1579 – 81," *Catholic Historical Review* 87: 185 – 213.

McMillin, Scott and Sally-Beth MacLean. 1998. *The Queen's Men and their Plays.* Cambridge: Cambridge University Press.

Marotti, Arthur F. 1995. *Manuscript, Print, and the English Renaissance Lyric.* Ithaca, NY: Cornell University Press.

Marotti, Arthur F. 2000. "Manuscript Transmission and the Catholic Martyrdom Account in Early Modern England," in Arthur F. Marotti and Michael D. Bristol, eds., *Print, Manuscript, and Performance: The Changing Relations of the Media in Early Modern England.* Columbus, OH: Ohio State University Press, pp. 172 – 99.

Marotti, Arthur. 2005. *Religious Ideology and Cultural Fantasy: Catholic and Anti-Catholic Discourses in Early Modern England.* Notre Dame, IN: University of Notre Dame.

Marprelate, Martin, *pseudo.* 1589. *Hayany Worke for Cooper.* London.

May, Steven W. 1999. *The Elizabethan Courtier Poets: The Poems and Their Contexts.* Asheville, NC: Pegasus Press.

Miscellanea 32. 1932. London: Catholic Record Society.

Monson, Craig. 1997. "Byrd, Catholics, and the Motet: The Hearing Reopened," in Dolores Pesce, ed., *Hearing the Motet.* Oxford: Oxford University Press, pp. 348 – 74.

Norbrook, David. 1994. "Rhetoric, Ideology, and the Elizabethan World Picture," in Peter Mack, ed., *Renaissance Rhetoric.* New York: St Martin's Press.

Parmiter, Geoffrey de C. 1988 – 9. "The Imprisonment of Papists in Private Castles," *Recusant History* 19: 16 – 38.

Parsons, Robert. 1594. *A Conference about the Next Succession to the Crowne of Ingland*. [Antwerp.]

Patterson, Annabel. 1994. *Reading Holinshed's Chronicles*. Chicago: University of Chicago Press.

Peck, Linda Levy. 1982. *Northampton: Patronage and Policy at the Court of James I*. London: George Allen and Unwin.

Razzi, Anthony W. (unpublished paper). "Gorboduc and the Early Elizabethan Polity."

Shell, Alison. 1999. *Catholicism, Controversy, and the English Literary Imagination, 1558 – 1660*. Cambridge: Cambridge University Press.

Walsham, Alexandra. 1993. *Church Papists: Catholicism, Conformity and Confessional Polemic in Early Modern England*. Woodbridge and Rochester: Boydell & Brewer.

Chapter 3

Royal Marriage and the Royal Succession

Paul E. J. Hammer

In August, 1578, Elizabeth I made a grand ceremonial visit to Norwich, the second-largest city in her realm, as part of a progress through East Anglia (Dovey 1996). Over the course of her six-day stay at Norwich, the queen was entertained with a busy schedule of public speeches, performances, and hunting trips. On the evening before her departure from the city, she was treated to an entertainment written by Henry Goldingham in which a procession of classical gods greeted her and bestowed symbolic gifts. The final – and hence most prominent – gift was a gold arrow from Cupid, who told the queen: "Shoote but this shafte at King or Caesar: He / And he is thine, and if thou wilte allowe" (B. G. 1578: sig. Eiii^v). Given the presence among the queen's company of ambassadors from France who had come to England to discuss Elizabeth's new interest in reviving the possibility of her marriage to the duke of Anjou, younger brother to the king of France, the significance of Cupid's device for securing a royal husband would have been lost on no one in the audience, least of all the queen herself. However, several of the other entertainments written and staged for the queen by Thomas Churchyard over the previous few days had offered a very different theme. This was most obvious in Churchyard's "device" on Tuesday August 19, which portrays Cupid after being "thrust out of Heaven" and confronted by "Dame Chastitie" and her maids Modesty, Temperance, Good Exercise, and Shamefastness. Dame Chastity and her maids evict Cupid from his coach, spoil "him of his counterfeyte Godhead and cloke and ... [take] away his bowe and his quiver of arrowes," reducing him to a state of vagabondage and the company of Wantonness and Riot (Churchyard 1578: sig. Di^r). Elizabeth's progress through East Anglia had the effect of demonstrating royal support for a Protestant reaction against recusancy in the region, and it is perhaps significant that Cupid seems to be associated with Catholicism. Like the notion of a "counterfeyte Godhead," the judgment of a Philosopher character – "Vayne Venus and blind Cupid both, and all the ragment rowe / And rabble of Gods, are fayned things" (ibid.: sig. E1^r) – seems to allude to the idolatry of which Catholics were routinely accused. More importantly, however, the entertainment turns into a paean to the magical and, more specifically, royal qualities associated with chastity itself: "Chast life may dwell alone … And sitte and rule in regall throne … Chast life a pretious pearle, doth shine as bright as sunne; / The fayre houre-glasse of dayes and yeares, that never out will runne" (Nichols 1823: II, 197). In contrast to the support for Elizabeth's pursuit of a match with Anjou that Goldingham's show implied, Churchyard's entertainment urged upon Elizabeth the attractions of foregoing marriage altogether in favor of "chast life."

The broader significance of the events at Norwich in August, 1578, can be gauged by the fact that this seems to be the first occasion when Elizabeth was openly encouraged by her subjects to consider abandoning the prospect of marriage in favor of an idealized, lifelong chastity. As John N. King has argued, representations of Elizabeth I cast her as an unmarried but nubile young woman until the early 1580s and as a perpetual virgin endowed with magical powers thereafter, with the intervening period of 1579–82 (when she pursued the prospect of marriage with Anjou) constituting a "liminal moment in the development of Elizabethan iconography" (King 1990: 55). However, one can go further, as Susan Doran has done, and argue that the creation of the image of Elizabeth as the Virgin Queen – with the soldier-poet Churchyard at its leading edge – was initially driven by a desire to counter the possibility that she might proceed with the French Match (Doran 1995). In other words, what is often termed the "cult of Elizabeth," with its myriad forms of extravagant praise for sacred female virginity, originated as a politically partisan construction by those who found the prospect of a French Catholic consort more immediately threatening than the political uncertainty that must ultimately accompany the queen's continued lack of a husband and heir. In this light, King's "liminal moment" was actually a period of political struggle in which conflicting views of royal marriage were played out across a range of different media. It is significant that a detailed description and texts of Churchyard's Norwich entertainments were hastily printed in London by a servant of Sir Christopher Hatton to serve as "a mirror and shining glasse, that al the whole land may loke into, or use it for an example in all places (where the Prince commeth) to our posteritie heereafter for ever" (Churchyard 1578:

sig. Aii^v). The political fashioning and national dissemination of this new "example" for entertaining Elizabeth shows that the "Virgin Queen" was an image that was being consciously imposed upon her. Although she later felt able to take up the mantle of Virgin Queen, and perhaps enjoy it to some degree, this role was not of her own devising or even reflective of her own impulses. The notion that Elizabeth was "always her own free woman," even in matters as intimate as her own iconography, is therefore as much of a romantic fiction as the much-repeated Jacobean myth that she always aspired to live and die a virgin because she saw her coronation in 1559 as a form of marriage to her kingdom (King 1990).

As Susan Doran shows in her authoritative study of Elizabeth's various courtships, the basic reason why the queen failed to marry was not for want of trying, but because she could not find a husband who was politically acceptable to a large enough proportion of the English political elite (Doran 1996). Elizabeth was perhaps unfortunate in succeeding England's first spinster queen, her older half-sister Mary I. Mary's marriage to Philip of Spain in 1554 not only triggered an almost-successful rebellion (Wyatt's Rebellion), but also sparked a widespread fear that England was being sacrificed to foreign interests, stirring a specifically anti-Spanish English patriotism that the all-English Elizabeth (her mother, unlike Mary's, being as English as her father) was able to capitalize on throughout the forty-five years of her reign. Mary's reinstitution of Catholicism (which Elizabeth promptly reversed) and intense persecution of Protestants also linked foreign marriage to fears of a revived Catholic Inquisition and the destruction of the freshly reconstituted Protestant England – fears that were exacerbated by the Protestant perception that the kings of Spain and France were bent upon the destruction of all Protestants, beginning with those in the Low Countries and France. The prospect of Elizabeth's marriage to a foreign Catholic prince consequently proved very difficult and stirred profound emotions among many of her subjects, while Protestant candidates either lacked sufficient prestige for a marriage alliance with one of the great crowns of Europe or brought awkward political baggage of other sorts, such as the prospect of entanglement in the bitter rivalry between Sweden and Denmark. Domestic candidates avoided the dangers associated with a foreign match, but raised even thornier problems of how subjects would react to the elevation of a former subject to royal status – especially as a wife was theoretically required to be obedient to her husband.

Most troublesome of all, in this regard, was the long-running suit of Robert Dudley, who was created earl of Leicester in 1564. Dudley was probably the love of Elizabeth's life and their intimacy in the opening years of her reign sometimes provoked scandalized comment both at home and abroad. However, the mysterious death of Dudley's wife in September, 1560, excited claims that she had been murdered to clear the way for his pursuit of the queen. The following month, Elizabeth seemed to confirm speculation about the seriousness of their relationship by ordering that a patent be drawn up to give Dudley the noble title that was necessary to make him a serious contender for her hand – only to change her mind at the last minute and slice the patent into pieces with a penknife. Dudley's subsequent attempts to prove his political worth, and win Spanish endorsement of his suit, by privately discussing with the Spanish ambassador the vexed issue of English participation in the Council of Trent only brought him further embarrassment and allowed him to be cast by his enemies as dangerously soft on Catholicism – and willing to do anything to marry the queen. This hostile interpretation seemed all the more compelling to those who opposed Dudley's suit because it revived memories of the unsuccessful attempt by his father, John Dudley, duke of Northumberland, to assume control over the crown on the death of Edward VI in 1553 by marrying his son Guildford Dudley to Jane Grey, the female heir nominated by the dying boy-king in preference to his half-sisters Mary and Elizabeth. In the eyes of his enemies, Dudley's pursuit of Elizabeth's hand in the early 1560s seemed like a fresh attempt to bring the crown of England into the hands of the Dudley family by marrying its female possessor.

Dudley's best chance to marry Elizabeth had passed by the middle of 1561, but the bond between them encouraged him to sustain his hopes and to work against the overtures of foreign suitors. For her part, Elizabeth's possessive attitude toward her "Sweet Robin" can be gauged by her extraordinary proposal in 1564 that he should marry the widowed Mary Queen of Scots, but that they should all live together at Elizabeth's Court in a kind of royal ménage à trois (Guy 2004: 193). By 1575, Leicester and Elizabeth were both aged 42 and the notion that they remained would-be suitor and potential bride was wearing thin. In July of that year, Leicester hosted the queen in extravagant fashion at his newly rebuilt seat of Kenilworth Castle in Warwickshire. This visit, which lasted eighteen days and involved the queen and her court in hunts, bear baiting, dancing, and a whole series of entertainments, provided Leicester with an unparalleled opportunity to dramatize the unresolved questions inherent in his relationship with Elizabeth (Frye 1993: 56–96). Having refrained from remarriage for so long (despite a quasi-matrimonial liaison with Douglas Sheffield over several years, which resulted in the birth of an illegitimate son in August, 1574), Leicester needed to know where he should look to find a mother for an heir to his earldom – to Elizabeth or elsewhere? Leicester also felt frustrated by his courtly life at a time when it seemed that urgent military action was needed to prevent Spain's reconquest of the Low Countries, which threatened dire consequences for the Protestants there and future danger to England itself. Questions about both of these issues could be read into the entertainments staged at Kenilworth, which combined a mix of classical mythology and conspicuous Arthurian themes, with the latter implying both a mythic royal lineage for Leicester himself and a symbolic basis for English intervention in the Low Countries. Although the team of writers employed by Leicester to write the various entertainments offered a complex series of messages, their main thrust seems to have been a request that Elizabeth should either take the earl's continuing interest in marrying her seriously or release him to serve as a knight errant in defense of the Protestant cause abroad. Unfortunately, Kenilworth failed to resolve the uncertainty. It is perhaps symbolic that the device in which Leicester's suit was to be most fully explored, the masque of the nymph Zabeta (for [Eli]zabet[h]a), was delayed and ultimately cancelled because of bad weather. In the end, its author, George Gascoigne, was forced to dress up as "Sylvanus, king of the woods" and tell the queen the story of what had been intended by running alongside her as she rode out hunting (Nichols 1823: I, 515).

Gascoigne had a fresh opportunity to advertise Leicester's concerns to the queen when she visited Woodstock, the house of Sir Henry Lee, two months later. The earl's concerns were refracted in the tale of Hemetes the Hermit, which told of the love of Contarenus ("of estate but meane, but of very great value") for Gandina, the sole and much-sought-after heiress of a rich dukedom, and of the resort of Loricus "to travell and to armes" after being rebuffed by his lady-love. Significantly, the tale concludes with Loricus being advised by the Sibyl to follow his "noble" knightly purpose: "Hercules had by his labour his renowne, and his ruyn by his love" (Nichols 1823: I, 558–63). By September, 1575, therefore, it seems that Leicester wanted Elizabeth to recognize that his suit for her hand was finally over and to release him to serve in the Low Countries. If so, he was disappointed.

Elizabeth's unwillingness to intervene openly on behalf of the Dutch thwarted Leicester's ambitions for another full decade. The earl's own dynastic need for a wife and an heir – an echo, in miniature, of the problem that Elizabeth's continued spinsterhood posed for the realm – ultimately forced him to take matters into his own hands by secretly marrying the dowager countess of Essex in September, 1578, during the same royal progress that included the visit to Norwich. Significantly, Leicester's new bride was named Elizabeth, was a close cousin of the queen, and looked somewhat like a younger and prettier version of her. Elizabeth never fully forgave the new countess of Leicester for this marriage, even after the earl's death in September, 1588, and the countess' prompt remarriage to the politically unthreatening Sir Christopher Blount in March or April, 1589. Despite the efforts of her son, Robert Devereux, second earl of Essex, to effect a belated reconciliation, the dowager countess of Leicester remained persona non grata at court (Hammer 1999: 33–4).

Elizabeth's inability to secure a politically acceptable husband and bear a child meant that the succession to the English throne remained uncertain and threatened the realm with a potential civil war between rival claimants upon her death. For contemporaries, the latter seemed a highly plausible, even likely, outcome. Mary had been forced to take up arms to eject "Queen Jane" from the throne in 1553, and Elizabeth herself had quietly prepared for similar action if her claim to the throne had been contested in 1558. In the absence of a candidate who could command the broad political support that Mary and Elizabeth had enjoyed in the 1550s, it seemed likely that opposing claimants to Elizabeth's throne would have no choice but to demonstrate their right to succeed by seeking God's judgment in battle, as Henry Tudor had done in 1485. Elizabeth's continued unmarried status therefore put the realm a heartbeat – or, rather, the lack of a heartbeat – away from a new version of the Wars of the Roses. It was no coincidence that Elizabeth faced extreme public pressure to find a husband during the Parliament of 1563, following her near-death from smallpox the previous year. However, the events of recent decades meant that Elizabeth's death without an accepted heir would provoke not just civil war, but – still worse – intestine wars of religion like those that were then wracking France and the Low Countries. The experience of Mary's reign had also shown that even Mary's passionate commitment to re-Catholicizing England counted for little if that policy could not be sustained into the next generation on the throne. English Protestants feared that the apparent act of God that had spared them from further persecution by Mary's death in 1558 might equally well result in a new return to those dark days if they earned divine disfavor and Elizabeth were succeeded by a Catholic. Elizabeth herself took a different lesson from her experiences during Mary's reign, remembering how Mary's failed pregnancy had given her, Elizabeth, political power (albeit of a dangerous kind) as England's obvious sovereign-in-waiting, and had encouraged acts of disrespect and disloyalty to Mary by subjects who were impatient for her death. By repeatedly refusing to name a successor and thereby formally identifying the holder of the reversionary interest in the crown, Elizabeth sought to avoid such erosion of her own authority in favor of a "rising sun." Every attempt to discuss openly what might happen after her death was firmly quashed.

Elizabeth's uncompromising refusal to name an heir in compensation for the lack of a husband and child of her own was not simply motivated by her unwillingness to be confronted with "my own winding-sheet" (Guy 2004: 157). Elizabeth's stance was also complicated by the legal and political problems that hedged about her most logical choice as successor, Mary Stuart, Queen of Scots. Mary was foreign-born and the heir of a Tudor line (from Henry VIII's elder sister Margaret) that had been excluded from the succession by the Act of Succession of 1544 and Henry VIII's will of 1546. As the husband of the dauphin of France (who reigned as Francis II during 1559–60), Mary's claim to the English throne had also been advanced by France in direct competition to Elizabeth's in 1558, raising the prospect of full-scale war between the two countries. Through her mother, Mary was also a member of the Guise family, whose public image was built around militant Catholicism and who were deemed chiefly responsible by Protestants for the Wars of Religion being fought in France. Not only, therefore, did Elizabethan England lack an official heir to the throne, but the leading candidate for that status was seen by a large part of the realm's political elite as a totally unacceptable choice as sovereign, raising fears of a return to Catholicism and foreign domination of English affairs. The result was what Patrick Collinson has termed an "Elizabethan exclusion crisis," which lasted for some twenty-seven years (Collinson 1994a). This made Mary Queen of Scots a target for Protestants on both sides of the Anglo-Scottish border and resulted in one of the most important fictional creations of the sixteenth century – the so-called "Casket Letters," which seemed to prove Mary was an adulterer and complicit in the murder of Lord Darnley, her second husband and father of her son James, in 1567. As John Guy has argued in his magisterial biography of Mary Stuart, it was no accident that the originals of these notorious letters mysteriously disappeared. Seemingly created by adding brief interpolations to genuine letters written by Mary, the "Casket Letters" were concocted to justify her deposition from the Scottish throne (from which she was forced to abdicate in favor of her son) and to provide grounds for putting her on trial for murder – an option that Elizabeth refused to countenance. Although the letters were "discovered" in Scotland, Elizabeth's own secretary of state, Sir William Cecil, seems to have had a hand in suggesting some of the necessary changes to the Scottish forgers (Guy 2004: 396–436). Cecil consistently acted as an enemy to Mary and even sought to sabotage his own sovereign's efforts to bring Mary into a new queen-to-queen dynastic settlement, which might have resulted in Mary becoming Elizabeth's successor. By giving tacit prior approval for Rizzio's murder and helping to set in motion the events that resulted in Darnley's murder, Cecil quite deliberately destroyed Mary's rule in Scotland, shattering Elizabeth's own plans in the process (Guy 2004: 247, 287–9).

Cecil has enjoyed a historical reputation as Elizabeth's most loyal adviser and, in his later incarnation as Lord Burghley (the title bestowed upon him in 1571), is often portrayed by modern scholars as an almost avuncular figure of stability and political prudence. This image obscures the ruthlessness needed to survive as a top-level politician in the sixteenth century, let alone for the forty-year span that Burghley enjoyed. However, the covert campaign of Cecil and his friends against Mary also underlines how the "Elizabethan exclusion crisis" often encouraged England's Protestant officials to shape their actions according to what they believed to be in the queen's best interests, rather than according to her actual wishes. As long as their hands were not tied by receiving an explicit command from the queen (which could not legitimately be disobeyed), councilors and other royal officials repeatedly interpreted royal policy in terms of what they thought was most appropriate to be done in the queen's name. Patrick Collinson has described this attitude toward the government of the realm as embodying the "monarchical republic" of Elizabethan England (Collinson 1994b: 31–57). This meant that Elizabeth's councilors, and their various advisers and adherents in both county and central government, tried to find ways of protecting the crown of England from what they believed was the queen's failure to fulfill her royal duty to ensure certainty over the royal succession, even if they had to utilize the language of republicanism to justify their conduct. In 1570, the Lord Keeper, Sir Nicholas Bacon, argued that the queen's continuing failure to marry must ultimately forfeit the obedience of even her most loyal subjects, "for that the naturall care in the moste parte of them that have possessions and families ... [is] to see to the preservacion of them selves, their children and posteritie that must folowe her life" (Collinson 1994b: 50). However great their own personal devotion to Elizabeth, the yearning for certainty about the holding of property, the priority attached to defending Protestant-ism, and the need for unbroken royal authority to safeguard against any revival of the social unrest that had been revealed in the popular tumults of 1549 sometimes forced the queen's politically active subjects to be royalists by talking like republicans.

Ironically, when Elizabeth at last made a really determined effort to pursue a royal marriage in the late 1570s, her choice of royal consort, the duke of Anjou, alienated many of those who had previously pressed her most eagerly to marry (a point that she was publicly proclaimed to "greatly mislike, yea, and marvel" at; L. E. Berry 1968: 150). By marry-ing Anjou and forming a deep Anglo-French alliance, Elizabeth hoped to control French involvement in the Dutch Revolt, which was threat-ening to grow at the expense of English influence in the Low Countries. Given her age, it seemed unlikely that Elizabeth would have a child, despite the pious hopes expressed by Burghley in his memoranda on the subject. In the view of English critics of the match, a more likely scenario was that pregnancy might prove fatal to Elizabeth, while Anjou himself was seen as a Trojan horse for French interference in England and the revival of Catholicism. For courtiers, the prospect of a royal consort setting up his own household as a second center of political influence at court offered exciting prospects to those who hoped to hitch their stars to a rising sun, but it brought the likelihood of disastrous political exclusion for Leicester and many others whose careers had been built upon the queen's special favor or aggressive anti-Catholicism. The result was a political struggle that not only invented the persona of the Virgin Queen, but explored the implications of marriage for a female sovereign in a mercilessly public way.

Perhaps the most striking feature of the polemics relating to the Anjou Match was the way in which the immense importance of the matter – and the fear of Anjou's opponents that they were losing the argument – drove high politics into plain public view and made it the subject of common discussion. The failure of Bishop Cox's attempt to dissuade the queen by presenting her with a Latin tract against the match on the first Sunday of Lent was therefore followed by a host of libels and ballads disseminated in the streets of London and, most famously, *The Discoverie of a Gaping Gulf whereinto England is Like to be Swallowed by an other French Mariage, if the Lord Forbid not the Banes, by Letting Her Majestie See the Sin and Punishment thereof,* written by John Stubbe (or Stubbs) (L. E. Berry 1968: 1–93). The full title of this work gives some sense of why it was so politically explosive. Stubbe not only described Anjou himself as "foule," the queen mother of France as a Jezebel, and the duke's train as "the scomme of all France, which is the scomme of Europe," who will batten on to England "like horseleaches, by sucking us to fill theyr beggerly purses," but also characterized the intended marriage as a profane act that would bring divine retribution and ensure that "both she and we poore soules, are to be mastered and, which is worse, mistrised to." Elizabeth was angry enough at the common ballads, but Stubbe's work drew special fury because its author was a gentlemen of substance who seemed to be peddling arguments that had already been made to her more privately by some of her leading councilors. The book was soon suppressed, but Elizabeth chose to make an example of Stubbe, ensuring that his right hand was publicly amputated for sedition – using an old law of Mary's reign that had been chiefly aimed at Protestant critics of that queen – after an attempt to have him condemned for treason failed. The punishment of Stubbe (who famously held up his bloody stump and called out "God save the queen!") was a public relations disaster for Elizabeth and supporters of the Anjou Match. For the many other writers who were engaged in the great debate, however, Stubbe's fate was a warning either to refrain from venturing into print (with its connotations of popular politics) or to utilize more indirect means of expression. A riposte to Stubbe by Lord Henry Howard, a supporter of the Match, was therefore restricted to limited circulation in manuscript, a form of coterie publication that was more consonant with genteel pretensions (L. E. Berry 1968: lix, 155–94). Philip Sidney's artful "A letter to Queen Elizabeth touching her marriage with Monsieur," which seems to have been composed in response to a request by his uncle Leicester for a new, courtierly argument against the Match in August, 1579, used the same technique. Although Sidney's "Letter" survives in a large number of manuscript copies, most of these actually date from the 1620s and 1630s (Woudhuysen 1996: 151–2). This makes it difficult to judge how widely the "Letter" was read during the heat of the Anjou Match controversy, but it serves to underline how documents relating to Queen Elizabeth – especially when written by a famous figure such as Sidney – enjoyed an active political afterlife during the two decades or so before the Civil War.

Sidney adopted an alternative and deliberately allusive approach to the Anjou Match for his pastoral epic, *Arcadia*, which was probably written in 1580. As Blair Worden has shown, this highly sophisticated work dramatizes the personal and political anxieties that Sidney experienced during the Anjou Match and the broader crisis then apparently facing international Protestantism (Worden 1996). A heavily revised but incomplete version of the work was subsequently printed in 1590 (four years after Sidney's death), while a composite of the two versions was published in 1593. The full text of the original, or *Old Arcadia*, circulated only in manuscript until modern times (Woudhuysen 1996: 299–355). Allusiveness was also the strategy adopted by Edmund Spenser in *The Shepheardes Calender*, which was registered for publication in December 1579 by the same publisher who so nearly lost his hand for publishing *The Gaping Gulf*. This complex poem in pastoral mode has long intrigued readers, and encouraged endless speculation, by such features as its dedication and "Argument" signed only as "E. K." and by its dense allusions, only some of which seem obvious. Spenser was then serving as a secretary to Leicester, and something of the frustrations felt within Leicester House (the earl's London residence) during late 1579 and early 1580 can perhaps be gauged from shorter poems that Spenser wrote about this time, especially "Prosopopoia, or Mother Hubberd's Tale." This is a satirical fable about how an ambitious Fox and Ape unscrupulously advance themselves in the world, ultimately even stealing the crown from the sleeping Lion – a crime that triggers the intervention of the gods and results in their eternal punishment. Part of this story seems to allude to the Anjou Match (Elizabeth jokingly referred to Anjou's agent, Simier, as her "ape"), while the character of the Fox was widely interpreted as an image of Burghley and seemed to imply that the latter hoped to use Anjou as his dupe to "steal" the crown from the careless Elizabeth (the Lion). It is unclear whether Leicester actually shared such a hostile view of Burghley's support of the Match (or, indeed, whether Burghley was really quite as supportive of the Match as he appeared – Stubbe had some interesting ties to him). Some critics have suggested that Leicester's preferment of Spenser to act as Lord Grey's secretary in Ireland shortly afterwards may even indicate some embarrassment over the poem (L. E. Berry 1968: lv). Whether such speculation is accurate or not, "Prosopopoia" and other poems by Spenser were "disperst abroad in sundrie handes" as manuscript copies during the 1580s, before partly revised versions were collectively printed as *Complaints: Containing Sundrie Small Poemes of the Worlds Vanitie* in

1591. With Leicester dead and Burghley increasingly sensitive about his dominance of the Privy Council, this proved to be an impolitic decision by Spenser, which may have cost him the chance for greater patronage than the £50 royal pension that he received after publishing the first three books of *The Faerie Queene* in 1590.

The intense controversy over the queen's intended marriage to Anjou also found expression in other forms, such as the song of *The Moste Strange Wedding of the Frogge and the Mouse* and *The Battle of the Frogs*, a Latin poem licensed for printing in January, 1580 (Doran 1996: 168). Although Elizabeth nicknamed Anjou her "frog" and he returned the joke by giving her numerous little gold and enamel jewels in the shape of frogs (Arnold 1988: 75–6), such works seem to have avoided serious complaint from supporters of the Match or the charge of rabble-rousing that had cost Stubbe his hand. The struggle over the queen's marriage was also expressed through rival portraits of Elizabeth. In late 1580, Elizabeth pointedly wore a French-style gown when she sat for a French painter for a portrait that was destined for the French queen mother (Arnold 1988: 122). On the other hand, the years of the Anjou Match also saw the production of a series of portraits of Elizabeth holding a sieve, a symbol of female virtue through chastity and a visual representation of the emerging new "Virgin Queen" image (Strong 1987: 95–107). These "Sieve Portraits" are also strongly associated with notions of a Roman-style imperial destiny for England (the original sieve-bearer, Tuccia, was a Roman Vestal Virgin – one of those upon whose chastity the continued favor of the gods toward Rome rested). The most elaborate and famous of these portraits (now held in Siena), painted c. 1580, seems to show Sir Christopher Hatton in the background, while the details on the imperial column to the queen's right tell the tragic story of Dido, whose pursuit of passion and failure to accept the imperial destiny embodied in the hero Aeneas brought her own destruction – a cautionary tale for an Elizabeth who had not yet shaken off Anjou or embraced the "Virgin Queen" destiny being thrust upon her by opponents of the French Match. Perhaps significantly, the same story also features in the "November" eclogue of *The Shepheardes Calender*, which "E. K." claimed to be the high point of the whole work, where Colin Clout sings a long dirge for Dido.

In the end, Elizabeth decided that the political costs of marrying Anjou were too high to justify proceeding with a full marriage treaty, especially when Henry III of France rejected English overtures to expand it into a broader Anglo-French military alliance. In effect, this meant the final abandonment of any hope that she would ever marry. Not surprisingly perhaps, she continued to resist making this decision final for as long as possible, although diplomatic maneuvering may also have helped to draw out events. In November, 1581, during Anjou's second visit to England, Elizabeth even kissed the duke publicly, pledged to become his wife, and gave him a ring, only to claim the next morning that she intended only financial support for his impending campaign in the Low Countries. Nevertheless, a decisive hint about the queen's intentions was given in a two-day tournament performed to entertain a high-powered French delegation on May 15–16, 1581, when "Four Foster Children of Desire" tried to capture the Fortress of Perfect Beauty (a symbolic representation of the chaste Elizabeth), which was protected by a host of knightly defenders. Significantly, the four attackers included two courtiers who had supported the French Match and two who had equally conspicuously opposed it (one of them being Philip Sidney, who seems to have played an important role in devising the show). At length, the defeated attackers were to "acknowledge this fortress to be reserved for the eie of the whole world, farre lifted up from the compasse of their destinie" (Nichols 1823: II, 328). Not only did the elaborate spectacle enact the final exhaustion and composing of the bitter arguments at court, but it reinforced the image of an Elizabeth "farre lifted up" by virtue of her royal chastity.

The failure of Elizabeth's French Match marked the end of the most intense and politically charged debate over royal marriage and succession during her reign. Its failure not only ensured that Elizabeth would have to become the "Virgin Queen" but also returned attention to the problems posed by Mary Queen of Scots, which had taken on a new form after the latter's flight to England in 1568. Mary's continued presence within the realm encouraged various plots by some of her English Catholic supporters to free her from detention and even to set her on the throne in Elizabeth's place with the aid of foreign troops. The queen's allegedly miraculous survival of these Catholic plots made her an iconic Protestant heroine, despite growing disenchantment with her religious policies (Walsham 2003: 151). Nevertheless, the fear that one of the plots might eventually succeed created waves of pressure on Elizabeth from her largely Protestant councilors and courtiers, and from royal officials across the realm, to solve the problem by trying and executing Mary. Elizabeth barely resisted these public demands in 1572 after the Ridolfi Plot. By the early 1580s, however, the likelihood of imminent Catholic invasion seemed to be rising and the queen's sympathy for Mary weakened. In 1584, Elizabeth came under even greater pressure when the Privy Council orchestrated ceremonial signings by leading Protestant gentlemen across the realm of the Bond of Association, a document that pledged signatories to take bloody revenge on those deemed responsible should the queen be killed. Mary and her largely Catholic supporters were the obvious targets. Ironically, the result would have been an English Protestant equivalent of France's notorious St Bartholomew's massacres of 1572 – which English Protestants had always claimed as definitive proof of the barbarism of international Catholicism. After a series of Catholic conspiracies were exposed in the mid-1580s, Mary was finally implicated in the so-called Babington Plot of 1586. The demands from England's political class to solve the Mary Stuart problem permanently now became overwhelming. Step by step, Elizabeth acceded to the demands for a trial and for Mary's death. In the end, Elizabeth chose to claim that Mary was executed in February, 1587, because the Privy Council executed the death warrant that she had signed but had not definitively released. The rumpus saw the junior secretary of state, William Davison, tried and imprisoned for releasing the warrant, while Lord Burghley and other leading councilors escaped with brief interludes of royal disfavor. The Privy Council undoubtedly seized upon this opportunity to expedite Mary's death before Elizabeth could remove their room for maneuver by issuing a formal pause to proceedings, but Elizabeth's own actions were much less innocent than her public professions of anger and regret proclaimed. As her councilors realized, she was determined to see Mary dead, but she also wanted to escape blame for executing a former sovereign who still had the strongest claim to be considered her heir. When Sir Amias Paulet refused Elizabeth's request that he poison Mary (no doubt anticipating a rather more severe version of the treatment later meted out to Davison), casting collective blame upon the Privy Council for their excessive zeal became the queen's alternative route to her own public exculpation.

The execution of Mary Queen of Scots effectively ended the "Elizabethan exclusion crisis," but it also complicated the question of the succession. Mary's son, James VI of Scotland, was the most obvious successor to her claim and Elizabeth consistently treated him as her protégé, although she adamantly refused to confirm him as her chosen heir. This caused James much frustration and gave some faint hope to potential domestic candidates, such as the sons of Edward Seymour, earl of Hertford, who had inherited the claim of

Jane Grey. However, Hertford's sons were officially deemed illegitimate and they lacked credible support. By contrast, James's appeal
within England was strengthened by his apparent Protestantism and
by the emergence in 1586–7 of a new Catholic contender, Philip II of
Spain (Rodriguez-Salgado 1991). After years of cold war between
them, England and Spain became locked in an open conflict in late
1585, which would last until the end of Elizabeth's reign. In characteristic Habsburg manner, Philip sought to bolster his cause in this
struggle by laying claim to the English throne on both religious and
dynastic grounds. Philip's religious justification was grounded upon
Elizabeth's excommunication by a papal bull in 1570, while his dynastic claims were based upon the alleged superiority of his double line
of descent (through the families of both his father and his mother)
from the late fourteenth-century house of Lancaster compared to that
of the Tudors. Philip's claims therefore reactivated old debates about
the rightful heirs to the English crown after the deposition and murder of Richard II in 1399, meaning that Elizabeth's death or loss of
power would threaten the realm literally as well as metaphorically
with a revival of the Wars of the Roses.

Philip's claim – which he subsequently assigned to his daughter, the
Infanta Isabella – was most famously argued in *A Conference about the
Next Succession to the Crowne of Ingland*, which was published in Antwerp
in 1594 by "R. Doleman" (a pseudonym for the English Jesuit Robert
Persons). This book caused a storm when copies began to circulate in
England during 1595, because its detailed analysis of all the potential
claimants to the throne (complete with elaborate discussion of their
family trees) shattered Elizabeth's prohibition of such discussion – a
policy that she had recently enforced by imprisoning the MP Peter
Wentworth for trying to stir up debate on the matter at the Parliament
of 1593. Ironically, Wentworth used his time in the Tower (where he
died in 1597) to write a response to the Doleman tract, "A Discourse
Containing the Author's Opinion of the True and Lawful Successor to
her Majesty." This work, together with his earlier plea for certainty on
the succession, "A Pithie Exhortation to her Majestie for Establishing
her Successor to the Crowne," were smuggled to Scotland, where they
were printed in Edinburgh in 1598 as part of James's efforts to foster
English support for his claim to the succession. Another product by the
king's printer in that year was *The True Lawe of Free Monarchies: Or the
Reciprock and Mutuall Dutie betwixt a Free King, and his Naturall Subiectes*,
an anonymous work that was actually written by James himself. At
least in part, this defense of the divine right of kings was a counter to

another highly controversial element of the Doleman tract – its insistence on a contractual view of monarchy, which asserted that only a "just" sovereign (by which the author clearly meant, but did not quite specify, a Catholic sovereign) could legitimately rule England. Even more explicit in its engagement with Doleman was a third publication by James's printer in 1598, *A Treatise Declaring, and Confirming Against all Obiections the Just Title and Right of the Moste Excellent and Worthie Prince, Iames the Sixt, King of Scotland, to the Succession of the Croun of England.* Issued under the pseudonym "Irenicus Philodikaios," this pointedly inveighed against the Spanish claim as one that had been "forged by some fugitive *Persons* of our own nation" (p. 3: emphasis added).

As many scholars have noted, English literature in the 1590s refracted contemporary anxieties about the succession and the debate over rival dynastic claims through the extraordinary profusion of works that explored incidents in English history or succession crises set in foreign countries. In part, this reflected the way that the Spanish claim, in particular, made English history of the fourteenth and fifteenth centuries directly relevant to the question of Elizabeth's successor. George Peele's *Edward I,* for example, casts Edmund Crouchback, brother of the king and the original earl of Lancaster, as a Judas, while Elinor, the Spanish Infanta who became Edward I's wife, is shown as adulterous (contaminating claims of descent) and bent upon imposing a brutal tyranny upon England (Axton 1977: 93, 101–2). Peele's play therefore attacks Philip's Lancastrian credentials and emphasizes the hispanophobia that was such a staple of Elizabethan patriotism. Indeed, the pull of this patriotism was sufficiently powerful that it even made many English Catholics hostile to the Spanish claim, shattering any hope of Catholic unity. Focusing on the past also allowed writers to meditate upon the country's uncertain future under the cover of writing history. This pose was most notoriously questioned in the investigation surrounding John Hayward's *The First Part of the Life and Reign of King Henry IV,* published in 1599. Although the book proved a sell-out in its large first edition, Hayward and his work were subsequently subjected to extremely intense scrutiny by the Privy Council, because they were seen as potential sources of evidence that could be used to support charges of treason or sedition against Robert Devereux, second earl of Essex. Essex's factional enemies on the Council believed that Hayward's dedication of the book to the earl as great "both in present judgement and in expectation of future time," and the book's subject matter – the deposition by a popular nobleman of an heirless sovereign who fought a costly war in Ireland – reflected Essex's desire to test public support for his designs upon the crown. In fact, although there were serious grounds for suspicion about the behavior of Hayward and Essex, the latter's chief concern seems to have been to ensure James's recognition as Elizabeth's heir (Hammer forthcoming).

Although the queen managed to stifle open discussion of the matter, the last years of Elizabeth's reign witnessed intense debate about the succession, albeit in somewhat veiled form or through the circulation of private manuscripts or books printed abroad. At the same time, royal image-makers sought to deny Elizabeth's own mortality by playing upon the magical qualities associated with her image as the "Virgin Queen." This was evident in the extravagant praises heaped upon Elizabeth (for example, in the elaborate set of associations developed around the figure of Cynthia) and in visual representations of her, which showed her as either ageless or actually becoming younger with time, as in Nicholas Hilliard's "mask of youth" images (Strong 1987: 146–51). Despite such flattering fictions, Elizabeth could have been under no illusion that her leading subjects were positioning themselves for the next reign, many of them quietly responding to James's propaganda campaign from Scotland. Nevertheless, the succession could easily have provoked the civil war that had been so long predicted, because James's chief supporter in England, Essex, was on the losing side in a prolonged power struggle that wracked the Elizabethan regime during the late 1590s (Hammer 1999: 167–71; Stafford 1940: 198–224). If Essex had not been driven to his own destruction in February, 1601, some of his rivals at court might have been forced to back another candidate for the throne (as Essex had believed they were doing) in order to protect themselves from the revenge they feared would follow an Essex-engineered Stuart succession. In the event, Essex's fall ended the danger that James's claim might become a partisan issue in the manner of the Anjou Match, and cleared the way for the earl's former enemies to stage-manage James's accession to the throne upon Elizabeth's death in March, 1603.

The accession of James created a union of crowns between the kingdoms of Scotland and England (which in turn held the crown of Ireland and principality of Wales), encouraging the king to launch his ill-fated project to remake his dominions as "Britain." James's arrival in England also marked the first time that the realm had had a royal family in the traditional sense since the latter days of Henry VIII's reign almost sixty years earlier. This meant not only that there was a royal court that

included official households for the queen consort and the heir apparent, but also that the reversionary interest in the crown – Prince Henry,
who was formally installed as Prince of Wales a few months after his
sixteenth birthday in 1610 – assumed its traditional form of a son who
became increasingly determined to become a different sort of king from
his father. In contrast to James's desire to be the great peace-maker of
Christendom, Prince Henry aspired to become the chivalric leader of
international Protestantism. These conflicting ambitions might have
caused a clash over Henry's marriage. James sought to marry his daughter Elizabeth to a Protestant prince, but he was determined to marry his
son to a Catholic princess, ideally a Spanish Habsburg. This strategy of
religious and political triangulation was partly accomplished with the
spousal of Elizabeth to Frederick V, Elector Palatine, the most presti-
gious German Protestant prince. However, Spain showed little interest
in Henry, and James's hopes of forcing an Italian Catholic bride upon his
son (despite the unresolved problems of religion) were dashed by the
prince's sudden death in November, 1612 (Strong 1986: 80–3). The
wedding of Elizabeth and Frederick was therefore delayed until Valen-
tine's Day, 1613. During the interim, the court was treated to some
twenty plays performed by the King's Men, Shakespeare's company –
including (perhaps) the premiere of *The Tempest*. The wedding itself was
celebrated in grand style (including a water battle between "Christians"
and "Turks" on the Thames) and made great play of Protestant and
anti-Habsburg themes. The ambassadors from the various Habsburg
territories conspicuously boycotted the festivities (Parry 1981: 95–107).

Despite the stridently Protestant connotations of Princess Elizabeth's
marriage, James still aspired to a Catholic bride for his surviving son,
Prince Charles. Although rival offers were made by France and Spain
in 1614, efforts to secure Charles's marriage were stepped up after
1618, when the prince turned 18 and the Bohemian Revolt sparked
a full-scale religious conflict that would become the Thirty Years War.
Elector Frederick's attempt to establish himself as the Protestant king
of Bohemia soon proved a disastrous failure and provoked a Spanish
invasion of the Palatinate itself. While English Protestants raged at the
military success of Catholic forces on the Continent and talked of
religious war, James instead threw his energies into pursuing a Spanish Match for Charles, hoping that it would secure the return of the
Palatinate to Frederick and Elizabeth without open resort to arms. This
divergence between royal policy and the perceptions of many of the
king's subjects ensured that the Spanish Match fueled popular mistrust
of James and raised fears about the future implications of the marriage,

especially after the king sought to mollify Spain by suspending operation of England's penal statutes against Catholics in 1622 (Cogswell
1989: 118). The volume of public outpourings against the Match far
exceeded the polemics that had been stirred by Elizabeth's Anjou
Match, and scandalous libels against individuals (especially the royal
favorite, George Villiers, marquess of Buckingham) also seem to have
been more conspicuous than in 1578–82. Many of the attacks on the
Spanish Match and subsequent government policy pointedly utilized
Elizabethan history to emphasize the dangers of wooing – instead of
confronting – England's inveterate Catholic enemy. The polemicist
Thomas Scott, for example, followed his *Vox Populi, or Newes from
Spayne* (1620) and *An Experimentall Discoverie of Spanish Practises*
(1623) with titles such as *Robert Earle of Essex his Ghost, Sent from Elizian
to the Nobility, Gentry, and Communaltie of England* (1624) and *Sir Walter
Rawleighs Ghost, or Englands Forewarner: Discouering a Secret Consultation,
Newly Holden in the Court of Spaine* (1626).

The Spanish Match took its most bizarre turn in 1623, when Prince
Charles and Buckingham slipped out of England and rode across
France to press the case for the Infanta's hand in person. Although a
marriage treaty was agreed, Charles increasingly found himself becoming a sort of latter-day duke of Anjou during his six-month stay in
Spain – extravagantly entertained, but frustrated in his hopes of turning the promises of a royal wedding into reality and, ultimately, becoming an expensive guest who had outstayed his welcome. By the
time Charles and Buckingham left Spain, it was clear that a marriage
would not bring a return of the Palatinate, and both sides were intent
upon escaping from their earlier promises (Pursell 2002; Redworth
2003). Although their return brought wild celebrations that England
had escaped the prospect of a future Spanish Catholic queen, Charles
and Buckingham quickly sought redemption for their Spanish humili-
ation by seeking a marriage alliance with the equally Catholic French
royal house. Their twin goals were to win Charles a wife whose family
prestige would fully match that of the Infanta and to create a grand
anti-Habsburg military alliance, opening the way for the recovery of
the Palatinate and the humbling of Spain by force of arms. Negotiations during 1624 finally secured a royal bride for Charles in the form
of Henrietta Maria, the 15-year-old sister of Louis XIII of France.
However, despite Buckingham's personal intervention at the French
court, the French refused to expand the dynastic alliance into a military one (Shimp 1981). The failure of the Spanish Match therefore
drove James and Charles into accepting a French Match in the very

circumstances that had ensured that Elizabeth abandoned her own French Match, even though this decision cost her any realistic chance of ever marrying or of continuing her dynasty.

When the new King Charles married Henrietta Maria in June, 1625, he gained a wife, but not an international ally. Indeed, Charles soon found himself at war with his new royal brother-in-law. To many of the king's subjects, their new French queen also seemed barely any better than the Spanish alternative, and her refusal to attend Charles's coronation in February, 1626, on the grounds of her Catholic faith only seemed to confirm this opinion. While the events of the previous half-century had repeatedly shown how formidable were the difficulties in contracting any royal marriage during this age of religious conflict, the tragic course of Charles's reign would also show that a royal wedding by itself was not sufficient to solve those problems.

References and Further Reading

Arnold, J., ed. 1988. *Queen Elizabeth's Wardrobe Unlock'd: The Inventories of the Wardrobe of Robes Prepared in July 1600* .... Leeds: Maney.

Axton, M. 1977. *The Queen's Two Bodies: Drama and the Elizabethan Succession.* London: Royal Historical Society.

Berry, L. E., ed. 1968. *John Stubbs's Gaping Gulf, with Letters and Other Relevant Documents.* Charlottesville, VA: University of Virginia Press for the Folger Library.

Berry, P. 1989. *Of Chastity and Power: Elizabethan Literature and the Unmarried Queen.* London: Routledge.

Churchyard, T. 1578. *A Discovrse of the Queenes Maiesties Entertainement in Suffolk and Norffolk.* London. *STC* no. 5226.

Cogswell, T. 1989. "England and the Spanish Match," in R. Cust and A. Hughes, eds., *Conflict in Early Stuart England: Studies in Religion and Politics, 1603–1642.* London: Longman, pp. 107–33.

Collinson, P. 1994a. "The Elizabethan Exclusion Crisis and the Elizabethan Polity," *Proceedings of the British Academy* 84: 51–92.

Collinson, P. 1994b. "The Monarchical Republic of Queen Elizabeth I," in P. Collinson, *Elizabethan Essays.* London: Hambledon, pp. 31–57.

Doran, S. 1995. "Juno versus Diana: The Treatment of Elizabeth I's Marriage in Plays and Entertainments, 1561–1581," *Historical Journal* 38: 257–74.

Doran, S. 1996. *Monarchy and Matrimony: The Courtships of Elizabeth I.* London: Routledge.

Dovey, Z. 1996. *An Elizabethan Progress: The Queen's Journey into East Anglia, 1578.* Stroud: Sutton.

Frye, S. 1993. *Elizabeth I: The Competition for Representation*. Oxford: Oxford University Press.

G., B. 1578. *The Ioyfull Receyving of the Queenes Most Excellent Maiestie into hir Highnesse Citie of Norwich*. London. *STC* no. 11627.

Guy, J. 2004. *"My Heart is My Own": The Life of Mary Queen of Scots*. London: Fourth Estate.

Hackett, H. 1995. *Virgin Mother, Maiden Queen: Elizabeth I and the Cult of the Virgin Mary*. New York: St Martin's Press.

Hammer, P. E. J. 1999. *The Polarisation of Elizabethan Politics: The Political Career of Robert Devereux, 2nd earl of Essex, 1585–1597*. Cambridge: Cambridge University Press.

Hammer, P. E. J., forthcoming. "The Smiling Crocodile: The Earl of Essex and Late-Elizabethan 'Popularity'," in P. Lake and S. Pincus, eds., *The Public Sphere in Early Modern England*. Manchester: Manchester University Press.

King, J. N. 1990. "Queen Elizabeth I: Representations of the Virgin Queen," *Renaissance Quarterly* 43: 30–74.

Levin, C. 1994. *The Heart and Stomach of a King: Elizabeth I and the Politics of Sex and Power*. Philadelphia: University of Pennsylvania Press.

Nichols, J. 1823. *The Progresses and Public Processions of Queen Elizabeth*, 3 vols. New York: Burt Franklin reprint of 1966.

Parry, G. 1981. *The Golden Age Restor'd: The Culture of the Stuart Court, 1603–1642*. Manchester: Manchester University Press.

Pursell, B. C. 2002. "The End of the Spanish Match," *Historical Journal* 45: 699–726.

Redworth, G. 2003. *The Prince and the Infanta: The Cultural Politics of the Spanish Match*. New Haven: Yale University Press.

Rodriguez-Salgado, M. J. 1991. "The Anglo-Spanish War: The Final Episode in the 'Wars of the Roses'?" in M. J. Rodriguez-Salgado and S. Adams, eds., *England, Spain and the Gran Armada, 1585–1604*. Edinburgh: John Donald, pp. 1–44.

Shimp, R. E. 1981. "A Catholic Marriage for an Anglican Prince," *Historical Magazine of the Protestant Episcopal Church* 50: 3–18.

Stafford, H. G. 1940. *James VI of Scotland and the Throne of England*. New York: Appleton-Century.

Strong, R. 1986. *Henry Prince of Wales and England's Lost Renaissance*. London: Thames and Hudson.

Strong, R. 1987. *Gloriana: The Portraits of Queen Elizabeth I*. London: Thames and Hudson (Pimlico edition of 2003).

Walsham, A. 2003. " 'A Very Deborah?' The Myth of Elizabeth I as Providential Monarch," in S. Doran and T. S. Freeman, eds., *The Myth of Elizabeth*. Basingstoke: Palgrave Macmillan, pp. 143–68.

Worden, B. 1996. *The Sound of Virtue: Philip Sidney's Arcadia and Elizabethan Politics*. New Haven and London: Yale University Press.

Woudhuysen, H. R. 1996. *Sir Philip Sidney and the Circulation of Manuscripts, 1558–1640*. Oxford: Clarendon Press.

Chapter 4

Patronage, Licensing, and Censorship

Richard Dutton

Patronage was one of the essential motors of early modern society, affecting far more than literature (Lytle and Orgel 1981; MacCaffrey 1961; Peck 1982). In a heavily hierarchical world, where property and power lay mainly in the hands of an aristocratic elite, the path to advancement for any educated man lay in securing the support of a noble patron – support in the form of employment, money, extended hospitality, or recommendation to others able to supply these. "Patronage, broadly defined, was the central social system of the era. It dominated political life and permeated the structure of the church and universities. Its influence on the economy was enormous, and the assumptions behind it were reflected in religious thought, in cosmological speculation, and in the organization and daily detail of family life" (Evans 1989: 23).

The effects of patronage were so wide-ranging because it was not understood as a one-way trade. The suitor looking for advancement offered service to his patron. If the patron accepted this service and rewarded it, it added to his own prestige. This was especially so if the reward lay not in his own gift, but in that of his own superior, especially the monarch. In such a case, the patron was further tied to the crown for the honor accorded in granting his request, just as the suitor was tied to the patron for his good offices: it was an endless cycle of reciprocal indebtedness, binding the parties together, reinforcing loyalties. It generated something akin to clan bonding, to the ties of an extended family: movie depictions of the Mafia perhaps give us a darkly colored version of what it was like.

Problems arose because there were too many suitors and not enough rewards to go round. This was particularly acute at court, the nub of patronage, which increasingly attracted far more suitors than it had posts and perquisites to dispense. Hence in the factional rivalries of the

1590s between the earl of Essex and the Cecils (Lord Burghley and his son, Sir Robert Cecil), tension often surfaced over patronage: who could secure most from the queen for themselves or their clients. In the later years of James's reign, the tension focused on resentment at the near-absolute control of court patronage wielded by his greatest favorite, the duke of Buckingham. The malcontent figures in so many Jacobean tragedies – like Flamineo in *The White Devil* or Bosola in *The Duchess of Malfi* – represent a real phenomenon: men of merit whose expectations of patronage have been thwarted, or who have been made to take on unpalatable work. Deflores in *The Changeling* is another: born a gentleman, he has no independent wealth, has failed to find a patron, and has slipped into the ranks of mere employment.

Writers like Webster and Middleton understood the men they depicted, because their own concerns would have been similar. Literature intersected with patronage in a variety of ways. Few lived by writing alone: books were still luxuries, selling in small numbers, and making little profit for their authors. Yet aptitude in writing might be a valuable commodity: demonstrating command of language and its affective powers, it displayed knowledge, wit, and understanding – all the skills and qualities of a humanist education that the ruling class in Renaissance England so valued. So writing might be a recommendation to patronage, perhaps to some post as a tutor or a secretary, a clerk or a clergyman – and so to greater things beyond.

John Donne is a case in point. However much his poetry is fired by personal experience and imagination, there is always an element in it of self-display (Marotti 1986). His outrageous conceits, conspicuous learning, and witty argumentation impressed the circles among whom his poems circulated in manuscript (which for some had a higher cachet than print, not being sullied with mercenary motives), and thereby came to the attention of potential patrons. Poetry would not have been his sole recommendation (he had, for example, also served on naval expeditions with the earl of Essex) but would have helped. Donne found a promising position with Lord Keeper Egerton in 1597/ 8, and rose in favor until he secretly married his patron's niece, Ann More, without the family's permission.

When the truth emerged in 1602 he was not only dismissed by Egerton but briefly imprisoned: he had committed a fundamental affront to the quasi-kinship bonds of the system. This put Donne in the patronage wilderness for over a decade. He tried to cultivate new patrons with his poetry, most notably Lucy, countess of Bedford, who was particularly receptive to literary talent, being also patron (among others) to Samuel Daniel and Ben Jonson. He addressed verse epistles to her; "Twickenham Garden" refers to her estate and the "Noctural, Upon St Lucy's Day" plays on her name. This was one context where women might contribute to the processes of patronage. Lady Bedford herself could only offer modest cash rewards and hospitality at her husband's estates, including their grand house on the Strand. But as the closest English friend of Queen Anna she had considerable influence. Yet even she failed to secure Donne a position in that household. In 1608 he tried for the secretaryship in Ireland, supported by the king's favorite, Lord Hay, but failed (the king specifically remembered the scandal of his marriage), as he did the following year when he sought to be secretary of the Virginia Company.

Donne enjoyed limited success in 1611–13, attaching himself to the household of Sir Robert Drury, for whose dead daughter he wrote "An Anatomy of the World" and the "Anniversaries." But he never achieved the major state position he sought. The king, however, admired Donne's works of religious controversy, especially *Pseudo-Martyr* (published 1610), and made it known that he could only expect advancement in the Church of England. This was not an easy option for a man from a deeply Catholic family, but in 1615 he took holy orders and became a royal chaplain, and in 1621 dean of St Paul's. In joining the church, Donne completed a striking trio. In the late 1590s, three young men made names by writing snarling verse satires: Joseph Hall, John Marston, and Donne. By 1615 all of them were in the church.

Donne's case shows how literature might help a man to a career That of his friend Ben Jonson shows how literature was on the point of becoming a viable career in itself. But for this Jonson had to exploit every facet of patronage available to a writer. Certainly he courted aristocratic patrons like Lady Bedford, offering verse that eulogized them for living up to the ideals of their stations in life (see *Epigrams* 76, 84, and 94): cynics, of course, called it flattery. He spun out the modest rewards and hospitality from this by pursuing multiple patrons, including at least two with whom he lived for a time, Sir Robert Townshend and Lord Aubigny, a cousin of the king. Over time, indeed, Jonson courted so many patrons that he seemingly minimized his dependence on any one of them. And in printing his poems – in the artfully structured collections, *Epigrams* and *The Forest*, within the great 1616 folio of Jonson's *Works* – he reversed some of the debt inherent in patronage relations. In the *Works* scores of patrons – the king and queen and others of the royal family, great ministers like Robert Cecil (now earl of Salisbury), luminaries of the court, down to a very personal "patron," William Camden, the great historian and Jonson's master at Westminster School – all appear in glowing cameos, in poems or entertainments, or in dedications of items to them, preserved for posterity honoring Jonson's genius.

Yet the apparent transcendence of the laureate poet is largely an illusion. Below the confident surface of some of the most celebrated of Jonson's eulogies, those to the extended Sidney family, we can still see patronage pressures at work. His praise of Sir Robert Sidney's estate, "To Penshurst," paints an idealized portrait of poet–patron relations:

> Here no man tells my cups, nor, standing by,
> A waiter, doth my gluttony envy,
> But gives me what I call, and lets me eat ...
> There's nothing I can wish, for which I stay.
>
> (ll. 67–75)

Sidney, brother of the dead Philip, presides over an Edenic world, where the poet enjoys his hospitality, with slightly grotesque self-indulgence. The self-made poet rubs shoulders with aristocrats, but is never quite their equal (Wayne 1984). Jonson also praises Sidney's son in *The Forest*, his daughter, Mary (see *Epigrams* 103 and 105, and the dedication of *The Alchemist*), and her husband ("To Sir Robert Wroth"); he repeatedly honors Philip Sidney's own daughter, Elizabeth, countess of Rutland. Most critically, he praises their much grander cousin, the immensely wealthy William Herbert, earl of Pembroke (see *Epigram* 102), also dedicating to him the whole collection of *Epigrams* and the text of his tragedy, *Catiline*, in the *Works*.

In the *Epigrams* he brings together two of his poems for the earl of Salisbury (63 and 64), but follows them immediately with "To My Muse":

> Away, and leave me, thou thing most abhorred,
> That hast betrayed me to a worthless lord.

The implication that Salisbury was that "worthless lord" is irresistible. Jonson could hardly have risked the inference when Salisbury was alive (he died in 1612) but repudiates his patronage now, justifying himself with the reflection that "Whoe'er is raised / For worth he has not, he is taxed, not praised" (ll. 15–16) – a comfortable doctrine, which releases the patronized poet from final responsibility for his words. Yet even as Jonson celebrates his escape from Salisbury's patronage, he records myriad ties to the political world that succeeded him. By 1616 Pembroke was a major figure at court and Lord Chamberlain. So the centrality of the Herberts and Sidneys in the *Works* is no innocent celebration of their generosity as literary patrons: it marks Jonson's involvement in the new political realities (Butler 1993; Brennan 1988). Pembroke was a more congenial patron than Salisbury ever had been, with a genuine interest in literature and drama; he gave Jonson £20 yearly to buy books and secured him an honorary MA at Oxford. But even at the height of his prestige Jonson remained trapped within the social and political patronage nexus.

This is never more apparent than in that patronage from which Jonson profited more than any of his contemporaries: in commissions to script occasional shows and entertainments. This began early in the new reign, with an entertainment for Queen Anna and Prince Henry at Althorp on their journey south; perhaps Lady Bedford was instrumental. The city of London employed Jonson, with Thomas Dekker, to devise pageants for James's delayed royal entry in March, 1604: *The Magnificent Entertainment*. He also scripted a *Panegyre* for the opening of Parliament and an *Entertainment at Highgate* for the Lord Mayor's welcome to the king. Such events might bring Jonson £20, perhaps twice as much as he might earn for writing a play (a fee plus profits of an early performance), and far more than he could expect for a poem. He was in regular demand for such commissions over the next few years.

The greatest prize was to write masques for the court, each worth a handsome £40. Queen Anna was fond of such theatricals and sponsored most of those in the early years of the reign. Jonson missed out to Daniel for *The Vision of the Twelve Goddesses* (1604), but secured the commission for *The Masque of Blackness* in 1605. Thereafter hardly a year of the reign passed without Jonson scripting at least one court masque, usually staged with elaborate magnificence by Inigo Jones. But *Blackness* suggests how Jonson's invention was circumscribed by his patron's tastes: the queen herself decided that she and her ladies would appear in black-face as negroes, a conceit not well received at court. Jonson did his best to build a suitable fable around it. *The Masque of Queens* (1609) shows how his authorship and her authority blurred together. The Venetian ambassador reported home that: "So well composed and ordered was it all that it is evident the mind of her Majesty, the authoress of the whole, is gifted no less highly than her person" (Jonson 1925–52: X, 457).

Renaissance patrons were deemed the "authors" of any works they commissioned, subsuming the talents of the artists and artisans employed. And in the printed text Jonson defers to this:

And because her Matie (best knowing, that a principall part of life in these Spectacles lay in theyr variety) had commaunded mee to think on some Daunce or shew, that might praecede hers, and have the place of a foyle, or false-Masque; I ... therefore, now, devis'd that twelve Women, in the habite of Haggs, or Witches ... should fill that part; not as a Masque, but a spectacle of strangenesse, producing multiplicity of Gesture, and not unaptly sorting wth the current, and whole fall of the Device. (Jonson 1925–52: VII, 282)

So Jonson credits Queen Anna with inventing the anti-masque, a feature of masquing that he himself brought to perfection. How comfortable was the proud and opinionated Jonson about subordinating his talents to the tastes of his powerful patrons? It tells us something that *Epicene* (1610) features a group of domineering aristocratic female "collegiates"; and when Epicene herself proves anything but silent and compliant, her "husband" exclaims: "She is my Regent already! I have married a Penthesilea" (Jonson 1925–52: V, 3.4.56–7). Penthesilea, the mythic queen of the Amazons, was a role Jonson had respectfully devised for Lady Bedford in *The Masque of Queens*.

If Jonson indeed chafed under the direction of his noble patrons, it was as nothing to his relations with the public stage, where his career started. The theatres of late Elizabethan England were a new phenomenon, challenging old forms of artistic patronage, as their key patrons were the paying customers. Jonson's relationship with them was always fraught. We see his scornful and defiant response to the disastrous first performances of *Sejanus, Catiline,* and *The New Inn*; and everywhere in prologues, inductions, and choruses we find him determined to prescribe the terms under which audiences should receive his plays, rather than trust them as "understanders" (a frequent pun, mocking the taste of those who paid least and literally stood in the pit beneath the stage: Barish 1973; Sweeney 1985). When the opportunity presented itself, Jonson avoided theatrical patronage altogether. After 1605 his output dwindled to a play every two or three years. When in 1616 the king granted him an annual pension of 100 marks (as, in effect if not in name, poet laureate), Jonson ceased writing plays. He only started again in 1625 when Charles I put an end to his regular masques.

Jonson, then, exploited patronage opportunities to make a living by his writing, rather than as a passport to other employment. But this almost changed when, in 1621, he received a reversion to the post of Master of the Revels: that is, he would have acquired it if others with prior claims had died before him, though in fact they did not. The

Master of the Revels is central to our understanding of theatrical licensing, and it is helpful to see how he relates to patronage. When Edmund Tilney was confirmed in the post in 1579, he owed it to his distant cousin and patron, Sir Charles Howard, latterly the Lord Admiral (Streitberger 1978). Tilney had displayed his literary talents to the court with *The Flower of Friendshippe* (1568), a discourse on marriage tactfully dedicated to the queen, but that was nothing without Howard's influence.

Howard, who long maintained an interest in theatricals, then held a watching brief for the ailing Lord Chamberlain; the Master was an official in the Chamberlain's office, mainly charged with providing entertainment at court. The Chamberlain had a proprietary interest in the post, but the right to confer it remained with the queen. As Tilney flourished, many suitors buzzed around for the next reversion. A sadly disappointed one was the dramatist and author John Lyly, client of the earl of Oxford, who bemoaned to the queen how she had said he "should aim all his courses at the Revels (I dare not say with a promise, but with a hopeful item of the reversion), for which these ten years I have attended with an unwearied patience" (Hunter 1962: 85–6). King James conferred the reversion on Sir George Buc, a historian of some distinction – but more importantly both a client of Lord Admiral Howard and a man who had done diplomatic service for Robert Cecil. Again, the serving Chamberlain was ill. Buc succeeded Tilney in 1610, and the reversion passed in 1612 to Sir John Astley, a client of Lord Chamberlain Suffolk; he in turn succeeded Buc when the latter went mad in 1622. But in effect he sold the post in 1623 to Sir Henry Herbert, brother of the poets Edward and George Herbert. Herbert was, more critically, a lesser kinsman of Lord Chamberlain Pembroke, who certainly secured him this position, as he doubtless secured the reversion for Jonson. There is some irony in Jonson so nearly achieving this appointment, since the Master of the Revels was also principal licenser for the acting companies in the London region (Dutton 1991). And no one's plays had more disturbed the peace than the early Jonson's (Riggs 1989: 32–4, 99–106, 122–6).

Licensing – whether in the form of authorizing institutions like trade guilds to regulate their own field of business, or granting monopoly trading rights, or allowing the actors to perform, or permitting books to be printed – was as characteristic of early modern society as patronage, and in many respects its counterpart. Everything hinged on the ultimate authority of the crown. In return for money, or simply as a cheap way of rewarding service, the crown would delegate part of its authority to favored groups and individuals, who would thereby profit from an exclusive advantage. Such licensing reinforced the hierarchical social fabric, tying license-holders (and beyond them their clients) into the circle of privilege and authority. But the granting of monopolies also generated resentments, becoming one of the bitterest bones of contention between Elizabeth, James, and their Parliaments.

For the actors, licensing had both good and bad points. It allowed their profession to survive and indeed flourish, in the face of widespread objections to it as a threat to public order, as a breeding ground of vice and disease, and as an affront to God. Conversely, it set strict conditions on who might perform, and what, as well as where and when they might do so. How this developed from conditions of patronage is apparent in the requirement that all acting companies must have a patron: without one they were deemed to be vagabonds or masterless men, a growing problem in the era, against whom increasingly savage legislation was passed (Beier 1986). By 1598 such patrons had to be members of the House of Lords; from 1594 companies allowed to act regularly near London and at court were virtually restricted to those patronized by members of the Privy Council (Lord Chamberlain, Lord Admiral, and, from 1601, the earl of Worcester, Master of the Horse); in 1603/4 they passed into royal patronage as the King's, Prince Henry's, and Queen Anna's Men.

The precise significance of "patronage" in this context remains elusive, since a patron did not normally pay his actors: they fended for themselves commercially (White and Westfall 2002). Yet they wore their patrons' liveries, prayed for them at public performances, and might invoke their authority if problems arose. Patrons who opted for this role (by no means all eligible aristocrats did) seem to have felt that their association with a successful troupe reflected well upon them, carrying marks of their standing around the country, and acquiring extra kudos when the troupe performed at court. Whether patrons took an active interest in what their troupes performed, or whether their repertoires deliberately promoted their interests, is imperfectly understood. The Queen's Men (an ultra-prestigious troupe created in 1583 at the instigation of the earl of Leicester and Sir Francis Walsingham) certainly had a repertoire that promoted English nationalism and Protestant ideology (McMillin and MacLean 1998). More contentiously, Shakespeare's plays for the King's Men have been described as "one of the master oeuvres of European patronage art" (Kernan 1995: xxiii), while opinion remains divided whether earlier plays such as *A Midsummer Night's Dream* and *The Merry Wives of Windsor* relate to the affairs of the Hunsdon Lord Chamberlains who were his company's patron at the time.

Such patronage did not in itself regulate the day-to-day business of theatre, especially in London. This is where the Master of the Revels came in. As early as 1574 the patent of Leicester's Men required that their plays should have been "sene and allowed" by him before performance: such "allowance" rendered a play fit to be performed at court, a standard that could hardly be challenged by local authorities around the country (Chambers 1923: II, 88). They would, of course, pay for this license. In 1581 Edmund Tilney received a Special Commission, from which wider licensing powers developed. This authorized him

> to warne commaunde and appointe in all places within this our Realme of England, aswell within francheses and liberties as without, all and every plaier or plaiers with their playmakers, either belonging to any noble man or otherwise, bearinge the name or names of using the facultie of playmakers or plaiers of Comedies, Tragedies, Enterludes or whatever other showes soever, from tyme to tyme and at all tymes to appeare before him with all such plaies, Tragedies, Comedies or showes as they shall in readines or meane to sett forth, and them to recite before our said Servant … whom we ordeyne appointe and aucthorise by these presentes of all suche showes, plaies, plaiers and playmakers, together with their playing places, to order and reforme, auctorise and put downe, as shalbe thought meete or unmeete unto himself. (Chambers 1923: IV, 285–7)

This was primarily to help Tilney provide entertainment at court at a reasonable cost: it gave him catch-all powers to call upon the resources of the acting companies that had only recently taken up semi-permanent residence at theatres like the Theatre and the Curtain (Streitberger 1978).

But it also meant that Tilney had a special relationship with those companies. Against the protests of the city authorities, he was seen as their protector, self-interestedly perpetuating the myth that public performances were rehearsals to play before the queen. At the same time, when competition to perform at court became excessive, it was Tilney who was authorized to create the Queen's Men, with leading figures from other troupes; they thereafter had sole entrée to court for several years. Licensing brought with it privileges, but only under conditions acceptable to authority. The star of the Queen's Men waned with the deaths of their backers, but arrangements after 1594 were prompted by similar considerations. It is not unlikely that the

Chamberlain's and Admiral's Men were put together, as the Queen's Men had been, by Tilney. While Shakespeare, to take the prime example, was clearly a dramatist of the commercial theatre, he was so within the very specific constraints of a licensing regime represented by the Master of the Revels. Within that regime he made antithetic choices to Jonson's, tying himself to the Chamberlain's Men as their "ordinary poet" (contracted dramatist) as the mainstay of his career, and only apparently contemplating aristocratic patronage (as in dedicating *Venus and Adonis* and *The Rape of Lucrece* to the earl of Southampton) in 1593/4 when plague closed the theatres.

All companies within Tilney's sphere submitted their playbooks to him for "allowance" before performance. This involved censorship, but also conferred on the company exclusive right to perform a play – a form of copyright. As a censor, Tilney was looking for several things: anything of specific offense to his superiors at court, or to the representatives of friendly foreign powers; anything that might provoke public disorder; anything that looked too closely at government affairs, and particularly the religious controversies of the day. When he found any of these, he exerted his authority firmly. At the head of the manuscript of *Sir Thomas More* he wrote: "Leave out the insurrection wholy with the Cause ther off & begin with Sr Tho: Moore att the mayors sessions with a reportt afterwardes off his good service don being Shrive [Sheriff] of London uppon a mutiny Agaynst the Lumbardes only by A Shortt reporte & nott otherwise at your perilles. E. Tyllney" (Dutton 1991: pl. 7). Tilney was uneasy about the depiction of public rioting, especially aimed at aliens resident in London: the issue was a fraught one in the early 1590s. Yet he seems indifferent to More's status as a Catholic martyr to Tudor tyranny for refusing to accept the Act of Supremacy. The play treads delicately around those issues; Tilney tinkered only occasionally. He shows no sign of having tried to police a strict conformity to "approved" views, or to have interrogated very closely the intentions of dramatists, so long as they were discreet and stopped short of overt dissent or offense.

We can see the line normally drawn in the office-book of Sir Henry Herbert, much of which (unlike those of his predecessors) has survived. In January 1631 he wrote: "I did refuse to allow of a play of Messinger's, because itt did contain dangerous matter, as the deposing of Sebastian king of Portugal by Philip the <Second,> and ther being a peace sworen twixte the kings of England and Spayne" (Bawcutt 1996: 171–2). So he refused to license a play that was overtly hostile to the king's foreign policy with Spain. Yet five months later he licensed *Believe as You List*, which is transparently the play he had turned down, but re-set in classical antiquity. There is no reason to suppose this was an oversight. The new play was not *overtly* offensive to anyone who mattered: it discreetly veiled its anti-Spanish sympathies behind a plausible historical facade, putting it on the right side of the line Herbert policed. There is another telling marker in Herbert's record of Charles I's reaction to another play by Massinger, entitled *The King and the Subject*: "readinge over the play at Newmarket, [he] set his marke upon the place with his owne hande, and in thes words: 'This is too insolent, and to bee changed'. Note, that the poett makes it the speech of a king, Don Pedro kinge of Spayne, and spoken to his subjects" (Bawcutt 1996: 204). This concerned royal taxation without parliamentary sanction, a highly sensitive issue. Herbert might simply have cancelled the passage, or banned the entire play. But he tried to make it playable after consulting the king, allowing it on condition that "the reformations [be] most strictly observed, and not otherwise," including that the title be changed; and no one suggested punishing Massinger. The king's dry response reflected the attitude of most aristocrats to such matters. They were used to regular insolence from the lower orders, and would not condescend to confront it; only occasionally did something "too insolent" evade or pass through the censorship that was meant to contain it.

Many of the era's famous theatrical scandals occurred in circumstances over which Masters of the Revels had no control, which is a measure of their effectiveness. When Jonson and Chapman were imprisoned for *Eastward Ho* (1605), and threatened with judicial mutilation, it was not simply that the play satirized James's Scottish courtiers – one of whom, Sir James Murray, complained to the king. The play had not been licensed, which put it altogether outside the protective frame of authority. In his predicament, Jonson wrote to seven powerful courtiers: Salisbury, Suffolk, Montgomery, Pembroke, two unnamed lords (one Aubigny?), and an unnamed lady (Bedford?) – invoking the entire umbrella of patronage that he normally relied upon for sustenance. The Children of the Queen's Revels, who staged the play, were uniquely given Samuel Daniel as a licenser in 1604, instead of Tilney. These "little eyases" generated successive scandals until, on the king's orders, they were wound up in 1608. The furore over *The Game at Chesse* (1624) was very different. This was licensed by Herbert in the normal way, but its frank depiction of deteriorating Anglo-Spanish relations was wildly popular and proved diplomatically embarrassing. Relations were nearly but not quite exhausted, so when the Spanish ambassador complained, the king and Privy Council had to go through the motions of stopping the play and seeking out responsible parties (Dutton 2001).

Timing also had a bearing on the most visible censorship to have affected Shakespeare's plays. This is the deposition scene in *Richard II* (4.1.145–308 in modern editions). It does not occur in any of the three quartos published in Elizabeth's reign, but was first printed in 1608. Its absence is not immediately apparent in the earlier versions: it does not leave a gaping gap. The Bishop of Carlisle warns of the dangers of deposing Richard and is arrested for his pains, and Bolingbroke promptly announces the date of his coronation – the deposition an implicit political reality. When the Abbot of Westminster then laments the "woeful pageant" they have "here beheld," it refers to this brisk realpolitik. Only in the 1608 text does it refer to Richard's ritualized self-deposition: it has even been argued that the scene is really an *addition* in a Jacobean revision of the play. Most scholars agree, however, that it was indeed a cut from Shakespeare's original text, raising three distinct questions: who made it, when, and why? Perhaps Tilney made the cut when he first licensed the play for performance, around 1594/5. But the play *ought* to have undergone a second censorship, by a clerical licenser for the press (see below), when it was first printed in 1597. This, however, is one of many works not entered in the Stationers' Register, the only record of such licensing, so we cannot be sure it happened.

Many have found this cut baffling, given that the scene largely registers Richard's poetic self-pity. In the play as published, Richard is clearly deposed even though we do not see the event, and is even murdered on stage. By far the most convincing explanation is that proposed by Cyndia Clegg, who argues that it is the political framework around the scene that made it so sensitive (Clegg 1997b). The first cut line is Northumberland's request to his fellow peers: "May it please you, lords, to grant the Commons' suit?" (l. 145); when Richard balks at reading aloud his offenses, he insists: "The Commons will not then be satisfied" (l. 262). So the whole proceeding is being conducted under the authority of Parliament: the peers represent the House of Lords, working in consort with the House of Commons. This suggests that Parliament has the authority to depose a monarch, which no monarch of the era would have conceded. What made this such a charged issue in the 1590s was the uncertainty surrounding Elizabeth's successor: no one knew who this would be, or by what authority the decision would be made. Anxieties were fomented by

A Conference about the Next Succession, by the Jesuit Robert Parsons and others; although proscribed, it circulated in England after 1595. By 1608, with James securely on the throne, and three children to provide for the succession, such matters were innocuous constitutional niceties; in 1597 someone clearly decided they were safer not aired.

Much has been made of the fact that the Chamberlain's Men were hired to perform a play of Richard II, probably Shakespeare's, on the eve of the Essex Rebellion in February, 1601. But in licensing terms, the actors did nothing wrong: it was an "allowed" play, performed in their usual theatre. When one of the company, Augustine Phillips, was examined he talked of it purely as a commercial event, claiming they had required a £2 fee to stage an old play that had lost its audience appeal. No action was taken against them. Indeed, they quickly played again at court – on the eve of Essex's execution. But another text concerning Richard II shows us both how works were licensed for the press, and how this quite anodyne process could become altogether more dangerous if events conspired against it. This was Dr John Hayward's *The First Part of the Life and Reign of King Henry IV*.

The book was entered in the Register of the Stationers' Company on January 9, 1599. The Stationers had the monopoly of printing in London, and this entry secured copyright to its publisher, John Wolfe. It also records that the book had been duly authorized by Samuel Harsnett, a domestic chaplain of the bishop of London. Under a Star Chamber decree of 1586 the authority for licensing most printed books fell to the archbishop of Canterbury and the bishop. Though sometimes cited as evidence of a wish for tight ideological control, this was not in origin government policy. It was actually brought in at the request of the Stationers' Company, who paid good money to get it through the Court of Star Chamber (Clegg 1997a). As Edward Arber observes, the "Star Chamber decree ... was undoubtedly promoted, not by the Government, but by the principal Stationers chiefly as a protection for their own literary property as an article of commerce" (Arber 1875–9: III, 17; cf. II, 807–12). Arber is surely right: a more clearly defined and circumscribed system of licensing (than the various measures applied since the time of Henry VIII) had the double virtue of promoting good relations with the authorities and preserving the Stationers' privileges.

There are analogies here with the collusive supervision of the acting companies through the Master of the Revels. The authorities could move with ruthless energy if the system of authority itself was abused, as happened with the Martin Marprelate pamphlets (1588–90), which attacked the church and were printed on unlicensed presses. But, for the most part, the system worked smoothly and uncontentiously during the 1590s, with a degree of informality that the Hayward case itself underlined. By the late 1590s, it was common for works – usually trivia like ballads – to be published without clerical authorization, merely under the warrant of the wardens of the Stationers (Blayney 1997). The bishops occasionally issued licenses personally (especially for works of theology), but usually relied on deputies. The supervision of these clerical censors devolved mainly on the bishop of London, and licensing duties became informally associated with posts in his gift. So Harsnett, Bishop Bancroft's client, became involved, issuing his first license in August, 1598. Licensing would occupy only a part of his time. Apart from regular clerical duties, he was already following Bancroft's prosecution of the Puritan John Darrell for performing fraudulent exorcisms, of which Harsnett was to write a satirical denunciation. He licensed only another nine books before putting his hand to Hayward's *Henry IV*. It then took fully eighteen months for the consequences of that signature to unfold.

The book was published in February, 1599, a month after being licensed; between licensing and publication it acquired a florid dedication, in Latin, to the earl of Essex (signed by Hayward), and a Preface to the Reader, signed "A. P." Wolfe later claimed that he and Hayward jointly dedicated it to Essex, when the book was already finished, since it dealt with military matters in Ireland such as Essex himself was about to undertake; and that he had personally taken it to Essex for his approval, Hayward being ill. The book was an immediate success, selling over 500 copies in three weeks and causing much comment (Chamberlain 1939: I, 70). But Essex belatedly objected to Archbishop Whitgift about the dedication, perhaps fearing it might be misconstrued. Whitgift ordered the Wardens of the Stationers to remove it from remaining copies, which they did, and the edition quickly sold out.

By April 8, however – after Essex had left for Ireland – Wolfe planned a further printing, and approached Hayward for a fresh text; Hayward obliged, adding an Epistle Apologetical protesting the innocence of his intentions, and 1,500 copies were printed by May 28 (Dowling 1930: 221–2). Bancroft seized the lot and burned them privately; Wolfe was imprisoned for two weeks, though no charges were brought. No explanation was offered, but the unspoken subtext to the whole affair was the status and the (real or supposed) ambitions of the earl of Essex. Cyndia Clegg has plausibly argued that Whitgift acted out of personal loyalty to Essex, whom he sought to shield during his absence, rather than out of his duty as a censor (Clegg 1997a: 204–10). The Essex affair also seems to have been central to the notorious Bishops' Ban of June 1, 1599, in which several contentious works were called in and burned (notably those of Harvey and Nashe); other satires and epigrams were forbidden, and all histories were to be referred to Privy Council members for approval. (These latter measures, rather typically, seem hardly to have affected anything in practice.)

This might well have been the end of the Hayward affair, had not Essex's career then taken the disastrous turn it did. But the Irish campaign was an unmitigated failure, and he returned to court (late September, 1599), against the express orders of the queen. The fortunes of Hayward and his book then shadowed those of Essex. The queen and her advisers stopped short of prosecuting Essex for treason, though they sought grounds for doing so – and Hayward's book was one place they looked. Lord Chief Justice Popham drew up notes for "Interrogatories ... to be administered to Dr Hayward." Highlighting a number of possibly charged historical inaccuracies and inventions, he headed his questions with "Who made the preface to the reader?" and "Wherein he conceives that book might be not only precepts but patterns for private direction and for matters of state, and instruct young men more shortly and old men more fully?" The preface, that is, seemed to alert readers to topical applications of what followed, while the history itself raised issues (taxation, Ireland, relationship between monarch, state, and subject) more pertinent to the end of the sixteenth century than that of the fourteenth, and that Hayward could not substantiate from his sources. Popham also shrewdly queried: "When he first resolved to set it forth, and at what time he began it?" (Green 1869: 404–45).

The dedication was the nub of the issue, since it was construed as inciting casual readers to approach the history from a very precise, contemporary perspective. Essex – addressed "Magnus siquidem es, et presenti judicio, et futuri temporis expectatio" ("Since you are great, both in the judgment of the present time, and in the expectation of the future") – stood out as Bolingbroke to Elizabeth's Richard II. But the authorities probably wanted to establish something even more damning: that there had been complicity between Essex and Hayward over it (perhaps even that A. P. was Essex himself), so that criminal conspiracy could be added to other charges Essex might face. Indeed the queen apparently insisted that Hayward was not the true author but was shielding "some more mischievous person." At bottom, the authorities wanted parallels between the book and recent affairs to prove Essex was *consciously* modeling himself on Bolingbroke, and that this explained his treacherous behavior in Ireland.

The most compelling evidence for this explanation lies in papers outlining an outright charge of treason against Essex (Green 1869: items 32 and 33, dated July 22, 1600). This charge, though never brought to court, involved counts of conspiracy with Jesuits and agents of the pope, and of treasonous complicity with the Irish rebel Tyrone. The last item claimed that "Essex's own actions confirm that intent of this treason. His permitting underhand that treasonable book of Henry IV to be printed and published; it being plainly deciphered, not only by the matter, and by the epistle itself, for what end and for whose behalf it was made" (Green 1869: 453–55). To those contemplating prosecuting Essex, his involvement with Hayward's book stood on a par with negotiating with Jesuits and Irish rebels.

But Essex was not prosecuted at this time, only censured in private proceedings. Now, however (July 11, 1600), Hayward was summoned before the Court of Star Chamber. Dudley Carleton linked this prosecution to a cat-and-mouse game with Essex: "My Ld of Essex remains prisoner, but at his owne custody. the Q. had given him liberty to go into the cuntrie, but recalled it againe upon the taking of Dor Haywood who for writing Henry the forth was comitted to the tower" (Dowling 1930: 212). Sir Edward Coke summarized the case against Hayward:

> in proof that the Doctor selected a story 200 years old, and published it last year, intending the application of it to this time, the plot being that of a King who is taxed for misgovernment and his council for corrupt and covetous dealings for private ends; the King is censured for conferring benefits on hated favourites, the nobles become discontented, and the commons groan under continual taxation, whereupon the King is deposed, and in the end murdered. (Green 1869: 499)

The Lords sent Hayward to the Tower – where he still was at Christmas, 1602, though apparently released before King James reached London in May, 1603. On January 22, 1601, as the Essex affair neared its tragic end, Hayward was examined again in the Tower, and was surprisingly candid about changes he had made in his history. But Essex's uprising on February 8 ended the authorities' interest in a mere book.

The prosecution of Hayward was a shot in a war of nerves – striking at Essex at one remove, and suggesting to people at large a wider background of disloyalty. The book was scrutinized almost from its publication, but was only found to be treasonable when it was politically convenient that it should be so. It attracted attention not for itself, but because it might provide evidence of *Essex's* treason. In his own defense Hayward made Harsnett's licensing an issue, arguing that a book that was properly "allowed" could hardly be illegal – an authorized reading precluded subsequent and more prejudicial ones. Coke wrote menacingly to Harsnett, whose reply is intensely revealing (Brownlow 1993: 175–7). He writes as a man in fear of his life, recognizing that Coke was looking to implicate Hayward in a conspiracy and that he (Hayward's fellow student at Cambridge) was in danger of being implicated too. So he defends himself with every argument he can muster: that Hayward did not, contrary to normal practice, present and defend his book in person, but left word that it was only "a cantel of our Englishe chronicles phrased and flourished over onelie to shewe the Author his pretie Witt"; that Harsnett's own "approbation" was not a true license but only a recommendation to the bishop (doubtless true, but normally irrelevant); that Hayward lied in saying Harsnett had passed it as published – in fact "it was heddlesse without epistle, preface, or dedication at all," leading Harsnett to conclude it was indeed "a meer rhetoricall exornation ... to shewe the foyle of the Author his witt"; most desperate of all, Harsnett, declaring himself an innocent divine, claims to have licensed the book without reading it.

He may have calculated that it was better to plead guilty to negligence than be convicted of collusion with Hayward. How plausible was this? How many books at the time were actually licensed unread? How open to abuse was it that there were twelve different licensers, and that authors usually had discretion about which they approached? The fact is we do not know. But the whole business of Hayward's *Henry IV* underlines a recurrent truth about licensing and censorship in the period, whether for print or for the stage: that for the most part these were *inclusive* processes, calculated to keep writers, dramatists, publishers, and players within the circle of authority, rather than to exclude them from it. Normally it took exceptional circumstances *beyond the writing itself* (such as the Essex affair) to generate real scandal.

Richard Dutton

References and Further Reading

Arber, Edward, ed. 1875–9. *A Transcript of the Registers of the Company of Stationers of London; 1554–1640 A.D.*, 5 vols. London: privately printed.

Barish, Jonas A.. 1973. "Jonson and the Loathèd Stage," in W. Blissett, Julian Patrick and R. W. Van Fossen, eds., *A Celebration of Ben Jonson*. Toronto: University of Toronto Press, pp. 27–53.

Bawcutt, N. W. 1996. *The Control and Censorship of Caroline Drama: The Records of Sir Henry Herbert, Master of the Revels 1623–73*. Oxford: Clarendon Press.

Beier, A. L. 1986. *Masterless Men: The Vagrancy Problem in England, 1560–1641*. London: Methuen.

Blayney, Peter W. M. 1997. "The Publication of Playbooks," in John D. Cox and David Scott Kastan, eds., *A New History of Early English Drama*. New York: Columbia University Press, pp. 383–420.

Brennan, Michael G. 1988. *Literary Patronage in the English Renaissance: The Pembroke Family*. London and New York: Routledge.

Brownlow, F. J. 1993. *Shakespeare, Harsnett, and the Devils of Denham*. Newark, DE: University of Delaware Press.

Butler, Martin. 1993. "Jonson's Folio and the Politics of Patronage," *Criticism* 35: 377–90.

Chamberlain, John. 1939. *Letters*, 2 vols. Ed. N. E. McClure. Philadelphia: American Philosophical Society.

Chambers, E. K. 1923. *The Elizabethan Stage*, 4 vols. Oxford: Clarendon Press.

Clare, Janet. 1990. *"Art Made Tongue-Tied By Authority": Elizabethan and Jacobean Dramatic Censorship*. Manchester: Manchester University Press.

Clegg, Cyndia Susan. 1997a. *Press Censorship in Elizabethan England*. Cambridge: Cambridge University Press.

Clegg, Cyndia Susan. 1997b. " 'By the Choise and Inuitation of Al the Realme': *Richard II* and Elizabethan Press Censorship," *Shakespeare Quarterly* 48: 432–48.

Clegg, Cyndia Susan. 2001. *Press Censorship in Jacobean England*. Cambridge: Cambridge University Press.

Dowling, Margaret. 1930. "Sir John Hayward's Troubles over his *Life of Henry IV*," *Library* (4th ser.), 2: 212–24.

Dutton, Richard. 1991. *Mastering the Revels: The Regulation and Censorship of English Renaissance Drama*. Basingstoke: Macmillan.

Dutton, Richard. 2000. *Licensing, Censorship and Authorship in Early Modern England: Buggeswords*. Basingstoke: Palgrave.

Dutton, Richard. 2001. "Receiving Offence: *A Game at Chess* Again," in Andrew Hadfield, ed., *Literature and Censorship in Renaissance England*. Basingstoke: Palgrave, pp. 50–71.

Evans, Robert C. 1989. *Ben Jonson and the Poetics of Patronage*. Lewisburg, PA: Bucknell University Press.

Finkelpearl, Philip J. 1986. " 'The Comedians' Liberty': Censorship of the Jacobean Stage Reconsidered," *English Literary Renaissance* 16: 123–38.

Green, Mary A. E., ed. 1869. *Calendar of State Papers, Domestic Series … 1598–1601*. London: Her Majesty's Stationery Office.

Hunter, G. K. 1962. *John Lyly, the Humanist as Courtier*. London: Routledge.

Jonson, Ben. 1925–52. *Ben Jonson*, 11 vols. Eds. C. H. Herford, Percy Simpson, and Evelyn Simpson. Oxford: Clarendon Press.

Kernan, Alvin B. 1995. *Shakespeare, the King's Playwright: Theater in the Stuart Court 1603–1613*. New Haven: Yale University Press.

Lytle, Guy Fitch and Stephen Orgel, eds. 1981. *Patronage in the Renaissance*. Princeton: Princeton University Press.

MacCaffrey, Wallace T. 1961. "Place and Patronage in Elizabethan Politics," in S. T. Bindoff et al., eds., *Government and Society: Essays Presented to Sir John Neale*. London: Athlone Press, pp. 95–126.

McMillin, Scott and Sally-Beth MacLean. 1998. *The Queen's Men and their Plays*. Cambridge: Cambridge University Press.

Marotti, Arthur. 1986. *John Donne: Coterie Poet*. Madison: University of Wisconsin Press.

Patterson, Annabel. 1984. *Censorship and Interpretation: The Conditions of Reading and Writing in Early Modern England*. Madison: University of Wisconsin Press.

Peck, Linda Levy. 1982. *Northampton: Patronage and Policy at the Court of James I*. London: George Allen and Unwin.

Riggs, David. 1989. *Ben Jonson: A Life*. Cambridge, MA: Harvard University Press.

Streitberger, W. R. 1978. "On Edmond Tyllney's Biography," *Review of English Studies* (n.s.), 29: 11–35.

Sweeney, John Gordon III. 1985. *Jonson and the Psychology of Public Theater*. Princeton: Princeton University Press.

Wayne, Don E. 1984. *Penshurst: The Semiotics of Place and the Poetics of History*. Methuen: London.

White, Paul W. and Suzanne R. Westfall, eds. 2002. *Shakespeare and Theatrical Patronage in Early Modern England*. Cambridge: Cambridge University Press.

Chapter 5

Humanism, Rhetoric, Education

Peter Mack

The aims of this chapter are to introduce part of the cultural and educational history of the English Renaissance, to analyze the training in reading and writing provided in Elizabethan grammar schools and universities, and to read some texts from the period 1580–1620 using the categories that contemporary readers learned to apply. I shall start with some working definitions, then describe the impact of humanism on Tudor education, next propose a list of skills that constitute Elizabethan communicative competence, before using this list of reading and writing skills to analyze texts by Sidney, Shakespeare, and Bacon. The issues raised in this chapter are considered in more detail and with fuller documentation in Mack (2002).

Fourteenth-and fifteenth-century Italian humanism was an attempt to reintroduce classical standards of Latin composition, by study and imitation of classical authors, by learning Greek, and by reviving classical rhetoric. In place of the inelegant but effective Latin that had been the medium of church business and university life in the Middle Ages, the humanists aimed to write stylish and impressive Latin like Cicero and the best of the classical Latin writers. Humanism was an important intellectual motive force of the Italian Renaissance, a broader movement that thought of itself as reviving literature and the visual arts. Rhetoric was the classical training in writing. It involved five distinct skills: invention, finding the arguments, stories, and ideas of a piece; disposition, putting them into the most effective order; style, expressing the ideas in the most effective language; memory, memorizing the speech; and delivery, including voice and gesture. Medieval and Renaissance rhetoric, which were more directed to written compositions, tended to concentrate on the first three of these skills.

In the later fifteenth century some Englishmen (like other northern Europeans) traveled to Italy to acquire the new humanist learning.

In the early sixteenth century famous Continental humanists like Erasmus and Vives spent time in England. Thomas More, whose most famous work, *Utopia* (1516), was composed in a witty neoclassical Latin, was the most internationally famous English humanist. From the foundations of St Paul's School (1509) and Corpus Christi College Oxford (1517), a group of new schools and colleges (together with reformed syllabuses in some older institutions) produced the classically educated young men who formed the most lasting impact of humanism in England. The schools that were lost with the dissolution of the monasteries were replaced by newly established town grammar schools, which were given humanist curricula. Thomas Cromwell promoted reform of the universities in the direction of the new classical learning in order to produce a new, non-clerical cadre of government servants and to educate a learned clergy to further the Reformation. At the same time as many new schools were founded, the number of students attending the two English universities (Oxford and Cambridge) increased. Learning enjoyed great prestige and the sons of wealthy country families, who would formerly have been educated at home or in a neighboring great house, began to attend university even though many of them did not take degrees. Power in Queen Elizabeth's council resided not so much with the hereditary barons as with the university-educated men of the middling sort (like the Cecils and the Bacons). Education came to be seen as a requirement for political influence, even at a local level. Humanist training in arguing and speaking enabled a person to be heard in public debate, and taught him the form and the content of what the elite social group would regard as persuasive speech.

School and University Curriculum

Many of the new schools were provided with detailed (if at times overoptimistic) lists of the books to be studied in each class. Teachers' manuals, surviving textbooks, and a few student notebooks also provide us with some idea of how grammar-school boys were educated. Putting this information together is a task of historical imagination and scholars differ as to how much weight should be given to different types of evidence. (Some highly privileged girls received a humanist education at home, but they could not attend school.)

Tudor grammar-school syllabuses (Baldwin 1944: I, 122–4, 310, 342–51; Mack 2002: 12–14) suggest a reasonably uniform curriculum that focused on three main elements: the Latin language, which was the basis for all further learning, Latin literature, and composition. Pupils were taught to read and speak Latin by learning grammar texts, proverbs, and dialogues by heart. They showed their knowledge of grammar by varying the number, gender, and tense of the sentences they had learned. Looking at these dialogues and exercises, though, it soon becomes clear that the potentially tedious learning by heart and drilling in different versions was enlivened by a spirit of play. When Erasmus provides a list of greetings to learn by heart they soon move into the inventive, the insulting, and the absurd ("Greetings, you consumer of quarts. Greetings to you, you bottomless pit and devourer of cakes ... Good luck to you with your baldness. Good luck to you with your crooked nose"; Thompson 1965: 558). Pupils learnt that language-learning was an opportunity for linguistic play and competitive ingenuity as long as grammatical correctness was maintained. It is unlikely that Greek was taught much outside London and the university cities.

In Latin literature, grammar-school pupils typically studied a range of important Latin genres through the best examples of each (Terence for comedy, Virgil's *Eclogues* and *Aeneid* for pastoral and epic, Cicero's *De officiis* for moral philosophy, Sallust or Caesar for history, Horace for lyric poetry, and Ovid for mythology). Alongside the Bible these authors provide us with the basic background reading required for serious study of Renaissance literature. Tudor elementary literature teaching focused on grammar and vocabulary, using the best Latin writers as models for the pupils in their own speaking and writing of Latin. Teachers were instructed to provide introductions to the books, conveying information about author, genre, structure, teaching, and style. Pupils were expected to notice their authors' use of rhetorical techniques (especially the figures of rhetoric) and to record memorable phrases and examples in their notebooks. Pupils were taught to read with an appreciation of the skills of their authors in exploiting the common fund of stories and techniques.

Literature teaching fed Latin composition, for which there were three main textbooks: a letter-writing manual, Aphthonius' *Progymnasmata* (or *Exercises*), and Erasmus' *De copia* (*On the Abundant Style*). Pupils learned to write letters in Latin by imitating the shorter letters of Cicero. Then they studied a manual that set out the contents of many different genres of letter. The *Progymnasmata* gave detailed recipes for writing in a range of genres (including fable, commonplace, comparison, speech for a character, description, proposal of a law). These school exercises could also be regarded as components of longer works that the pupils might later write. Erasmus' *De copia* (apart from Latin grammars the most successful school textbook in six-teenth-century Europe) offers a method of supercharging texts, either by varying their words (using figures of rhetoric) or by adding to the material, for example by dividing into parts, discussing the causes and effects of something, or describing every detail of its appearance. A copious style would give special verbal and emotional emphasis to an important section of a text. *De copia* shows pupils how to write descriptions and use commonplaces, examples, and maxims. It teaches them how to use a commonplace book to collect material from their reading. Elizabethan grammar-school syllabuses did not generally include a comprehensive treatment of rhetoric, but pupils were taught the figures of speech and many other rhetorical techniques.

Recent studies of Oxford in the sixteenth and seventeenth centuries have shown that students pursued a wide range of subjects under the direction of their individual tutors, alongside their required studies in classical literature, rhetoric, and logic (McConica 1986: 693–721). In rhetoric students studied some of Cicero's speeches (and sometimes some of Demosthenes') and at least one rhetoric textbook. In logic they usually prefaced Aristotle's *Organon* with a study of one of the human-ist introductions to dialectic (such as those by Agricola, Melanchthon, and Ramus). Turning away from medieval logic's concern with intri-cate problems of semantics, humanist dialecticians emphasized the use of logic in constructing persuasive arguments in good neoclassical Latin. They focused on the topics of invention (see below), the forms of argumentation, and the logical structure of texts.

To obtain a degree students had to participate in disputations. A Renaissance disputation often began with a speech by one of the participants (the respondent). The other participant (the opponent) then made an argument against the respondent's view. The respond-ent repeated the substance of this argument and denied it. The oppon-ent then made another argument, which the respondent repeated and replied to, either agreeing or denying the argument (and perhaps giving a reason). The opponent aimed to force the respondent either to agree to the opponent's first argument or to contradict himself. The opponent would often make arguments that appeared irrelevant to the question at issue (but that could later be shown to be connected). The respondent needed to take careful account of the implications of either agreeing or disagreeing with a particular argument. The respondent often distinguished different senses of the words that the opponent put to him, agreeing with them in one implied sense but disagreeing in another. The whole exercise called for great mental and verbal agility on the part of the participants (Mack 2002: 58–66, 71–3). Disputations between eminent scholars were often staged as intellectual entertainments for important visitors to the university, such as the queen and her court. The practice of disputation had a considerable impact on the way in which debates were conducted in the privy council and in Parliament (Mack 2002: 176–252).

Skills Promoted by Humanist Rhetorical Education

The rhetorical and dialectical skills learned at school and university can be considered (in line with the first three parts of rhetoric) as part of: invention, contributing materials that a pupil might use; disposition, the organization of texts read and composed; or presentation, concerning style, emphasis, or approach to an audience. These categories distinguish practical levels of analysis. One might begin by noticing the style and angle of approach of a work, before analyzing its structure and material. Conversely an analysis of content will help in understanding how material has been adapted for a particular audience.

Under invention I shall discuss moral sentences, narratives, descriptions, examples, commonplaces, and arguments. Many of the teaching strategies of the grammar school made pupils learn and use moral sentences. Their elementary readers on which they were drilled were short moral sentences (such as "Help your friends," "Know yourself," "A liar needs to have a good memory") from the *Distichs* attributed to Cato and from Culmann's *Sententiae pueriles* ("Latin Sentences for Boys"). Teachers pointed out moral sentences in their commentaries on more advanced texts. Pupils were taught to collect pithy sentences under moral headings in their commonplace books. They were provided with reference books like Erasmus' *Adagia*, which discusses the meaning and use of hundreds of Latin and Greek proverbs. The *Progymnasmata* exercise of the chreia elaborates a moral sentence from an author into a short composition by praising the author of the maxim, explaining its meaning, finding arguments from cause, contrary, comparison, example, and testimony, and adding an epilogue (C8). Moral axioms are ubiquitous in Renaissance discourse. Because they are so central to grammar-school education (Crane 1993), we can assume that audiences would have noticed the way writers used them.

The connection between moral axiom and illustrative narrative was taught through the second of the elementary readers, the Latin version of Aesop's *Fables*. Pupils' reading of Cicero's *De officiis* would have drawn particular attention to the way in which illustrative stories were used. School commentaries on Virgil's *Aeneid* and Ovid's *Metamorphoses* discuss the ethical conclusions to be drawn from particular episodes. The *Progymnasmata* include both fables and narratives among the composition exercises for the student. These exercises provide criteria, both of content (person, action, time, place, means, cause) and of handling (clarity, brevity, plausibility, propriety of diction) with which pupils could analyze historical stories (B8^v). Expository narratives were often required as parts of letters.

Aphthonius' *Progymnasmata* classify descriptions according to subjects: persons, things, times, and places. Descriptions of persons should proceed from the head to the feet. Descriptions of things should include their antecedents, their contents, and what results from them (Aa8). Lorichius' commentary, which accompanies most sixteenth-century editions of Aphthonius, makes many cross-references to the discussion of description in Erasmus' *De copia*, book two. Erasmus associates description with the technique of enargeia, bringing something before the eyes of the audience by vivid description in order to move their emotions. Vivid descriptions need to be full. Above all they must contain telling detail. They can be enhanced with comparisons, similes, contrasts, and by the use of striking adjectival clauses. In describing persons one can rely on the characteristics of particular occupations and ages, adding touches of individuality. It is very important to devise appropriate speech and dialogue for a described person. Descriptions involving a catalogue of external features are rare. Places described include rivers, countries, and towns. Descriptions of time concentrate on times of day, such as dawn, dusk, or night, or the seasons, especially spring and autumn (Erasmus 1978: 577–89). Brief descriptions can make an emotional point in an argument, as when Francis Bacon in the Parliament of 1593 (Hartley 1995: 109–10) argued against a new tax by describing the gentlemen selling their plate and the farmers their brass pots in order to pay it, or longer descriptions can be elaborated for their own sake in works intended mainly to give pleasure. Both Aphthonius and Erasmus direct their readers' attention to a number of descriptions from classical literary texts.

Elizabethan speeches and plays are full of historical examples. Some grammar-school teachers used epitomes of history organized according to the chief deeds and sayings of each emperor. Erasmus' *De copia* described ways to use and collect examples (Erasmus 1978: 606–39). The commonplace book helped pupils to collect from their reading significant examples under moral headings. For the university student, the example was one of the forms of argument, drawing a general conclusion from a single instance. Examples could be made more forceful through extended description or detailed narrative. In the Parliament of 1572, the bishops assembled sixteen pages of exemplary arguments from scripture in favor of Mary's execution, while the laymen produced fourteen pages of arguments from civil law, backed up with historical examples (Hartley 1981: 274–90). These examples could be assembled very quickly, but they had no effect on the queen. They were a good way of embellishing a case, but they did not carry much weight in determining the political issue. Because they were trained to quarry their own reading for re-usable examples, Elizabethan readers would have been particularly alert to the way in which their contemporaries made logical or emotional use of examples.

A commonplace is a multi-purpose elaboration of a subject, for example a praise of the benefits of peace or an evocation of the horror of murder, which can be inserted into a speech or a narrative. Cicero says that such passages may be used either to establish a point or to arouse the emotions of an audience (*De inventione*, II.xv.49). Aphthonius, who treats it as a form belonging to the prosecutor, provides a very detailed recipe for a commonplace, which should begin with an argument from the contrary and continue with exposition, comparison, elaboration of a moral axiom, rejection of pity, and finally a series of arguments to show that the action proposed is legal, just, useful, possible, and honorable and that it should happen. Lorichius adds that commonplaces are composed on topics that often arise in human affairs, such as fame, wealth, honor, life, death, virtue, prudence, justice, and so on. He connects the preparation of commonplaces with the use of the commonplace book (M4^v–O6^r).

The commonplace book was a blank exercise book with a moral heading at the top of each page. When pupils came across striking sentences or examples in their reading, they would enter them under an appropriate heading. When Hamlet calls for his tables to enter the thought "one may smile and smile and be a villain" (I.5.107–8), he presumably intends to enter it under "hypocrisy." When the student needs to write on a particular topic, the quotations in the commonplace book will provide useful material. As pupils read they would be asking themselves whether what they were reading merited inclusion and, if so, under what heading. This mental habit would have made it easier for them to follow the scattered discussion of particular issues in some Renaissance plays (for example "nature" or "need" in *King Lear*). Commonplaces and commonplace books contribute to the development of the Renaissance form of the essay.

Erasmus' methods for producing abundance (*copia*) of material draw on the arguments generated by the topics of invention, which were studied in the university logic course. The topics of invention are a set of headings (such as definition, genus, cause, contrary, comparison), which can be used to find ideas and arguments related to a subject. So arguments about love might mention the genus (the emotions) or refer to its causes (sight, acquaintance) and contraries (hatred). Agricola and his followers showed how the topics helped find materials that could be built into arguments. Agricola urged his readers to develop an understanding of the nature and subtypes of the individual topics and of the force of arguments derived from them. By using the topics to classify the arguments that they found in texts, students could learn about how good writers used particular types of argument.

Under disposition I shall discuss different genres, disputation, and dialectical reading. Whereas classical rhetoric proposed the four-part oration (introduction, narration, proof and refutation, conclusion) as the model for all types of text, grammar-school pupils had experience of a range of different genres. Letters were subdivided into many different genres whose structure was analyzed both in the letter-writing manuals and in the commentaries on Cicero's letters. The *Progymnasmata* described a range of minor genres that could be practiced in their own right or included as sections of longer texts. Teachers' introductory lectures discussed the genre and the structure of texts. Commentaries analyzed the structure of speeches in the *Aeneid* and in Terence's comedies. In his *De inventione dialectica*, Agricola pointed out the variety of structures used in classical literature and argued that the appropriate structure for a new composition will depend on a consideration of the writer's persona, aim, subject matter, audience, and occasion (Agricola 1539: 412–20, 449–50). Some Renaissance texts follow closely the expectations of a particular genre; others play with such expectations by variations of structure and content.

The rules of disputation required the respondent to outline the argument made by the opponent before replying to it. This way of organizing a reply influenced formal debate and other forms of writing. In Parliament a speaker usually outlined the two or three main points made in the previous speech and formulated his own speech as a response to those points. In the Privy Council, too, speeches often began by summarizing what had already been said and taking a new approach to some of the issues. The memoranda that Cecil and others made in preparation for meetings usually took the form of lists of arguments for and against a proposition, with replies to each of the arguments set out. Essays too often set out an initial position that is then modified in some of its detail. Disputation encouraged students to distinguish between different meanings of a word, refusing a statement in one sense of a term and accepting it in another, and to define terms carefully for the purpose of particular arguments.

As part of his teaching of humanist dialectic, Rudolph Agricola outlined a method of analyzing the argumentative structures underlying a text. He and his followers showed that Cicero's speeches could be understood to have simple, overarching logical structures. So Agricola analyzes Cicero's *Pro Milone* as a hypothetical syllogism: "whoever takes part in an ambush may lawfully be killed. Clodius took part in an ambush and was therefore lawfully killed" (Agricola 1539: 242). Much more complicated arguments were required to support each part of the overall argument. Humanist commentators also analyzed the arguments underlying speeches from the *Aeneid* and short poems by Virgil and Horace. Logical readings could be applied to a whole text (as in William Temple's Ramist analysis of Sidney's *Apology for Poetry*) or could be combined with an appreciation of the generic structure of a comedy or a sermon.

The following aspects of presentation will be discussed: figures of speech, style, amplification, and the approach to an audience. Some of the syllabuses of grammar schools include a handbook of the figures and tropes. The notebook of the Elizabethan schoolmaster John Conybeare includes a fourteen-page summary of them extracted from Susenbrotus' *Epitome troporum ac schematum* (1541). Schoolmasters were instructed to point out the use of rhetorical figures when they read texts, and discussions of some figures appear in *De copia* and Lorichius' commentary on it. Although modern readers find that there are too many figures of rhetoric, there is not much doubt that Elizabethan students knew many of the names and examples by heart; and being able to name them makes it possible to notice and discuss the different ways they are used.

The doctrine of the figures of speech rests on the idea that there is a simple form of language that can be embellished by the use of the figures. Poets know, by contrast, that figures like metaphor make intelligible thoughts that could not be expressed without them. There is an immense variety in the figures and tropes, but it is perhaps not too great a simplification to suggest that there are three main types. Some of the figures involve patterns of repetition or balance of words or sounds. Often these bring elegance to the writing, but they sometimes also have a strong emotional effect. Anaphora places the same word at the beginning of a succession of phrases; antistrophe repeats the same word at the end of a series of clauses; complexio combines these two. Traductio or ploce repeats a word within the same clause. Chiasmus repeats two words (or ideas) in successive clauses, altering the order in the second (A ... B, B ... A). Climax links three or more ideas (or words) through successive repetition (A to B, B to C, C to D). Parison balances the structure of two paired clauses; isocolon balances their length; antithesis balances two phrases with contrariety ("Prosperity encourages vice, but adversity discovers virtue").

A second group (often called the tropes) works through a change or extension in the meaning of the words used, for example through metaphor, allegory, metonymy (a word is replaced by a logically linked word), and synecdoche (a part is substituted for a whole or vice versa).

A third group describes an attitude that lies behind a particular use of language. With correctio, a speaker deliberately corrects a word spoken and replaces it with another. Aposiopesis involves deliberate hesitation, breaking off with the sense of a sentence incomplete. With concessio, a speaker allows the truth of a counter-argument. In this group one could also include exclamation, internal dialogue, rhetorical question, apostrophe (breaking off to address another person, often with the initial exclamation "O"), and enargeia (vivid description).

Style consists of more than the figures. It is regulated by the three qualities of good style: correctness, clarity, and careful sentence construction. Classical authorities also distinguish three levels of style (high, middle, and low) based on the level of diction (choice of vocabulary in relation to subject matter), on the complexity of sentence structure, and on the intensity with which the figures of rhetoric are employed (*Ad Herennium*. IV.viii.11, xii.17–18). Sixteenth-century writers recognized a distinction between the elaborately balanced Ciceronian sentence, consisting of several subclauses (also known as cola, or colon in the singular) and the more terse and epigrammatic Senecan style (Croll 1966).

Amplification aims to make something seem more important in order to elicit a stronger response from an audience. Sometimes this is a result of richness of detail in a passage; sometimes of the richness of the style employed. Commentaries and marginalia often draw attention to amplification in a particular passage of a text. It seems that readers appreciated that some passages were more densely worked than others, and thought that understanding the reason for this would help them interpret the text. In grammar schools amplification was taught mainly from *De copia*, reinforced by teachers' comments on ornaments of style, proverbs, and comparisons. In *De copia* Erasmus mentions certain specific techniques of amplification drawn from Quintilian's account in *Institutio oratoria*, 8.4: incremental increase, augmentation through circumstances, comparison, reasoning, pretending not to be surprised, and the piling up of words and phrases with the same meaning. Amplification is sometimes achieved by adding synonyms and using many figures of rhetoric together (Erasmus 1988: 218–20). In a broader sense all the techniques described in *De copia* serve to increase the verbal density of the style (Cave 1979).

Although consideration of the audience is one of the hallmarks of rhetoric, rhetoric textbooks say relatively little about audiences. Grammar-school boys would have come across this primarily in the letter-writing manual. Erasmus discusses the importance of comparing the topic of the letter with the relationship between writer and recipient. Certain forms of expression are required in address to a superior or in preparing an awkward request. Some hints on handling different types of address occur in the sections on different types of letter (for example in discussing the different approaches to writing a letter of consolation). In reading Latin texts, according to Brinsley, pupils must always bear in mind the person speaking, the subject matter, the person being addressed, and the occasion or purpose of the speech (Brinsley 1917: 123–4). The question of the relationship between speaker and audience is addressed in another way by the issue of self-presentation, which comes to the fore in the exercise of ethopoeia in Aphthonius's *Progymnasmata*. Ethopoeia is a speech that expresses the feelings and behavior of a historical person or an imaginary character. Aphthonius provides the example of Niobe lamenting the deaths of her children. Lorichius explains that the exercise is useful in adapting one's expression and material to different emotional states. The calm and prudent man speaks in a different way from someone who is frightened or angry (Y8⁻–Z7ʳ). Self-presentation also becomes a subject for investigation in the exercise of writing a letter appropriate to character from history or epic. An approach to the audience will be indicated by the style chosen, by the self-presentation of the speaker or writer, by the passages chosen for emphasis, and by the way in which an audience is implied in the text.

The rhetorical skills of humanist education that have been described in the last few pages were developed through a reciprocal exploration of reading and writing. Reading provided material for composition and writing exercises, and textbooks encouraged a reading from within the techniques of writing. Part of the response of an educated Elizabethan to a piece of writing was an aesthetic response of craftsmanly admiration or disdain. Grammar-school training provided society with a common set of criteria for what would count as acceptable and persuasive discourse. It encouraged certain expectations about the effect and appropriateness of particular techniques. But there was also an expectation that these techniques would be the subject of innovative play, that people would make new combinations from among the techniques, or would astonish their audience by using a technique associated with a particular genre for entirely different purposes. Such training created expectations that reasons for actions would be given, that questions could be asked, and that the language in which ideas were expressed would have an impact on its success. In the last part of the chapter I shall use the rhetorical skills Elizabethan students learned to analyze texts by Sidney, Shakespeare, and Bacon.

Sidney, *Astrophil and Stella*, Sonnet 5

It is most true, that eyes are form'd to serve
The inward light: and that the heavenly part
Ought to be king, from whose rules who do swerve,
Rebels to Nature, strive for their own smart.
  It is most true, what we call Cupid's dart,   5
An image is, which for ourselves we carve;
And, fooles, adore in temple of our hart,
Till that good God make Church and Churchman starve.
  True, that true Beautie Vertue is indeed,
Whereof this Beautie can be but a shade,   10
Which elements with mortall mixture breed:
True, that on earth we are but pilgrims made,
  And should in soule up to our countrey move:
  True, and yet true that I must Stella love.

Sonnets set up a range of generic expectations. From the example of Petrarch we expect that sonnets may have a *volta* or turn, in Petrarch usually placed at the main division of the sonnet between octave

Peter Mack

(the first eight lines, usually divided into two sets of four) and sestet (the final six lines). The rhyme scheme of Sidney's sonnet preserves the distinction between octave (abababba) and sestet (cdcdee) but adds the more English feature of a third quatrain and a final couplet. These structural features invite us to consider how the sonnet is divided up, what the role of the final couplet is, and the position and nature of the *volta*.

The chief structural markers of this sonnet, which can be considered as a type of anaphora ("It is most true," lines 1, 5; "True," lines 9, 12, 14), establish a stylistic context of logical argument. This is embellished with imagery derived from the languages of politics (lines 3–4), religion (lines 6–8), and Neoplatonic philosophy (lines 1–2, 9–11), culminating in a combination between philosophy and religion in lines 12–13. The address of the poem is initially impersonal, with small indications of fellow-feeling ("our," lines 6, 7, 13; "we," lines 5, 6, 12; in contrast to "who," "their," lines 3–4) between the speaker and his male audience (perhaps his fellow-debaters), but this is broken with the firm "I" of the final line, setting his own feelings against the shared wisdom he has summarized up to this point. The effect is that he is summarizing a series of arguments against love (perhaps he is admitting the strength of points made earlier in a disputation; perhaps he is summarizing a set of arguments in order to work out his own view, rather as Cecil used to) before asserting the contrary position: that in spite of all such reasons, he has to love Stella.

In spite of the pronounced *volta* in the final line, the poem presents no strong division in the speaker's self. Rather we are impressed with the brevity, ease, and smoothness of the exposition of received ideas before they are almost inevitably turned on their head. Some of the exposition makes use of axioms ("eyes are form'd to serve / The inward light"; true beauty is virtue; mortal beauty is only a shadow; we are pilgrims on earth) alongside imagery (light, dart, shadow, mixture, pilgrimage, return home). In the octave he develops the ideas of the primacy of the spiritual with arguments from contraries (if we concentrate on the earthly we are like rebellious subjects who will only harm themselves; by making a religion of Cupid we foolishly turn away from true religion), so the position taken in the final line is prepared (and disparaged) in advance. The turn to the personal and emotional is as conventional as the Neoplatonism, leading the audience to admire the delicacy of a poet who can touch so gracefully on so many ideas in such a short, well-mannered artifact. Above all this poem is a demonstration of Sidney's skill in elaborating conventional ideas. The logical frame of the poem (which may well recall disputation), rather than (as we might expect) providing the argumentative sinews of the poem, serves as an ornament, guaranteeing and enclosing Sidney's display of erudition. No one should underestimate the skill and knowledge required for such an assured performance.

Two Speeches from Shakespeare, *Hamlet*, Act I, Scene 2

> CLAUDIUS: Though yet of Hamlet our dear brother's death
> The memory be green, and that it us befitted
> To bear our hearts in grief, and our whole kingdom
> To be contracted in one brow of woe,
> Yet so far hath discretion fought with nature   5
> That we with wisest sorrow think on him
> Together with remembrance of ourselves.
> Therefore our sometime sister, now our queen,
> Th'imperial jointress of this warlike state,
> Have we, as 'twere with a defeated joy,   10
> With an auspicious and a dropping eye,
> With mirth in funeral and with dirge in marriage,
> In equal scale weighing delight and dole,
> Taken to wife. Nor have we herein barr'd
> Your better wisdoms, which have freely gone   15
> With this affair along. For all, our thanks.
> Now follows that you know ...
>
> (lines 1–17)

On the surface Claudius is the consummate politician. After the ceremonial of the court entry (clouded by the figure in black at the end of the procession) he takes command of the public arena, saying what needs to be said and dispatching business with confidence and aplomb. The markers of the speech suggest that we could read it almost as a single sentence ("Though ... Yet ... Therefore ... Now ... "), moving from a balanced consideration of factors to a rational conclusion and decisive action. Like a politician too he understands that the bare bones of the speech will not be enough, that he will need to elaborate appropriate gestures to public feeling and to reassure himself of the support of his followers (lines 14–16). Each element of the speech receives emphasis, with the greatest amplification attached to the marriage, which is the part of his narrative that requires most justification. On the simple outline "I have married my sister (in law)," Claudius elaborates the predicate first from a comparison of times (line 8), and then from position, as he enlarges "queen" with the more copious (not to say bombastic) "imperial jointress of this warlike state." Then he amplifies the circumstances of "taken to wife," with three expressions of the balance between hope and sorrow. "With mirth in funeral and with dirge in marriage," by assigning (with anaphora and isocolon) the unexpected mood to each ceremony, constitutes a sort of chiasmus. This linking of contraries is an example of the difficult rhetorical figure of synoeciosis. And yet the effect of the combination of figures is too artful. "Mirth in funeral" is a sign of inappropriate rather than well-tempered feelings. The two eyes that look in opposite directions can be read as signs of bodily indiscipline, even of madness, rather than the tempered and restrained display of appropriate emotion that Claudius craves.

Above all Claudius wants his audience to endorse his actions as fitting the norms of his society (an understandable desire in one who has transgressed them so outrageously). He wants to use the word "befitted" to confirm the appropriateness of his response to his brother's death, but the grammatical effect of lines 2–4 is to suggest that his grief of heart was required of him by circumstances rather than genuinely felt. The effect of the triple word play on "contracted," signifying the *agreement* in the nation and the idea of the nation *reduced* to a single body or even a single face, whose brow is *contorted* with sorrow, is diminished by being framed by the notion of expectation. Sorrow that is merely fitting or over-wise is probably not sorrow at all, especially when the yet green memory of his brother is matched "with remembrance of ourselves." Claudius' attempt to control his court's response to his accession and marriage, to insist on his prudent balance and moderation of expected emotions, is undone by the effect of his over-artful language. Later in the scene, he is too easily persuaded of the success of his amplified moral commonplaces on the appropriate and moderate response to the death of a father.

> HAMLET: O that this too too sullied flesh would melt,
> Thaw and resolve itself into a dew,   130
> Or that the Everlasting had not fix'd
> His canon 'gainst self-slaughter. O God! God!
> How weary, stale, flat and unprofitable
> Seem to me all the uses of this world!
> Fie on't, ah fie, 'tis an unweeded garden   135
> That grows to seed; things rank and gross in nature

Possess it merely. That it should come to this!
But two months dead – nay, not so much, not two –
So excellent a king, that was to this
Hyperion to a satyr, so loving to my mother   140
That he might not beteem the winds of heaven
Visit her face too roughly. Heaven and earth,
Must I remember? Why, she would hang on him
As if increase of appetite had grown
By what it fed on; and yet within a month –   145
Let me not think on't – Frailty, thy name is woman –
A little month, or ere those shoes were old
With which she follow'd my poor father's body,
Like Niobe, all tears – why, she, even she –
O God, a beast that wants discourse of reason   150
Would have mourn'd longer – married with my uncle,
My father's brother – but no more like my father
Than I to Hercules. Within a month,
Ere yet the salt of most unrighteous tears
Had left the flushing of her galled eyes,   155
She married – O most wicked speed! To post
With such dexterity to incestuous sheets!
It is not, nor it cannot come to good.
But, break, my heart, for I must hold my tongue. (lines 129–59)

Hamlet's first soliloquy falls into three sections: an exclamation about
his own wish for physical dissolution or death (lines 129–32); a description of the world (lines 132–7); and a history of recent events in
his family (lines 137–58), rounded off by an exclamation returning to
silence and the beginning of the speech (line 159). This history can be
subdivided into an account of his father, with his mother's reactions to
him (lines 137–45) and an account of his mother's speedy marriage
(lines 145–58). Although Hamlet does not provide the connecting
words that would make this explicit, the audience understands the
description and the history as justifications of the initial exclamation.
Hamlet wants no longer to exist, or to dissolve into dew, because he
sees the world as rotten; he sees the world as rotten because of the
behavior of his mother. No doubt all these feelings are made more raw
by having had to listen to his uncle's instructions on appropriate and
moderate reactions to death.

The dominating tone of the first part of the speech is exclamation
and extreme grief. Hamlet is here at his lowest point in the play. If
possible he would like to be dead or non-existent. Horatio's news from
the battlements, delivered at the end of this speech, in fact gives him a

reason to live and immediately arouses his curiosity, tinged with suspicion, and a desire to act. The epithets that Hamlet chooses to describe the "uses" of the world embody his weariness and disgust. There is nothing good in the world; it is an untended garden that has gone to seed, possessed only by whatever is rank and gross in nature. The untended garden is an image (properly domestic and familial) of a civilization that has been lost, a rationality that has given way before the basest appetites.

Hamlet's family narrative is marked by exclamation, amplification, and internal dialogue. These figures of thought all emphasize Hamlet's extreme emotional state, rendering him incapable of Claudius' logically articulated structures, making him speak almost with different voices, interrupting his sentences to correct his account of time (line 138) or to exclaim against the pain of remembering (lines 142–3). The amplification is conducted through comparisons (King Hamlet compared to Claudius is like the classical god of the sun compared to a lecherous half-human) and descriptions enhanced with causes (lines 140–2, 143–5). When he describes his mother, whose betrayal he feels more keenly because of their closeness, the emotion grows more intense as he takes a simple sentence ("within a month (145) she (149) married my uncle (151)"), breaking it up, amplifying each part in turn and then repeating the essence (lines 153, 156), emphasizing the speed and immorality of her action. The use of visual details (the shoes, the tears, the sheets) and of comparisons with grammar-school examples (Niobe, Hercules) and with animals (150–1), and the moral generalizations (frailty), could be used as textbook examples of the techniques of amplification. Shakespeare uses familiar rhetorical techniques to portray a mind almost unhinged by anguish, whipped up to a frenzy of feeling by dwelling on words, on pictures, and especially on the pressure of time ("within a month," "a beast ... would have mourn'd longer," "most wicked speed").

The soliloquy is a convincing portrayal of a mind at the end of its tether. At the same time it is an effective riposte to Claudius' self-interested portrayal of his own actions and his conception of filial duty. Hamlet's jesting response to Horatio, "The funeral baked meats / Did coldly furnish forth the marriage tables," effectively reverses the terms of Claudius' attempts to balance funeral and marriage. In the soliloquy the audience experiences Hamlet's feelings from the inside but also recognizes the obsessive, dangerous element in his thought. This speech plays an important part in Shakespeare's design of the whole play, laying the foundations linguistically and thematically for

Hamlet's most passionate speeches later in the play: his rejection of Ophelia and his tirade against Gertrude in the closet scene.

Bacon, "Of Revenge," "Of Adversity," from *Essays* (1625)

Like Bacon's other essays, "Of Revenge" probably originates in a set of quotations (from Solomon, Cosimo de Medici, and Job) and historical examples (Julius Caesar, Pertinax, and Henry III of France). Bacon begins the essay with a maxim of his own, in the form of a metaphor, and builds this pithy Senecan beginning into a longer, more measured sentence, developing a metaphor of nature running wild and needing to be restrained, and pairing clauses of near equal length.

> Revenge is a kind of wild justice, which the more man's nature runs to the more ought law to weed it out: for as the first wrong it doth but offend the law, but the revenge of that wrong putteth the law out of office. Certainly in taking Revenge a man is but even with his enemy, but in passing it over, he is superior; for it is a prince's part to pardon, and Solomon, I am sure, saith, "It is the glory of a man to pass by an offence." That which is past is gone and irrevocable, and wise men have enough to do with things present and to come; therefore they do but trifle with themselves that labour in past matters. There is no man doth a wrong for the wrong's sake, but thereby to purchase himself profit, or pleasure, or honour, or the like; therefore why should I be angry with another man for loving himself better than me? And if any man should do wrong merely out of ill-nature, why, yet it is but like the thorn or brier, which prick and scratch, because they can do no other.

Bacon's first argument rests on an equivocation of sense. Revenge is a sort of justice, but a justice that runs wild and usurps the place of law. Therefore law must extirpate revenge. Then he compares revenge with its contrary, forgiveness. Revenge makes you equal with an enemy but forgiveness makes you superior. This is confirmed with arguments from the agent (princes forgive) and from authority (Solomon). Then Bacon considers the person who might take offense and consider revenge. Wise men do not have time for brooding on the past. Wise people (like the readers) might also consider the motives for doing wrong: how can one be angry with people for preferring their own interests? Even malicious people are best considered as a useless annoyance rather than a threat. After making these arguments against revenge, Bacon makes an important distinction ("The most tolerable sort of Revenge is for those wrongs which there is no law to remedy"). Revenge may be more allowable where there is no prospect of justice through the law. Later he argues from history that public revenges are more likely to be successful than private ones. In conclusion he returns to the figure of the revenger, asserting with telling images that "a man that studieth Revenge keeps his own wounds green, which otherwise would heal and do well" and "vindictive persons live the life of witches." In the following essay too, "On Adversity," images from the experience of the senses make the strongest impact on the reader, leading up to the maxim that forms the climax to the essay.

> Prosperity is not without many fears and distastes and Adversity is not without comforts and hopes. We see in needleworks and embroideries it is more pleasing to have a lively work upon a sad and solemn ground, than to have a dark and melancholy work upon a lightsome ground; judge therefore of the pleasure of the heart by the pleasure of the eye. Certainly virtue is like precious odours, most fragrant when they are incensed or crushed: for Prosperity doth best discover vice, but Adversity doth best discover virtue.

The structure of Bacon's essays often comes from techniques associated with disputation: counter-argument, distinction of meaning, and topical invention; but their force derives from elements of amplification: comparison, visual detail, and moral axioms. By working within the form of the commonplace and by the stylistic combination of near proverbs with balanced clauses, Bacon projects an aura of inherited and impersonal wisdom that disarms opposition.

A sixteenth-century reading would have elaborated the moral lessons to be learned from these texts alongside the analysis of structure and rhetoric that I have provided. We cannot discard our own expectations of literary analysis and become sixteenth-century readers, but an awareness of their categories of reading can add to our readings and elucidate for us preoccupations of their writing (such as recurrent examples, images, or maxims). It can enable us to understand how early modern writers made their own combinations of the skills they had learned, working with their readers' expectations but also exploiting techniques for purposes never dreamed of by textbooks of rhetoric.

References and Further Reading

Agricola, Rudolph. 1539. *De inventione dialectica*. Cologne, repr. 1967, Nieuwkoop: De Graaf.

Aphthonius. 1575. *Progymnasmata*, with Lorichius' commentary. London.

Aristotle. 1991. *On Rhetoric*, trans. G. Kennedy. New York: Oxford University Press.

Baldwin, T. W. 1944. *Shakspere's Small Latine and Lesse Greeke*, 2 vols. Urbana: University of Illinois Press.

Brinsley, J. 1917. *Ludus Literarius*. Liverpool: Liverpool University Press.

Cave, Terence. 1979. *The Cornucopian Text*. Oxford: Clarendon Press.

Cicero. 1968. *Rhetorica Ad Herennium*, ed. H. Caplan. Cambridge, MA: Harvard University Press.

Conley, Thomas M. 1990. *Rhetoric in the European Tradition*. New York: Longman.

Crane, Mary Thomas. 1993. *Framing Authority*. Princeton: Princeton University Press.

Croll, M. W. 1966. *Style, Rhetoric, Rhythm*. Princeton: Princeton University Press.

Erasmus. 1978. *De copia*, trans. Betty Knott, in *Collected Works of Erasmus*, vol. 24. Toronto: University of Toronto Press.

Erasmus. 1988. *De copia*, ed. Betty Knott, in *Opera Omnia*, I-6. Amsterdam: North Holland.

Hartley, T. E., ed. 1981–95. *Proceedings in the Parliaments of Elizabeth I*. Leicester: Leicester University Press.

Kristeller, P. O. 1979. *Renaissance Thought and its Sources*. New York: Columbia University Press.

Lanham, Richard. 1991. *A Handlist of Rhetorical Terms*. Berkeley: University of California Press.

McConica, J. K. 1986 *History of the University of Oxford*, III: *The Collegiate University*. Oxford: Clarendon Press.

Mack, Peter. 1993. *Renaissance Argument: Valla and Agricola*. Leiden: Brill.

Mack, Peter. 2002. *Elizabethan Rhetoric: Theory and Practice*. Cambridge: Cambridge University Press.

Quintilian. 2001. *The Orator's Education* (*Institutio oratoria*), trans. D. A. Russell. Cambridge, MA: Harvard University Press.

Susenbrotus. 1953. *The Epitome Troporum ac Schematum*: text, translation and commentary by J. Brennan. PhD thesis, microfilm available from UMI.

Thompson, C. R. 1965. *The Colloquies of Erasmus*. Toronto: University of Toronto Press.

Vickers, Brian. 1988. *In Defence of Rhetoric*. Oxford: Clarendon Press.

Chapter 6

Manuscripts in Early Modern England

Heather Wolfe

Manuscripts in a Post-Print Age

Over a century after the invention of the printing press, manuscript production and circulation were healthier than ever, albeit forever altered by the possibility of an alternative medium. The restrictions on the print trade resulting from the Stationers' Company's monopoly on printing, along with strict licensing laws, ensured that manuscripts remained a vital form of communication, especially outside of London, Oxford, and Cambridge, the only cities where printing was legal. Some of the most subversive political and religious texts existed only in manuscript, which was seen as a more dangerous weapon than print because of the inability of the government to regulate it. The popular practice of circulating poetry in manuscript was largely fueled by the sense that the handwritten form lent a certain intimacy and exclusivity to a literary work. On a less glamorous level, individuals conducted domestic, legal, and business transactions almost entirely in manuscript. Antiquarians and local historians made transcripts of ancient manuscripts for posterity, for establishing precedents for use in the contemporary legal system, and for establishing ownership or inheritance of property or privilege. Deeds and receipts were handwritten, and manuscripts were the main form of record-keeping in Parliament and the courts of law. Professional scribes produced copies of parliamentary proceedings and newsletters, and penned letters and petitions for the illiterate. Recipes and medical remedies were collected in manuscript receipt books, while literary, historical, and religious extracts, in English and Latin, were collected in commonplace books. Manuscripts were sold alongside printed books in the shops of booksellers and stationers. The ink-spattered pages of early modern printed books, along with handwritten annotations in the margins and indexes on the blank endleaves, testify to the inseparability of reading and writing, and print and manuscript, in early modern England.

The instability and malleability of the manuscript text, as well as its incarnations and reincarnations in other media, mean that our conception of the handwritten *world* must encompass far more than the handwritten *word* if we have any hope of understanding the motivations and intentions of manuscript authors, compilers, and copyists, and the extent to which manuscripts were made for private use, informal circulation, profit, or patronage. In the early modern period, as now, individuals learned to negotiate and profit from different media for different purposes. Manuscript production and transmission played a crucial role in the commerce, exchange, control, and manipulation of information and knowledge, serving as both a complement and an alternative to print for both men and women. The climate in which handwritten documents were produced in Renaissance England was not unlike a symbiotic and osmotic sphere, with information flowing from speech to manuscript to print and back again in a continuous, cross-fertilizing cycle. The advent of print changed England's written topography dramatically, giving manuscript circulation a new, and ironically more privileged, position in the information matrix. Manuscripts reached and targeted more specialized audiences than printed documents, and depending on the number of copies needed, the length of the text, and the urgency to distribute it, "publication" by manuscript was often a more cost-effective form of dissemination than printing, since it could be done on demand with minimal initial investment. The possession of a literary or controversial manuscript delineated one's "membership" in an unofficial scribal community of like-minded individuals.

"Scribal publication," which Harold Love defines as "a movement from a private realm of creativity to a public realm of consumption," was a powerful form of communication in early modern England (Love 1998: 36). While the identities of most scribes, scriveners, writing-masters, clerks, and secretaries are largely lost to us, in their own lifetimes they were "every bit as vitally productive as printers and publishers" (Beal 1998: v). The majority of surviving manuscripts from the early modern period are in the hands of these copyists, a feature of manuscript culture that has forced scholars to reassess assumptions about authorship and circulation as they attempt to recreate narratives from patchy caches of manuscript texts and fragments, make sense of silences and absences, and compare texts, hands, and watermarks across an array of genres to reveal invisible networks and hidden connections.

Learning to Write

The predominant style of handwriting in the period 1580–1620 was Elizabethan secretary, a compact and efficient cursive script with a range of letter forms unfamiliar to the modern eye (especially c, h, r, s, and x). Italic, a more upright and unlinked script that originated in Italy, was employed by royalty and nobility when signing letters and official documents, in addition to being used for Latin quotations, proper names, and headings in literary manuscripts. A mixed hand, combining attributes from the secretary and italic scripts, came into use in the late sixteenth century as well.

Compared to today, writing in the early modern period was a relatively messy and arduous process requiring a number of supplies: quill pens (usually made from goose feathers), a penknife for cutting the quills, homemade ink stored in an inkstand or inkhorn, paper (made from the pulp of linen and rags), parchment (goat or sheepskin) or vellum (calfskin), pounce (a powdery substance sprinkled on the surface of the paper to prevent it from absorbing too much ink), sand (to help the ink dry), and scissors (for cutting paper). Until paper-making in England firmly took hold in the late seventeenth century, nearly all paper was imported from France, Italy, and elsewhere. Most manuscript receipt books contain at least one recipe for black ink, which was generally composed of gum arabic, rainwater, vinegar, and iron sulfate, which reacted with oak gall nuts (round protuberances on branches formed by the action of insects) to form a black compound (most manuscripts written in iron gall ink have now faded to a lighter brown shade).

The first writing manual to be published in England, *A Booke Containing Divers Sortes of Hands* (1570), was executed by the French writing-master Jean de Beauchesne and by 1610 had been reprinted five times. Like the manuals and copybooks that followed, Beauchesne's manual contained plates showing secretary, italic, calligraphic, and specialized court hands, and directions for the use and preparation of ink, paper, and quills. Heavily used and scribbled upon, most of these books now only exist in one or two surviving copies.

Manuscripts and Memory: Commonplace Books, Marginalia, and Writing Tables

The act of writing was largely intertwined with the acts of reading and remembering. Building on classical and medieval educational theory, humanists such as Erasmus, Montaigne, and Vives advocated the use of manuscript commonplace books as storehouses of knowledge (Crane 1993). With the explosion of printing in the Elizabethan and Jacobean periods, individuals needed a way to extract and compartmentalize *sententiae*, or pithy sayings and examples, from the ever-expanding supply of available texts. Creating manuscript filters helped individuals to tame unwieldy texts.

Armed with a classification system (letters of the alphabet, theological categories, or rhetorical styles, for example), a reader would add headings to his or her blank commonplace book and then gradually fill these headings with relevant adages and examples from his or her readings, sometimes adding a table of contents for quick reference. In grammar schools, students were taught to read with a sense of how a text could be usefully dissected into component parts for later use, ''gathering'' and ''framing'' rhetorical styles and classical models in order to improve their speaking and writing, whether through direct imitation or to provide ''matter'' for invention. The contents of commonplace books were likened to treasure-chests of jewels, garlands or posies of flowers, beehives of nectar waiting to be turned into honey, and food for thought, gathered together for digestion and rumination. The utility of the commonplace book was situated in the *act* of commonplacing, rather than the book itself; that is, reading, digesting, ruminating, and collecting matter helped to imprint it on the reader's mind, so that the resulting handwritten page was a trigger to allow him or her to be able to quickly retrieve the memory of the original encounter. Less structured than commonplace books were miscellanies and notebooks, which could be private or shared, and which had no hard and fast rules for content or arrangement. Surviving miscellanies contain information gathered from a wide range of printed and manuscript sources and genres, such as poems, sermons, letters, financial accounts, and cookery and medical receipts. It was not unusual for a commonplace book or miscellany to be a work in continual progress, started at both ends upside down from one another, and used and added to by successive generations.

Printed books bear witness to the process, and ubiquity, of commonplacing in other ways. Printers inserted manicules (pointing hands) in the margin and used italics to indicate memorable passages. It was not uncommon for individuals to personalize their printed books by adding their own notes to the margins, underlining passages, and marking text with a variety of symbols. Gabriel Harvey is perhaps the most extreme example of the consummate note-taker. Over 200 surviving printed books of his are crammed with manuscript notes in Latin, English, Italian, Greek, and other languages, and ornamented with a series of symbols designating particular types of subject matter. Harvey's Cambridge friends lampooned his compulsive note-taking in a Latin comedy, *Pedantius,* performed at Trinity College on February 6, 1581, in which Pedantius (Harvey) hopes to sell his books, "enriched with marginal annotations like precious gems or stars," for financial gain. Like other humanist-educated men and women, Harvey approached the printed page as a launching pad for the ideas housed in his mind. The layers of notes and the differences in ink shades indicate that Harvey read his books multiple times and with multiple goals, although he summarizes his overriding principle in a manuscript annotation in a printed collection of Italian jokes and mottoes: "Make most of such Examples, as may serue for Mines of Inuention; Mirrours of Elocution, & fountains of pleasant deuises" (Folger Library MS H.a.2, fol. 57^r).

"Writing tables," a form of erasable and portable (inkless) writing descended from the wax tablets of classical and medieval times, were used in the same way that we jot notes in Palm Pilots, Filofaxes, and Post-It notes when a more permanent form is either not convenient or not necessary (Stallybrass et al. 2005). Writing tables were temporary holding tanks where information was stored until its utility was past, or until it was transferred into a commonplace book or miscellany. Also known as table books, writing tables consisted of paper or vellum dipped in a plaster-like mixture called gesso and then coated with varnish or glue. The writing surface could be inscribed with a metal stylus or "pin," with a graphite pencil, or with iron gall ink, and erased with a damp sponge or finger. Initially imported into England in the 1520s–30s, the earliest example of writing tables produced in England is from the 1570s, when they started to be bound with 24-year almanacs. While fewer than thirty of these writing tables–almanacs now survive from the period between the 1570s and 1625, references to them in plays, prefaces, and elsewhere suggest that they were ubiquitous and ephemeral, printed in the thousands and discarded in the same way that we discard calendars and phone books. Merchants were most likely the primary users since the printed section includes calculations for wages and woodcuts of English and Continental coins. Manuscript notes in the few surviving copies record the dates of fairs in market towns, directions for curing horse ailments, mathematical calculations, and court testimony. In contrast, luxury blank table books in ornate bindings were novelty items for the aristocracy, particularly women, and were typically associated with poetry and private musings. Elizabeth I received writing tables with jeweled bindings as New Year's gifts on at least five occasions: in 1567, 1586, 1588, 1589, and 1591. Writers also used them for jotting down ideas, including Sidney, Peacham, and Montaigne (Stallybrass et al. 2004: 402–6). All of these examples bring to mind Hamlet's promise to the Ghost of his father in Shakespeare's play:

> Yea, from the Table of my Memory
> Ile wipe away all triuiall fond Records,
> All sawes of bookes, all formes, all pressures past
> That youth and obseruation coppied there,
> And thy commandement all alone shall liue,
> Within the booke and volume of my braine,
> Vnmixt with baser matter.
>
> (1.5.98–104)

Poetical Manuscript Miscellanies

In his address to the "general reader" of *Poly-Olbion* (London, 1612), the poet Michael Drayton complained of his disadvantage in printing poetry "at this time, when Verses are wholly deduc't to Chambers, and nothing esteem'd in this lunatique Age, but what is kept in Cabinets, and must only passe by Transcription." The early modern "cabinet" symbolized privacy and exclusivity, the site of one's most personal and treasured belongings, including jewelry, manuscript letters, devotions, and poetry. Drayton was one of the few poets from the period who went against the convention of "cabinetizing" one's poetry, shepherding his poems through multiple editions, "newly corrected" and "newly enlarged," between 1591 and his death. He was aware of the added responsibility that went along with unleashing his poetry on a public readership, however, compared to the easy give-and-take of manuscript circulation among friends. He wrote in the introduction to *Englands Heroicall Epistles* (London, 1597): "seeing these Epistles are now to the World made publique, it is imagined that I ought to bee accountable of my private meaning" (sig. A2). As the ensuing discussion shows, public and private meanings often had no relation to one another.

While poets did not eschew the print medium altogether, the primary form of transmission for a poem was in manuscript, and most manuscript poetry survives in miscellanies copied out in multiple hands, often seemingly indiscriminately mixed with other genres, usually lacking attribution, inconsistently titled, and rarely devoted to the work of a single poet. Poems were read, copied, and circulated within limited, amorphous, and often overlapping "coterie circles" of like-minded individuals "based on region, family, education (school and university), religion and politics," which usually did not extend beyond the gentry classes, and were particularly concentrated at the royal court, the universities, the Inns of Court, and aristocratic households (Love 2002: 109). Within these circles, poems would initially be transmitted orally, or individually on loose sheets enclosed in letters or grouped together in loose quires, which were then either collected and bound together or else copied into blank books, sometimes systematically, but usually as the collector received them. Marotti describes the most popular miscellanized poems as fitting roughly into three categories: "model epitaphs and elegies for either social superiors, equals, or inferiors;" "poems that express general cultural beliefs or moral truisms or both;" and "poems celebrating the lifestyle and shared values of a social or intellectual elite" (Marotti 1995: 129). The manuscript medium encouraged "incessant revision" by the author and appropriation, supplementation, or response from the reader ("compiler poetry"), as well as "answer poetry" from one poet to another (Love 1998: 53). In the 1570s and 1580s, vernacular love lyrics, influenced by Petrarch, took hold, along with Latin epitaphs, translations of classical verse, imitations of contemporary Continental humanists in the English vernacular, and original English sonnet sequences.

The majority of poems in miscellanies from this period lack attribution, their authors and compilers, with their "shared values and social pressures that influence the attribution decisions," engaging in a casual anonymity fueled by a "combination of ambition, discretion and nonchalance" (North 2003: 168, 161). Within a coterie circle, the level of social familiarity between poet and compiler would make attribution obvious and unnecessary, especially since the subject matter was perceived to be of greater significance than the identity of the poet. Paradoxically, in order to understand the inside jokes and subtle social dynamics of coterie poetry, a modern reader must both decode these seemingly invisible networks and then restore them to their original, "anonymous" state, without imposing our modern conception of authorship. While a poem might maintain its specific meaning and occasion among the original circle of readers, it could also acquire a more general appeal entirely separate from the circumstances of its original production as it spread from manuscript to manuscript, orbiting farther and farther away from its point of origin. Peter Beal

notes that transmission was "subject to the common process of manuscript culture whereby texts were liable to be copied, and sometimes
adapted, to suit the tastes, standards and requirements of *compilers* and
readers, rather than out of any sense of reverence for the sanctity of the
author's original" (Beal 2002: 124). For example, it is notoriously
difficult to establish the canon of Sir Walter Ralegh's poetry since
many of his poems, originally written for or about a particular person
or event, soon evolved into communal property because of the
universal truths and popular appeal of his observations.

Nicholas Breton, Thomas Carew, Richard Corbett, Sir Edward Dyer,
Henry King, Ralegh, William Strode, and Sir Thomas Wyatt are just
some of the heavily miscellanized poets whose names have been
largely forgotten because their poems circulated either primarily or
solely in manuscript in their lifetimes. The sonnets of Philip Sidney
did not appear in print until after his death, but during his life were
prized in manuscript by friends and acquaintances for a number of
reasons: because of their literary merit; because their author, a
knighted courtier, was an especially appealing figure; and because he
tried to keep them from widespread circulation (Woudhuysen 1996).
Although only three of his poems and a small number of epigrams and
miscellaneous verses were printed in his lifetime, the most popular
English poet in this period was John Donne. Over 5,000 scribal copies
of Donne's 200-odd poems survive in at least 260 manuscripts, with
some individual poems surviving in fifty or more manuscript copies
(only one poem survives in Donne's autograph). Many manuscript
collections of Donne's poetry can be linked to his friends, family,
patrons, and potential patrons between 1615 and 1620. Although his
poems started out being written for and inspired by an exclusive group
of friends, they were soon being copied and recopied at greater and
greater removes from him, both as individual poems and as poetic
groups (Beal 2002: 124). Despite the appearance of his collected poetry
two years after his death, Donne's poems continued to circulate widely
in manuscript, and some surviving copies of the 1633, 1635, and 1669
printed editions contain manuscript corrections that are presumably
based on more "authoritative" manuscript copies (Beal 2002: 125).

Like many other poets from this period, Donne was the author but
not the owner of his poems. In two letters to Sir Henry Goodyer, Donne
confesses his tangential hold on his oeuvre. In December 1614, Donne
confides in Goodyer "so softly, that I am loath to hear my self" that he
was "brought to a necessity of printing my Poems, and addressing them
to my L. Chamberlain" before he took holy orders (this printed edition

never came to fruition). This "unescapable necessity" has "cost me more diligence to seek them, then it did to make them," and to this end, he asks to borrow from Goodyer "that old book" with his poems. Donne seems to lament the more stringent expectations of print publication compared to manuscript circulation, worrying that Goodyer might have made use of all or part of one of Donne's verse epistles, which would prohibit Donne from using it himself, since its previous appearance "will be discerned, when it appears in the wholepiece" (*Letters to Severall Persons of Honour*, 1651: 196–8).

Ben Jonson, whose poetry circulated in both print and manuscript in his lifetime, and who was one of the first poets to exert control over the format and appearance of his poetry in print, nonetheless fancifully imagines the imminent manuscript trajectory of his epigram on Sir Kenelm Digby once it is delivered by Sir Kenelm's wife to "the Treasurer's board" and read aloud: "what copies shall be had / What transcripts begg'd? how cry'd up, & how glad, / Wilt thou be, *Muse*, when this shall them befall? / Being sent to one, they will be read of all" (*Workes*, London, 1640: lxxviii). Strangely enough, only four copies of this epigram are known to survive in manuscript, all but one post-dating its print publication (Beal 1980: 243).

Some of the earliest printed miscellanies were based on private manuscript miscellanies. Although by the time a poem appeared in print it was often stripped of its original social context and coded meaning, this did not reduce the popularity of print miscellanies. Richard Tottel's collection, *Songes and Sonnettes* (known as *Tottel's Miscellany*), was printed seven times between 1557 and 1587, and included the courtly poems of the already-deceased Henry Howard, earl of Surrey, and Sir Thomas Wyatt. Tottel decided "to publishe to the honor of the english tong, and for profit of the studious of Englishe eloquence, those workes which the vngentle horders vp of such tresure haue heretofore enuied." The "ungentle hoarders" of manuscript poems and the general readership of the same poems in print were two entirely different groups with different expectations and desires.

Manuscripts and Patronage: Presentation Manuscripts and Books as Gifts

As a young princess whose succession to the throne was less than certain, Elizabeth I presented manuscript books written in her own italic hand as New Year's gifts to her father Henry VIII (translations into Latin, French, and Italian of Catherine Parr's *Prayers and Meditations* in 1546), her stepmother Catherine Parr (a translation into English of Marguerite de Navarre's *Miroir de l'Âme Pécheresse* in 1545), and her brother, the future Edward VI (Bernardino Ochino's *Sermon on the Nature of Christ* from Italian into Latin in 1552). Elizabeth I had a strong appreciation of the power and beauty of the handwritten word, and her New Year's gift rolls record dozens of manuscript books given to her as gifts.

Manuscript books played an important role in the gift economy of early modern England, functioning as multi-layered forms of flattery critical for maintaining and advancing personal and professional relationships. More personal and unique than presentation copies of printed books (that is, printed books personally inscribed by the authors, translators, or publishers), presentation manuscripts were extensions of their givers' own hands, holding greater resonance because of the extensive time, ability, and resources involved. Usually recognizable by their dedications, presentation manuscripts also often had fine penmanship and paper, special bindings (embroidered, or stamped with the arms of the dedicatee, for example), and gilt fore-edges. Even if the dedication of a manuscript presentation copy did not directly present itself as a request for social, political, or financial advancement, the agenda would be implicitly understood by the recipient, since petitionary language was remarkably standardized within the patronage networks of Elizabethan and Jacobean England. Presentation copies made for self-advancement were especially popular under James I, when newcomers to court were jockeying for preferment.

It is difficult to measure the success rates of patronage-seekers who used manuscripts as gifts. Henry Peacham (1576?–1643?), a schoolmaster, musician, and artist, who dedicated emblem books, courtesy manuals, epigrams, essays, elegies, and pamphlets, in both print and manuscript, to James I and prince Henry, among others, admits in a printed dedication that "I never gained one halfe-penny by any Dedication that ever I made, save *splendida promissa*" (*The Truth of Our Times*, London, 1638: 39). Sir John Harington (1561–1612), godson of Elizabeth I, was perhaps slightly more successful due to his connections to the queen (he was granted the reversion of family lands in Nottinghamshire and the forfeited lands of a Catholic cousin, but other bids failed; Scott-Warren 2001: 212). One of the most prolific writers of verse and prose in Elizabeth's court, Harington devoted "extraordinary quantities of time, energy, patience, and money to the task of customizing individual copies of his books for presentation to particular individuals" (Scott-Warren 2001: 21). Penned both by himself and by professional scribes who emulated his hand, Haring-ton's manuscript books, like Peacham's, were dedicated to the usual suspects, including the king, Prince Henry, and Lucy, countess of Bedford. Harington also personalized copies of his printed works with manuscript annotations, dedications, and red-ruled borders. In an explicit bid to gain the trust and inheritance of his mother-in-law, Lady Jane Rogers, for example, he bound a copy of his *Orlando Furioso* (London, 1591) with fifty-two manuscript epigrams and a manuscript dedicatory epistle in which he disingenuously claims to have collected the epigrams "out of my scatterd papers." Harington supposes that his mother-in-law has seen them before, but asks her to "revew [sic] them againe, and remember the kynde, and sometime the vnkynde occa-sions, on which some of them were written." After recontextualizing these familiar epigrams, he then emphasizes her privileged access to two additional groups of epigrams: "because there was spare roome, I haue added a few others that were showd to our Soueraigne Lady, and some, that I durst neuer show any Ladie, but you two [his mother-in-law and wife]." He ends the dedicatory epistle with a request for her love and favor, couched in an analogy that is meant to remind her that his gift is to be treasured: "And so wishing you to lock me vp as safe in your loue, as I know you will lay vp this booke safe in your Chest" (Cambridge University Library, Adv. b. 9. 1; see Scott-Warren 2001: 99–146; Beal 1980: 121–57).

Esther Inglis (1571–1624) operated solely in the manuscript med-ium. The daughter of French Huguenot emigrants to Scotland, she was most likely trained in calligraphy by her mother, Marie Prescot. Around 1586 she made the first of at least fifty-eight decorated manu-scripts (dedicated to at least thirty-six different individuals) to further her and her husband Bartholomew Kello's affairs in London, Edinburgh, and the tiny parish of Willingale Spain, Essex, where her husband was rector. She employed an exquisite calligraphic flexibility (over forty different styles of handwriting) in transforming the Psalms, Proverbs, and other devotional texts into works of art, decorating many of her manuscripts with flowers, birds, and insects, as well as title-page borders, ornaments, emblems, and ornate initials copied from printed sources. Fifteen manuscripts are bound in velvet or silk, and thirteen of these are thought to have been embroidered in silk by her. Many of the dedications are written in French, the language of the Scottish court. Some of the dedications and preliminary poems are written by her father, Nicholas Langlois, and her husband, and some manuscripts include laudatory verses *to* her written in Latin and English, with titles such as "to the only Paragon, and matchless Mistresse of the golden Pen." She included self-portraits in nearly half of her manuscripts, mostly depicting herself in the act of writing, and in at least eight manuscripts she draws gold pens crossing each other on a crowned wreath with either the motto "Vive la Plume" or "Nil Penna Sed usus." Inglis made multiple copies of some works and dedicated them to different individuals – whether or not they thought they were the sole recipients is unknown.

On one level, Inglis's choice of recipients reveals her Huguenot roots and ongoing interest in the furthering of international Protestantism. Her dedicatees were primarily key Protestant figures in the royal courts, including Elizabeth I, James I, princes Henry and Charles and their friends, the earl of Essex and his close friend Sir Anthony Bacon, the earl of Somerset, Robert Sidney (brother of Philip Sidney), Sir Thomas Egerton, and Continental supporters of Protestantism such as Catherine de Bourbon, Prince Maurice of Nassau, Henri, duc de Rohan, and his mother, vicomtesse de Rohan. For example, Inglis hoped that Prince Maurice of Nassau would carry around her "petit livret," with its variety of handwriting to delight the sight and diversity of prayers to delight the spirit, as a weapon to provide "council and courage against the enemies of God and his religion" (Folger Library MS V.a.93, trans. from French; see Ziegler 2000).

Other dedications express Inglis's gratitude, or her hope, for preferment and financial assistance. Anticipating that her reputation would precede her, she addressed manuscripts to recipients both known and unknown, including Lady Erskine: "for although you have perchance neither seen nor heard of me, yet your noble and worthy Lord has both, and can best report of me, therefore have I sent this little offrand of mine to his Lordship to be delivered unto you" (Scott-Elliot and Yeo 1990: 52, my modernization). Inglis's March, 1599, gift of a manuscript book to Elizabeth I was accompanied by a letter from James VI recommending her husband to the queen. Kello's July, 1599, follow-up letter to Elizabeth I reminds her of her reaction to his wife's gift:

> I did understand by report of certain your Majesty's servitors, the work was very acceptable to your Majesty whereof indeed I could not but greatly rejoice, and so will the writer thereof when she shall hear your Majesty to have taken any small pleasure or delight in her handiwork ... It may therefore be your Majesty's princely pleasure to give order for my speedy dispatch. (Scott-Elliot and Yeo 1990: 35, my modernization)

These last two examples indicate that Inglis's gift books were not intended to work in isolation, but within a complex and hierarchical patronage network in England and Scotland and on the Continent, consisting of royalty, nobility, and other acquaintances in high places. Despite her efforts, Inglis died in debt. She was not wholly unrewarded, however: Prince Henry's account books show that she received £5 in 1609 for *A Book of the Armes of England done by me Esther Inglis*, and £22 in 1612 shortly after his death.

Manuscript Transmission of Subversive Texts

In 1588, Elizabeth I issued yet another proclamation declaring it treasonable to possess seditious books, this one in response to a papal bull against her issued by Sixtus V: "no person whatsoever shall convey, carry, or bring into any of her Majesty's realms or dominions any of the said bulls, or any transcript or copy thereof, or any the said libels, books, pamphlets, or writings, nor shall in any wise disperse or utter any of the same" (*STC* 8172). Elizabethan and Jacobean royal proclamations against seditious books and rumors took pains to emphasize the potency of these "texts" in print, manuscript, *and* speech. This potency is succinctly observed by the lawyer Sir Christopher Sibthorp, who ponders a "popish" adversary's decision to respond in manuscript to Sibthorp's *A Friendly Advertisement to the Pretended Catholickes of Ireland* (Dublin, 1622): "Seeing then that hee might have printed it; Why did he rather choose to divulge it in a Manuscript? Did he thinke, that by that course used, he might the more freely speake and write what he listed, and that no man would answere or reply unto it?" Sibthorp then proceeds to point out that "mens hearts may be poysoned, and seduced, aswell by Manuscripts, and written Bookes and Pamphlets, as by those that be Printed, especially after they be once scattered and dispersed," and re-emphasizes the porosity between the two media: "I see not but I may bee as bold to reply to his Manuscript, in Print ... as he made bold to answere a part of my Printed Booke, in a Manuscript" (*A Reply to an Answere, made by a Popish Adversarie*, Dublin, 1625: sig. C1ʳ).

Immediacy, a sense of secrecy and privileged access, and a mistrust of government-sanctioned print media were three key reasons for the scribal circulation of topical texts (Love 2002: 111). Individuals made their own copies of suppressed or subversive texts, and stationers' and scriveners' shops offered transcription services (Woudhuysen 1996:

52–66). At his 1585 trial, Philip Howard, earl of Arundel, allegedly left copies with his sister and a Catholic priest of his letter to Elizabeth I justifying his flight from England. The priest "caused divers coppies there of to be made by scrivenors & to be published & dispersed in sundrye partes of the realme." Attorney General Sir John Popham estimated at Arundel's 1589 arraignment that 500 copies were made of that "factious & traiterous letter" (Woudhuysen 1996: 52–3). Manuscript transmission of illegal texts allowed disenfranchised groups to communicate under the radar of censors and to quietly rally support. For example, English Catholics relied not only on printed books issued by secret presses in England or smuggled from the Continent, but also on manuscript copies of martyrdom accounts, devotional works, and casuistry manuals, a steady supply of which helped strengthen their convictions, which in turn led to greater financial support of the English Catholic mission.

Over thirty-seven manuscript copies (c. 1580–c. 1660) are known to be extant of Philip Sidney's 4,300-word *Letter to Queen Elizabeth*, written in 1579 when he was just 24 and not printed until 1663 (Beal 1998: 109–46, 274–80). The nephew of the queen's temporarily disgraced favorite, Robert Dudley, earl of Leicester (who angered the queen by concealing his marriage to Lettice Knollys), Sidney became the spokesperson for the aristocratic faction against the queen's proposed marriage to the French Catholic brother of Henri III, François, duc d'Anjou. While it was penned as a private letter to the queen – hoping his words "shall only come to your merciful eyes" – it is unknown whether or not he ever sent an original autograph version to her. He released this letter in manuscript with the calculation that it could very well stir up opposition among the queen's courtiers. Shortly after Sidney's manuscript first appeared, the Puritan John Stubbs printed a pamphlet, *The Discoverie of a Gaping Gulf whereinto England is like to be Swallowed by an other French Mariage* (London, 1579), which cost him and his publisher their right hands on November 3, 1579. After slowing in the first two decades of the seventeenth century, the *Letter*'s manuscript circulation surged again a half-century later in 1625–30, when it became apt fodder for those fearing the return to a Catholic monarchy. One of the *Letter*'s main scribes during this second period of copying has been dubbed "the Feathery Scribe" by Peter Beal because of the wispy, trailing strokes of his letter forms.

A subversive text's appearance in print in no way precluded its circulation in manuscript. Printed in either Paris or Rouen in 1584, the anonymous and venomous attack on the earl of Leicester, *The Copie of a Leter, Wryten by a Master of Arte of Cambrige to his Friend in London, Concerning some Talke … about some Procedinges of the Erle of Leycester and his Friends in England. Conceyued, Spoken and Publyshed … towardes her Most Excellent Ma. and the Realm, for whose Good Onely it is Made Common to Many,* was suppressed by the Privy Council soon after it arrived on English shores because of its potential to tarnish not only Leicester's reputation, but theirs and the queen's as well. Dozens of sixteenth-century copies survive, many emulating the title page of the 1584 edition. Falsely attributed to Robert Parsons but probably written by exiled Catholics in Paris, it was not printed in England until 1641 as *Leicester's Common-wealth.* Similarly, Edmund Spenser's condemnation of the queen's policy in Ireland, *A View of the Present State of Ireland,* was written in 1596 and entered into the Stationers' Register in 1598 "uppon Condicion that hee gett further aucthoritie before yt be prynted." Not surprisingly, it did not appear in print until 1633, but was copied widely both prior to, and after, its publication. Another widely copied text was *An Apologie of the Earle of Essex, against Those which Iealously, and Maliciously, Tax Him to be the Hinderer of the Peace and Quiet of his Country. Penned by Himselfe in Anno 1598,* printed covertly in London c. 1600 under the title *To Maister Anthonie Bacon,* and overtly in 1603. In 1598, Essex coyly claimed that he was not responsible for having his apology "published either in print or writing" (Woudhuysen 1996: 148, 152, 18). The interesting textual variants among seemingly identical "copies" of these various tracts show that they derived from a wide range of sources, which in turn sheds light on the diversity of professional and non-professional hands that contributed to the tracts' widespread dissemination and influence.

Manuscripts and the Theatre

Despite the critical role that manuscripts played in the theatrical world, and contemporary references to over 3,000 individual plays in the Elizabethan and Jacobean period, fewer than a dozen playhouse manuscripts survive from between 1580 and 1620. The majority of these manuscripts are anonymous, and none of them ever reached printed form. The survival of autograph copies of plays is almost nil; no printer's copies of plays have yet been discovered; and only a handful of stage plots and actors' parts survive. These, along with printed copies, private transcripts, and the diary of the theatre owners Philip Henslowe and his son-in-law Edward Alleyn, are the few sources available to scholars to reconstruct the day-to-day activities of the Renaissance stage.

Other types of extra-theatrical dramatic manuscripts are more prevalent. Fair copies of plays for presentation and for personal use, not connected with their performance, do survive, as do academic plays (largely in Latin or Greek) written and performed at Oxford, Cambridge, the Inns of Court, Westminster school, and Catholic schools at Douai and St Omer, manuscripts transcribed or adapted from printed play-texts, masques and other court entertainments, and closet dramas. William B. Long notes that "playbooks were of, by, and for the theater; they existed solely for use by players and theater personnel. It is only by occasional accident ... that any found their way to the printing house and thus to not only a vastly wider, but also a very, very different readership" (Long 1999: 418). A play-text could change dramatically in the evolution from authorial manuscript to licensed copy to performed "oral" text to fair copy to print copy. Printed versions of plays, often derived from flawed manuscript copies or memorial reconstructions, rarely represented the play-text exactly as it was performed. However, as the tangible residue of the performance, printed plays exerted great influence. In the preface to *The Malcontent* (1604) John Marston expresses his discomfort that "scaenes invented, meerely to be spoken, should be inforcively published to be read" (McKenzie 1990: 90).

How manuscript playbooks were produced and circulated for the theatre and for wider distribution is largely unknown. Companies or theatres probably employed scribes, who made copies of play-texts and part-books as needed, and bookkeepers, who were in charge of making revisions, adjustments, clarifications, and updates to playbooks in preparation for performance or revival. New manuscript evidence, along with a reappraisal of previously known playhouse manuscripts, has led scholars and editors to question the categories of play manuscripts set forth by W. W. Greg in the early twentieth century. It is now thought that Greg's distinction between "fowle papers" (the author's working papers, or drafts in which the text is for the most part "in the form the author intended it to assume"; Greg 1931: 31) and "fair copies" (cleaner copies ostensibly sent to the Master of the Revels for licensing or used for performance, often anachronistically referred to as "promptbooks") is inaccurately based on Greg's assumption that the untidiness and disorganization of surviving copies of plays meant that they were not the copies used for performance. However, Long's analysis and comparison of eighteen playhouse manuscripts dating between 1590 and 1637 indicates that these manuscripts moved much more seamlessly between playwrights, players, bookkeepers, scribes, and Masters of the Revels than previously supposed (Long 1999: 425–6). Paul Werstine, who has pointed out the undue influence on modern Shakespeare editors of Greg's "speculations" concerning manuscripts used by printers, as well as the irony that according to Greg's definition of foul papers, none is known to exist, argues for appreciating each dramatic manuscript "in its uniqueness," rather than formulating grand hypotheses based on slim evidence (Werstine 1997: 494).

However, the few surviving playhouse manuscripts do suggest two important features of manuscript culture in the theatrical world. First, the writing of plays, and the preparation of them for production, was largely a collaborative effort, and second, contemporary users of playhouse manuscripts (unlike modern editors and scholars) would not have been troubled by the presence of multiple hands, contradictory deletions and insertions, inconsistent speech headings, sporadic appearances of stage directions, unresolved narrative issues, and other signs of disorganization. When writing or copying a play-text, playwrights and scribes generally divided a page into four vertical columns by folding it lengthwise twice. Speech headings were generally written in an italic hand in the left column; the play-text, in a secretary hand, occupied the two center columns; while long prose lines extended into the forth column, along with exits and very infrequently, in italic, stage directions (Long 1999: 416). The different styles of handwriting allowed the users to distinguish quickly between text and paratext. Henslowe's *Diary* regularly records payments to multiple playwrights for work on a single play, or to one playwright for "mending" another playwright's text (Foakes 2002).

Given the ephemeral nature of playhouse manuscripts, it is not surprising that we have no record of Shakespeare's handwriting beyond six versions of his signature (three on his will, three on deeds). However, some scholars believe that Shakespeare's hand is the "Hand D" that contributes three revised leaves to *The Book of Sir Thomas More* (British Library, Harleian MS 7368). Written in 1592–3, during a period of anti-alien sentiment in London, the manuscript's original twenty-five pages (out of thirty-seven) have been identified as being a "fair copy" in the hand of Anthony Munday, while other pages have been added, others removed, and two pieces of paper pasted over deleted sections. As a result of its incendiary subject matter, the manuscript underwent particular scrutiny by Master of the Revels Edmund

Tilney, one of whose duties was censoring plays for public performance. Tilney advised the playwright(s) on the first page of the manuscript: "Leave out the insurrection wholly with the cause thereof and begin with Sir Thomas More at the Mayor's sessions with a report afterwards of his good service done being sheriff of London upon a mutiny against the Lombards only by a short report and not otherwise at your own perils" (modernized). Wanting to minimize allusions to rebellions against authorities, Tilney requests a more passive summary of the May Day Rebellion of 1517. In three other scenes, he advises the playwrights to "mend" and "alter" the text and has made deletions and corrections.

In addition to Munday's ("Hand S") and Tilney's hands, five other hands revise and add text. Two have been identified as Henry Chettle ("Hand A") and Thomas Dekker ("Hand E"), and it has been argued that a third hand possibly belongs to Thomas Heywood ("Hand B"). "Hand C" has not been identified. Like the other emending hands, "Hand D" appears entirely unaware of Tilney's advice, perhaps because he made his additions before Tilney read the manuscript. Scholars have speculated endlessly about the identity of "Hand D" and whether or not parts of the manuscript constitute either "foul papers" or a heavily corrected "fair copy." In viewing the manuscript as a literary work instead of a theatrical production, they lose sight of the importance of its original playhouse habitat, where its layers of contributions, corrections, deletions, inconsistencies, and contradictions would have been considered normal.

The earliest known manuscript copy of a Shakespeare play is a conflated and condensed version of *Henry IV* parts 1 and 2 made in early 1623 by the antiquarian Sir Edward Dering (Folger Library MS V.b.34). The first page of the play is in Dering's hand and the rest is copied by a scribe named Mr Carrington. Dering added corrections, additions, and deletions to the entire manuscript, reworking the staging and further condensing the scenes, but never entirely completing his revision. It is thought that Dering adapted the two parts of *Henry IV* from the 1613 quarto edition of part 1 and the second issue of the 1600 quarto edition of part 2; however, it has also been argued that the text might be based on a now-lost manuscript version of a single five-act play that pre-dates the two-part version. Two crossed-out cast lists in Dering's hand for John Fletcher's play *The Spanish Curate* (first published in 1647) appear on the back of a scrap containing one of his emendations to *Henry IV*. The lists include his own name and the names of other family members, neighbors, and even "Jacke of the buttery," suggesting that both plays were intended for private performance at Dering's country seat in Surrenden, Kent.

Thomas Middleton's *The Game at Chesse*, a satire on the Spanish monarchy and its representatives in England, is a telling example of a playwright's involvement in the manuscript afterlife of a banned play, and of the evolution of a play from a performed "text" to a static book designed specifically for reading. The stage in *The Game at Chesse* consists of a giant chessboard, on which James I and his Protestant court are the white chess pieces being played against their corrupt and sexually dissolute Catholic counterparts from Spain. The play enjoyed a nine-day run at the Globe in August, 1624, performed each night before an audience of roughly 3,000, until complaints from the Spanish ambassador caused the Privy Council to stop performances and ban the circulation of the play in print or manuscript. At the time of its performance and suppression, Middleton participated in the copying of at least six carefully written versions of the play, and was also likely involved in the production of three printed editions in 1624 and 1625. One of the manuscripts includes an added description on the title page in Middleton's autograph, "as it was acted Nine Days together," while a version in the theatrical scribe Ralph Crane's hand is dated August 13, a day before the play's final performance on August 14. Another was presented by Middleton as a New Year's gift to William Hammond on January 1, 1625, with the assertion in the dedication that "This which nor Stage, nor Stationers stall can showe, / (The Common-Eye maye wish for, but ner'e knowe)" (Folger Library MS V.a.231; V.a.234; Bodleian Library MS Malone 25). Was Middleton seeking to profit from the play's notoriety by making presentation copies of it? If he oversaw the production of the six manuscripts in such a short time-frame, then why are there so many versions? *The Game at Chesse* provides a valuable example of the infinite versions and possibilities in manuscript transmission, and both the easy malleability of a text under the author's own hand and others, and the clear attention to detail in each of the versions.

Conclusion

Donne represents the views of many of his contemporaries when he forgives his friend Dr Andrews for returning a manuscript transcript of a printed book that Donne had lent him, because Andrews's sons had tattered it: "What Printing-presses yield we think good store / But what

is writ by hand we reverence more" ("De Libro cum Mutuaretur ...,"
Poems, London, 1635: 278; trans. Blunden 1955: 11). The continued
primacy of oral communication in early modern England – in Parliament, in court, in schools, and in church – indicates the importance of
"presence" in establishing a text's authority, a presence that in early
modern England was still "greatest in speech, still implied by script, least
of all in print" (McKenzie 1990: 91, 96). The value placed on this
immediacy, presence, and authority is evident in the titles of hundreds
of printed works from this period that adopt the nomenclatures usually
reserved for speech and manuscript, such as Letters (or Copies
of Letters), Humble Addresses, Petitions, Remarks, Dialogues, and
Answers, to name a few.

As Marotti and Bristol state, manuscript communication creates "an
intimate, and interactive, bond between writer and reader," a world
"in which the roles of reader and writer are fused ... the whole
environment being one in which texts are malleable and social rather
than fixed and possessively individualistic" (2000: 5). Our modern
twinned notions of individual authorship and intellectual ownership
rub uneasily against the intentions and functions of early modern
manuscript cultures since, as we have seen, manuscript authorship
was largely diffused, and imitation and appropriation were commonplace. If anonymous poets and playwrights happily merged and
layered their hands and their ideas, circulating and sharing their writings without regard to "authorship," then we should only try to
unravel their identities in order to permit greater insight into the
workings of the complex webs of readers, writers, collectors, and
copiers, who have left behind thousands of manuscript leaves for us
to discover and ponder.

References and Further Reading

Beal, Peter. 1980. *Index of English Literary Manuscripts. Vol. 1: 1450–1625*.
London: Mansell.

Beal, Peter. 1998. *In Praise of Scribes: Manuscripts and their Makers in Seventeenth-Century England*. Oxford: Clarendon Press.

Beal, Peter. 2002. "John Donne and the Circulation of Manuscripts," in John
Barnard and D. F. McKenzie, eds., *The Cambridge History of the Book in Britain.
Vol. 4: 1557–1695*. Cambridge: Cambridge University Press, pp. 122–6.

Beal, Peter and Margaret J. M. Ezell, eds. 2000. *English Manuscript Studies
1100–1700. Vol. 9: Writings by Early Modern Women*. London: British Library.

Blunden, Edmund. 1955. "Some Seventeenth-Century Latin Poems by English Writers," *University of Toronto Quarterly* 25: 10–15.

Burke, Victoria E. and Jonathan Gibson, eds. 2004. *Early Modern Women's Manuscript Writing*. Aldershot: Ashgate.

Crane, Mary Thomas. 1993. *Framing Authority: Sayings, Self, and Society in Sixteenth- Century England*. Princeton: Princeton University Press.

Crick, Julia and Alexandra Walsham, eds. 2004. *The Uses of Script and Print, 1300–1700*. Cambridge: Cambridge University Press.

Foakes, R. A., ed. 2002. *Henslowe's Diary*. Cambridge: Cambridge University Press.

Goldberg, Jonathan. 1990. *Writing Matter: From the Hands of the English Renaissance*. Stanford: Stanford University Press.

Greg, W. W. 1931. *The Editorial Problem in Shakespeare*. Oxford: Oxford University Press.

Hobbs, Mary. 1992. *Early Seventeenth-Century Verse Miscellany Manuscripts*. London: Scolar Press.

Long, William B. 1999. " 'Precious Few': English Manuscript Playbooks," in David Scott Kastan, ed., *A Companion to Shakespeare*. Oxford: Blackwell, pp. 414–33.

Love, Harold. 1998. *The Culture and Commerce of Texts: Scribal Publication in Seventeenth-Century England*. Amherst: University of Massachusetts Press. (First edition, Oxford: Clarendon Press, 1993.)

Love, Harold. 2002. "Oral and Scribal Texts in Early Modern England," in John Barnard and D. F. McKenzie, eds., *The Cambridge History of the Book in Britain. Vol. 4: 1557–1695*. Cambridge: Cambridge University Press, pp. 97–121.

Love, Harold and Arthur F. Marotti. 2002. "Manuscript Transmission and Circulation," in David Lowenstein and Janel Mueller, eds., *The Cambridge History of Early Modern English Literature*. Cambridge and New York: Cambridge University Press, pp. 55–88.

McKenzie, D. F. 1990. "Speech – Manuscript – Print," *Library Chronicle of the University of Texas – Austin* 20: 87–109.

McKitterick, David. 2003. *Print, Manuscript, and the Search for Order, 1450–1830*. Cambridge: Cambridge University Press.

Marotti, Arthur F. 1995. *Manuscript, Print, and the English Renaissance Lyric*. Ithaca,NY, and London: Cornell University Press.

Marotti, Arthur F. and Michael D. Bristol, eds. 2000. *Print, Manuscript, and Performance: The Changing Relations of the Media in Early Modern England*. Columbus, OH: Ohio State University Press.

May, Steven W. 1991. *The Elizabethan Courtier Poets: The Poems and their Contexts*. Columbia: University of Missouri Press.

North, Marcy L. 2003. *The Anonymous Renaissance: Cultures of Discretion in Tudor-Stuart England*. Chicago: University of Chicago Press.

Schulz, Herbert C. 1943. "The Teaching of Handwriting in Tudor and Stuart Times," *Huntington Library Quarterly* 4: 381–425.

Scott-Elliot, A. H. and Elspeth Yeo. 1990. "Calligraphic Manuscripts of Esther Inglis (1571–1624): A Catalogue," *Papers of the Bibliographical Society of America* 84: 11–86.

Scott-Warren, Jason. 2001. *Sir John Harington and the Book as Gift*. Oxford: Oxford University Press.

Stallybrass, Peter, Roger Chartier, Frank Mowery, and Heather Wolfe. 2004. "Hamlet's Tables and the Technologies of Writing in Renaissance England," *Shakespeare Quarterly* 55: 379–419.

Werstine, Paul. 1997. "Plays in Manuscript," in John D. Cox and David Scott Kastan, eds., *A New History of Early English Drama*. New York: Columbia University Press, pp. 481–97.

Woudhuysen, H. R. 1996. *Sir Philip Sidney and the Circulation of Manuscripts, 1558–1640*. Oxford: Clarendon Press.

Ziegler, Georgianna. 2000. " 'More than Feminine Boldness': The Gift Books of Esther Inglis," in Mary E. Burke, Jane Donawerth, Linda L. Dove, and Karen Nelson, eds., *Women, Writing, and the Reproduction of Culture in Tudor and Stuart Britain*. Syracuse: Syracuse University Press, pp. 19–37.

Chapter 7

Travel, Exploration, and Empire

Ralph Bauer

Although travel writing has a long history in medieval Europe with the traditions of pilgrimage and knightly adventure, the notions that travel should serve the purpose of exploration – of learning about the physical world something not known before – and that travel writing should yield a naturalistic description of an unfamiliar physical landscape are the consequences of a distinctly modern ideology. The focus of medieval travel literature had been primarily on the self's inner spiritual advancement (or a good match after the knight's return), not on the exploration of the external world (see Zacher 1976; Howard 1980; Hall 1965; also Nerlich 1987). In most medieval travel writing, as in most medieval painting, therefore, the physical world surrounding the traveling subject was ignored, only sketchily depicted, or populated with the monstrosities from fable that modern psychoanalysts have seen as the archetypal symbols of a collective unconscious (see Jung 1967). If, in modern times, the emphasis in travel writing began to shift to the external world, it was because the subject's relationship to the physical world had itself begun to change. This change was due, in part, to transforming economic relations in early modern Europe, as inalienable land had increasingly become alienable and the local estate-based economies of the landed aristocracies were being superseded by inter-regional mercantile economies based on trade. The information about the physical world that was increasingly becoming of interest in interregional trade became imperative once these trading networks, stretching across continents and oceans, became formalized within political and administrative systems of protection, exploitation, and coercion – within the political geographies of early modern empires.

It is in the geopolitical context of early modern imperialism that the English literature of travel and exploration during the period under consideration here must primarily be understood. The so-called

European "Age of Exploration" had been precipitated after the capture of Constantinople by the Turks in 1453 had in effect cut off the European trade routes via the eastern Mediterranean, and European states found themselves looking for alternative routes to Asia. In 1498, the Portuguese Vasco da Gama had successfully opened such a route by circumnavigating Africa and landing in Calicut, thereby laying the groundwork for a permanent European colonial presence in India that formally ended only in 1961 – a decade after the end of British rule there. In 1492, the Italian Christopher Columbus's enterprise to sail to India for Spain via a western passage had ended on the shores of America, although he died believing that he had indeed reached Asia. In 1502, another Italian explorer sailing for Spain, Amerigo Vespucci, announced to Europe that the lands found across the Atlantic by Columbus were not Asia but rather a "New World." In 1520, Hernando Cortés conquered Mexico for Spain, and ten years later, the Pizarro brothers conquered the Inca Empire in South America. Meanwhile, the Portuguese Pedro Álvares de Cabral had landed in Brazil (in 1500), establishing there a permanent base that would serve as an important nexus for a budding Portuguese maritime empire between its Iberian base and its colonies in East and West India. In 1522, a Spanish fleet sailing under the Portuguese-born commander Ferdinand Magellan returned from the first circumnavigation of the globe to Seville (after Magellan himself had died in its course). Resulting from these developments, the geographic center of European activity in trade and exploration had begun to shift from the eastern Mediterranean and the Levant to the western Atlantic seaboard by the end of the sixteenth century – a shift reflected in the personal biographies of many of the Italian explorers, such as Columbus and Vespucci, as well as Giovannia da Verrazano and the Cabot brothers, who moved away from the former economic centers of the once powerful Italian city states in order to offer their services and navigational expertise to the western courts of Spain and Portugal.

By contrast, as English writers were sorely aware, England's voyages of exploration had by 1580 not yielded concrete profits to the nation at large – despite some impressive individual feats such as John Cabot's early voyages on behalf of the English crown (1497) and Sir Francis Drake's circumnavigation (1577–80) (see Williamson 1935; also Andrews 1967; Andrews et al. 1979). An English "empire" had therefore remained largely an elusive projection throughout the sixteenth century (see Knapp 1992; also Foss 1974). "I marvaile not a little," Richard Hakluyt the younger wrote in the dedication of his *Divers*

Voyages (1582) to Philip Sidney, "that since the first discovery of America (which is nowe full fourscore and tenne yeeres) after so great conquests and plantings of the Spaniards and Portingales there, that wee of England could never have the grace to set fast footing in such fertill and temperate places, as are left as yet unpossessed of them" (1582: "To the Right worshipfull," n.p.). The period from 1580 to 1620 therefore saw a concerted effort on the part of Englishmen to "catch up" with their neighbors on the Continent in the race for geographic intelligence and colonial toeholds. Yet, still from the vantage point of the 1620s – more than a century after the Spanish conquest of Mexico – the record of English ambitions overseas left much to be desired: Frobisher's attempts during the 1570s to find a northwest passage to Asia had ended on the stubbornly resistant North American mainland; the first attempt to establish an English colony in America, by Sir Humphrey Gilbert in Newfoundland in 1583, had literally ended in a storm; the first English colony actually established in the New World, under Sir Richard Grenville and Ralph Lane at Roanoke in 1585, had to be abandoned (despite some promising beginnings with the explorations of Amadas and Arthur Barlowe the year before); the second attempt, under John White in 1587, failed with the mysterious disappearance of the Roanoke colony in 1590; and the first colony that had lasted so far, Jamestown, had barely survived in the face of a string of disasters after its founding in 1607. In 1620, finally, a second colony called "Plymouth" was established further north by a band of religious "Separatists" who had arrived there via the Netherlands. But these religious enthusiasts seemed more interested in the particular advancement of their own small Protestant utopia and their personal spiritual salvation than in serving the mother country and in making good on their sponsors' expectations for profitable returns on their investments. By the end of the period under consideration here, the record of English overseas activities still told of incoherence, dissentions, starvations, plagues, ships wrecked, and investments lost (see Quinn 1955, 1965, 1974a).

Anxiously conscious of the causal connections between Spain's soaring political might in Europe and Spanish possessions, late sixteenth-century English promoters of exploration and empire invested substantial intellectual energies not only in encouraging Englishmen to engage in the colonial enterprise but also to make English explorations, hitherto conducted mainly in the form of "privateering" (see Andrews 1964), more useful to the nation at large. As a consequence, the period from the 1580s to the 1620s saw a proliferation of manuals aimed at prescribing, formalizing, and regularizing the content and style of travel histories by urging travelers to adopt a more systematic stance when reporting on their voyages, by placing less emphasis on their own personal actions and more on geographically or ethnographically useful information. It is "no marvaile," lamented Francis Bacon, if useful knowledge about the physical world had not advanced beyond the grotesque monstrosities contained in the books of Mandeville and Pliny, for most contemporary travel histories were "negligent, inequall, and as it were casuall observation." It was a "vain Tradition and from idle report; ... ignorant, dull, wild, and broken" (1987: 31). Thus, as early as 1575, Jerome Turler, in his *The Traveiler*, had proposed recommendations on "the maner, and order of traveling ... into straunge and forrein Countreys," in particular on "[w]hat things are to be considered in traveilinge," such as

> the lande what maner one it is, and ... the people that dwell therein, whether thy bee stronge or weake, many or fewe, the Lande good or bad; what Cyties there bee, walled or not walled; the soyle fertile or barreine; wooddie or champion; so That there bee five principal poyntes too bee considered in euerie Cuntrey: the fame, figure, bignesse, jurisdiction, and situation. (1951: 50)

Similarly, in 1606 Thomas Palmer published *An Essay of the Meanes How to Make our Trauailes, into Forraine Countries, the More Profitable and Honourable*, in which he addressed himself to remedying "the manifould errors and misprisions, that the greater sort of such as trauaile into forraine Countries, haue theretofore committed" and to giving a "perfect rule" on "how to make the trauailes of other men who for the good of this kingdom wherein they liue so happily, their better seruiue to his Maiestie" (1606: "Epistle," "To the Reader," n. p.). For this purpose, Palmer proposed a quasi-scientific taxonomy of travel, prescribing moral conduct for travelers in various situations and things to be taken account of in their narratives. He especially called upon the "General Voluntarie Trauailers" (meaning those who travel for curiosity, like aristocrats, not necessity, like soldiers) that before traveling they "counsaile and deliberate with themselves, whether they bee mooued with the iust pretence of doing good to the Common weale ...or whether their owne lusts and affections pricke them not forward" (p. 35). He chastised those who traveled for "the disordinate appetite of man, corrupt and vnsauorie (as Ambition, Sensualitie, vaine glorie, couetousnes, vanitie of knowledge, & such like." With regard to the content of travel accounts, he specified a number of topical heads in order to provide the traveler with an order to follow in making his (and in special cases her) observations, such as place names, population, situation, quantity, commodities, air, soil, rivers, springs, buildings, towns, fortifications, trade, farming, clothing, laws, religion, customs, government, and diplomacy (pp. 81–127). However, while Turler's and Palmer's poetics of natural history were still primarily intended as guides for the genteel traveler in Europe, who should have knowledge of the "Artes," such as astronomy, cosmography, geography, hydrography, geometry, arithmetic, and architecture, for traveling in "ciuill" Italy (Palmer 1606: 38, 44), during the seventeenth century these prescriptions became geared also toward commoners and merchants, who were increasingly regarded as vital in the projects of science (see Shapin 1994; also Solomon 1998). In fact, as Samuel Purchas pointed out in 1617, commoners' testimony was often preferable to that given by the educated and aristocratic traveler, for their minds were not adulterated by "theorie" and, thus, predisposed to deliver only the useful facts. "I mention authors sometimes of meane quality, for the meanest have sense to observe that which themselves see, more certainly then the contemplations and Theorie of the more learned. I would acknowledge the labour of the meanest" (Purchas 1617: "Epistle Dedicatorie," n. p.).

Responding to the need both to promote English initiative in the colonial venture and to make travel and exploration more "useful" to the nation at large, Sir Walter Ralegh initiated in 1587 the practice of adding a scientific and artistic staff when setting out on ventures of exploration and colonization. He hereby found an able person in Thomas Harriot, who had a reputation as a scientist and mathematician (as well as alchemist, sorcerer, and magician). Born in Oxford in 1560, Harriot had been a student at St Mary's Hall in 1577, and after graduating had joined the Ralegh household as a tutor in mathematics. When Ralegh was granted a patent to colonize Virginia and was preparing an expedition to that end, he therefore charged Harriot with the study of the Indians, the mapping of the domain, the listing of the natural resources, and the writing of a report of the colonizing venture. The product was what is today considered to be one of the most important exploration tracts of the English Renaissance, the *Briefe and True Report of the New Found Land of Virginia* (Harriot 1972). First published as a quarto volume without illustrations in 1588, it was republished at Frankfurt in Theodore de Bry's magnificent collection entitled *America* (1590). There the *Report* appeared in folio and richly illustrated by printed woodcuts that de Bry had prepared based on the water-color paintings of John White. As Harriot himself stated, the publication of the *Report* was mainly intended to counteract some of the "slanderous and shamefull speeches" that the English colonial enterprise had received after the recent failure of Grenville and Lane's colony at Roanoke. These slanderers had "done not a little wrong to many that otherwise would have also favored & adventured in the action, to the honour and benefit of our nation" (1972: 5). In order to restore the good reputation of that part of America that Englishmen regarded as providentially reserved for them, he provided an inventory of the economic potential of Virginia in its riches in natural resources and commodities. These he divided into three parts: first, "commodities [that] there already found or to be raised," such as silk worms, flax, hemp, spice, wood, metals, furs, and dyes; second, "commodities which wee know the countrey by our experience doeth yeld of it selfe for victual, and sustenance of mans life," such as maize, beans, squash, melons, roots, fowl, and fish; and, third, "such other commodities ... as I shall thinke behoofull for those that shall inhabite," which includes mainly an account of "the nature and manners" of the Native Americans. In order to make the strange customs of Virginia's Native American more intelligible to his English audience by showing that "the Inhabitants of the great Bretannie have bin in times past as sauuage as those of Virginia" (p. 75), the de Bry edition ended with a section of "Som Picture[s] of the Pictes which in the Old tyme dyd habite one part of the great Bretainne."

Although many of the "commodities" described by Harriot turn out to be wrongly identified, and though this second attempt at colonization that he chronicled would also fail with the disappearance of the second Roanoke colony, the lasting popularity of his account was instrumental in the formation of a cluster of the colonialist ideas that would later lead to the foundation of the Virginia Company in 1606, by reinforcing the rationale for colonization already laid out in Hakluyt's 1584 *Discourse of Western Planting*: the Protestant gospel would be "enlarged," commodities yielded, idle Englishmen employed, Spanish power bridled, and the English treasury enriched (Hakluyt1993: 57). Thus, Harriot's account and de Bry's woodcuts emphasized ethnographic details about Algonquin "enchantments" (Harriot 1972: 54) and "idol[s]" (p. 71), which inspired Harriot to "make declaration of the contents of the Bible; that therein was set foorth the true and onelie God, and his mightie woorkes" (p. 27). Harriot's attempts at conversion were apparently aided by the disastrous effects of what he called the "invisible bullets" of European diseases upon the Natives, who "could not tel whether to think us gods or men, and the rather because that all the space of their sicknesse, there was no man of ours knowne to die, or that was specially sick" (p. 20). Moreover, the apparent similarities between the present-day inhabitants of Virginia and Britain's Picts of "Old tyme" – patent in the "sauuage" customs of both, such as tattooing – reinforce the colonialist idea of a "New World" without history, according to which the European arrival in America represents the arrival of history, technology, Christianity, and so on (see Wolf 1982; Pagden 1993; Fabian 1983; Hulme 1986).

Finally, the *Report*, in its edition by de Bry, also evidences an increasing awareness of the commercial value and proprietary status not only of the exotic novelties therein described but also of the printed text describing them. Thus, in his preface to the section presenting the illustrations, Harriot, invoking his image as a magus, threatened potential plagiarizers and pirates of his book that "secret marks lye hiddin in my pictures, which wil breede Confusion unless they bee well observed" for the case that "any seeke to Contrefact thes my bookx, (for in this days many are so malicious that they seeke to gayne by other men labours) thow wouldest give noe credit unto suche counterfeited Drawghte" (1972: 41). Harriot's concern for his commercial property in the book was well founded. De Bry's collection went through numerous editions, each of which was separately published and sold in Latin, English, French, and German, bearing testimony to the close interrelationship between the history of printing and European imperialism in the New World (see Fuller 1995; also Johns 1998).

Travel collections, such as de Bry's *America* and Gian Battista Ramusio's *Navigationi et viaggi* (1556), had become increasingly popular in sixteenth-century Europe. (In fact, Harriot's *Report* was also included in the first and second editions of Richard Hakluyt's *Principal Navigations* – though without White's illustrations.) Many of the early collections published in England were actually editions of Spanish and Portuguese works translated by English promoters of empire, such as Richard Eden (1521–76), who had published Sebastian Münster's *Cosmographiae* (1550) as *A Treatise of the New India* in 1553, and Peter Martyr's *Décadas* as *The Decades of the Newe Worlde or West India* in 1555, and again (along with other documents) as *The History of Trauayle* in 1577. Similarly, the literary career of the great Elizabethan polymath and Anglican minister Richard Hakluyt (1552?–1616) had begun with his translations from Spanish and Portuguese narratives of the discovery and exploration of America, which he published in 1582 as the

Divers Voyages Touching the Discoverie of America, in order to incite the English spirit of adventure in emulation of the Spanish achievements in the New World. As had its foreign models, Hakluyt's works followed the "order of the map, and not the course of time" (1582: "Epistle Dedicatorie," n. p.), meaning that the travel narratives they contained were arranged according to geographic subject matter rather than chronology. But whereas the English translations from the Spanish and Portuguese travel compilations may have done much to excite English imperial ambitions to emulate the Spanish example, they had ultimately exalted the historical role that foreign explorers had played in the advancement of modern geographical knowledge, leaving Englishmen still without a record of their own nation's activities in this regard. It was due to this lack of a literary record, Richard Hakluyt argued, rather than to the actual sluggishness of Englishmen in the affairs of exploration and empire, that his nation suffered from disregard in the modern historiography of travel and exploration; and it was to redress this situation that he set out to work on his magnum opus, the 1589 *Principal Navigations, Voyages, Traffiques & Discoveries of the English Nation*. As he remembers in his address to the reader,

> I both heard in speech, and read in books other nations miraculously extolled for their discourses and notable enterprises by sea, but the English of all others for their sluggish security, and continually neglect ... either ignominiously reported, or exceedingly condemned ... Thus both hearing and reading the obloquie of our nation, and finding few or none of our owne men able to replie heerein: and further, not seeing any man to have care to recommend to the world, the industrious labors, and painefull travels of our countrey men: for stopping the mouthes of the reprochers, ... [I] determined notwithstanding all difficulties, to undertake the burden of that worke wherein all others pretended either ignorance, or lacke of leasure, or want of sufficient argument, whereas (to speake truly) the huge toile, and the small profit to insue, were the chiefe causes of the refusal. (1927: I, 2–3)

First published as a single volume in 1589 but swelling, in its second edition (1598–1600), to three gigantic volumes, *Principal Navigations* has aptly been called the "prose epic of the English nation" (Morison 1971–4: I, 555; Fuller 1995; also Helgerson 1992). Thus, volume I of the second edition collected 109 individual narratives relating to the north and northeast, from Arthur's expedition to Norway in 517 to Queen Elizabeth's embassies to Russia and Persia; volume II collected 165 voyages relating to the south and southeast, mainly to Turkey,

Tartary, Algiers, India, China, and Guinea; volume III, finally, presented 243 narratives about the New World, from the fabulous story of Prince Madoc's voyage in 1170 to the sixteenth-century voyages of Frobisher, Drake, Hawkins, Ralegh, and Harriot to the New World.

One of Hakluyt's principal goals in selecting and arranging his materials was to put England on the map in the history of travel and exploration. Thus, while many of the narratives dealing with Mediterranean travel were still cast within the generic mold of pilgrimage, their focus lay on the descriptions of the diversity of national customs and natural environs. These naturalistic descriptions were packaged in narrative plots that articulated an "English" national identity distinct from other nations', particularly in terms of a "Christian" identity as distinct from the Turks' and of a "Protestant" identity as distinct from the Spanish. In "The voyage of M. John Locke to Jerusalem" of 1553 (1927: III, 12–36), for example, the pilgrim-narrator consistently presents himself as the Protestant skeptic among his superstitious fellow travelers from other nations with regard to some of the sacred Catholic relics, such as a certain "holy Crosse" that allegedly "hath 3. drops of our lordes blood on it" – which, he dryly observes, "you must (if you will) believe it is so, for see it you cannot" (III,31). Especially powerful in the articulation of a distinctly English identity were hereby narratives that involved a captivity plot, such as the one entitled "The worthy enterprise of John Foxe an Englishman in delivering 266. Christians out of the captivitie of the Turkes at Alexandria, the 3. of Januarie 1577" (III, 38–50). This narrative relates the capture of the English ship *The Three Halfe Moones* by the Turks in 1563 after its departure from Portsmouth en route to Spain, the sufferings of the Christian captives at the hands of unspeakably cruel Turks, and the Englishman Fox's heroic leadership in winning their freedom after he had himself served as a galley slave for fourteen years. Upon their dramatic escape in a hijacked Turkish vessel and under hot pursuit by thousands of Turks, "John Fox was thrise shot through his apparel, and no hurt" by the special favor of God, whereas the Spaniard "Peter Unticaro, and the other two, that had armed them with the duckats, were slaine, as not able to weild themselves" (III, 46).

As the geographic focus shifts in the *Principal Navigations* from the Mediterranean to the New World theatre, the Catholic Spanish actors take on the roles of the cruel Turkish infidels in captivity narratives such as those of John Hortop (1927: VI, 336–53), Miles Philips (VI, 296–335), and Robert Tompson (VI, 246–62). For example, the narrative of John Hortop, a Lincolnshire powder-maker conscripted to John

Hawkins's fleet on his third voyage to the Indies in 1567, begins by relating the passage of Hawkins's fleet along the African coast to Sierra Leone in order to buy slaves before heading west. After a short stay-over in the Caribbean, Cuacao, and Rio de Hacha, the fleet sought refuge from stormy weather at San Juan de Ulloa, the principal port of New Spain. Unfortunately for Hawkins and his men, they were surprised by the Spanish *flota*, the silver fleet traveling annually between New Spain and Seville, which had returned early that year on occasion of the passage of the newly appointed viceroy Don Martin Henríquez. Some of Hawkins's ships were able to make their escape, but found themselves in such distress due to shortage of supplies that they were forced to set on shore parts of their crew in northern New Spain, Hortop among them. During the subsequent struggle to reach Panuco, the landed party was repeatedly harassed by Chichimec Indians and finally captured by Spanish forces and brought to Mexico City. After being imprisoned there for two years, Hortop was sent to Spain to serve various terms in prison, on the galleys, and in servitude to the king's treasurer. After twenty-five years, he was finally able to make his return to England after a vessel on which he was traveling was captured by an English ship in 1590. Hortop's first-person narrative of his ordeal was one of the earliest English accounts of interior Spanish America, and published independently as *Travails of an Englishman* (1590) before being included later in the second edition of the *Principal Navigations*. On the one hand, it describes many exotic novelties, such as monstrous fish, worms, and crocodiles, which seem to have been included in order to excite English curiosity about America. On the other hand, its portrayal of the Spanish national character as irrational, superstitious, cowardly, effeminate, and cruel lent legitimacy to England's own expansionist project. Similarly, the account of Miles Philips, an English merchant who had lived in New Spain since the 1550s and who had the bad luck to become caught up in the trials of the Hawkins crew, promised the reader "many special things of that country and of the Spanish government, but specially of their cruelties used to our Englishmen, and amongst the rest to him selfe for the space of 15 or 16 yeres together, until by good and happy meanes he was delivered from their bloody hands, and returned into his owne Country" (VI, 296). Philips's narrative contains one of the first English descriptions of an auto-da-fé, a spectacle of condemnation and penitence frequently staged by the Inquisition, in which the Englishmen were displayed to the public on Good Friday in 1575.

> [W]e were all brought into a court of the Inquisitors pallace, where we found a horse in a readinesse for every one of our men which were condemned to have stripes, and to be committed to the gallies … and so they being inforced to mount up on horsebacke naked from the middle upward, were caried to be shewed as a spectacle for all the people to behold throughout the chiefe and principall streets of the citie, and had the number of stripes to every one of them appointed, most cruelly laid upon their naked bodies with long whips … and so this horrible spectacle being shewed round about the citie, they returned to the Inquisitors house, with their backes all gore blood, and swollen with great bumps, and were then taken from their horses, and carried againe to prison, where they remained until they were sent into Spaine to the gallies, there to receive the rest of their martirdome. (VI, 322–3)

The larger meta-narrative underlying Hakluyt's arrangement of travel and exploration accounts found an apt culmination with the inclusion of what is perhaps the greatest piece of Elizabethan literature of travel and exploration – Walter Ralegh's *The Discoverie of the Large, Rich, and Bewtiful Empyre of Guiana*, which had been published independently in four separate editions in 1596 before being included in *Principal Navigations* (see Whitehead 1997: 10). Despite his fierce anti-Catholicism, Ralegh, like Hakluyt an indefatigable promoter and sponsor of English imperial ambitions, was enchanted with the Iberian model of universal conquest. During a reconnaissance mission to South America in 1594, Ralegh had seized Pedro Sarmiento de Gamboa, an official of the Spanish crown who had been charged with the fortification of Spain's South American main, who told Ralegh of the legend of El Dorado: the fantastic golden kingdom said to be hidden in the remote interior of South America. By the following year, Ralegh had mobilized a fleet of four ships and a crew of 300 men that included – in keeping with Ralegh's proto-scientific bent – an Oxford mathematician, Lawrence Keymis, in order to discover and conquer the fabulous city of El Dorado. During the passage, Ralegh captured Don Antonio de Berrio, the Spanish governor of Guiana who had led a number of earlier expeditions in search of El Dorado and who gave Ralegh a great deal of (more or less reliable) information about a golden city called "Manoa," which allegedly stood on a lake up the Orinoco River. Accompanied by some additional vessels and a crew of 100, Raleigh spent a month gathering provisions and then went up the Orinoco River until they reached the Caroni River, where Ralegh befriended a local cacique by the name of Topiawari, who gave Ralegh further geographic information. Newly inspired, Ralegh pressed on, but bad weather finally forced him to return to

Trinidad before finding Manoa, leaving two of his men behind and taking with him Topiawari's son. Ralegh now sailed up the Venezuelan coast, raiding some Spanish settlements there and losing a large number of his men in the process.

Although Ralegh had, upon his subsequent return to England, not found anything concrete worth writing home about, his *The Discoverie of the Large, Rich and Bewtiful Empyre of Guiana* teemed with magical expectations and possibilities about future exploits in Guiana. The evidence for such riches, however, was by and large confined to "signes" (Ralegh 1997: 125) that, often secret, had to be interpreted by the trained eye of the scientist. "[A]ll the rocks, mountains, all stones in the plaines, in woodes, and by the rivers sides" in Guiana were "in effect thorow shining, and *appeare* marveylous rich" (p. 125; my emphasis). Thus, Ralegh argued that Guiana possessed the "same" or even "more" riches than the Spaniards had found in neighboring Peru, (mis)identifying the Native Americans of Guiana as the remnants of the Inca Empire who had, under their ruler Manco Inca, withdrawn to Vitcos in the lowlands of Vilcabamba, as Ralegh had read in the Spanish chronicles of the discovery and conquest (pp. 136–7). For Ralegh, Guiana had

> *more* abundance of gold than any part of Peru, and *as many or more* great cities than ever Peru had when it flourished most. It is governed by the *same* laws, and the emperor and people observe the *same* religion and the *same* form and policies in government as was used in Peru, *not differing in any part*, and I have been assured by such of the Spaniards as have seen Manoa, the imperial city of Guiana, that for greatness, for the riches, and for the excellent seat, it far *exceedeth* any of the world, at least so much of the world as is known to the Spanish nation. It is founded upon a lake of salt water of 200 leagues long, *like unto* mare caspium. (pp. 136–7)

Not only was Guiana a second Peru, Ralegh argued, but the Indians were more than happy to accommodate English desires for gold, having become Queen Elizabeth's admirers and England's allies against a common, hated foe–the Spaniards.

> I made them understand that I was the servant of a Queene, who was the great Casique of the north, and a virgin, and had more Casiquie under her then there were trees in their lland: that she was an enemy to the Castellani in respect of their tyrannie and oppression, and that she delivered all such nations about her, as were by them oppressed, and having freed all the coast of the northern world from their servitude had

147

sent me to free them also, and with al to defend the country of Guiana from their invasion and conquest. I shewed them her majesties picture which they so admired and honored, as it had beene easie to have brought them Idolatrous thereof. (1997: 134)

Ralegh's claim that the English had arrived in the New World in order to restore an order more ancient, legitimate, and pure than the present usurpations and corruptions perpetrated by Spanish Catholics would have struck a chord with Protestant Reformist sensibilities, and echoed the Tudor ideology constructed by Elizabethans such as John Dee, who saw the Virgin Queen as the heir to and restorer of an Arthurian, mythical, and mystical 'British Empire' (a term Dee is credited with coining; see Sherman1995: 148–200). In Ralegh's *Discoverie*, this ideology is also reflected in the literary form in which he presents the account of his explorations. Thus, his pervasive use of defamiliarizing and untranslated Native American terms and place names in his *Discoverie* – seen by some modern critics as evidence of the "proto-ethnographical" bend of this text (see Whitehead 1997) – functions hereby in part as a rhetorical device supporting his historical argument: the English will not impose themselves upon the New World, as the Spanish conquerors had done, by linguistically appropriating the New World through translation, but rather restore the New World to its "legitimate" (Native American) order.

Not surprisingly, this story stood in need of some adjustments later, once the first English settlements in the New World had been founded, and especially when the American Indians on whose land they had been built showed themselves to be less than grateful to their Protestant English friends for having saved them from cruel Spanish Catholics. To be sure, already Hakluyt had known (as we have already seen) that "hammerous and rough masons" may at times be necessary in order to "square and prepare" the Native Americans for the colonial project. However, in comparison with the promotional travel and exploration narratives printed by the Elizabethan Hakluyt, the narratives published by Samuel Purchas in his compilations during the first two decades of the seventeenth century adopted an overall more militant "cant of conquest" that was in part designed, as the historian Francis Jennings has suggested, to rationalize England's own "invasion of America" (Jennings 1975: 77–82). Indeed, Purchas's collections, while following Hakluyt's general model, had a character that markedly differed from those of his Elizabethan predecessor. While Hakluyt had still been engaged in the establishment of a literary record of English explorations, as well as in the promotion of English expansionism, conducted largely by aristocratic individualists and the regimes of the great trading companies, Purchas was engaged in a redefinition of the imperial project within the geopolitical context of a centralizing Stuart monarchy (see Armitage 2000: 67; also Bauer 2003: 77–116).

The ideological difference between the works of Hakluyt and Purchas is manifest in the editorial style, content, and literary form of the travel and exploration narratives each chose to include in his collections. Purchas's career as a historian/collector had begun in 1613 with the first edition of a travel collection entitled *Purchas his Pilgrimage; or Relations of the World. And the Religions observed in all Ages and Places. Discovered, from the Creation unto this Present*, additional and gradually expanding editions of which appeared in 1614, in 1617, and (posthumously) in 1626. The two subsequent works, *Purchas his Pilgrim. Microcosmus, or the History of Man. Relating the Wonders of his Generation, Vanities in his Degeneration, Necessity of his Regeneration, Meditated on the Words of David* (1619) and *The King's Tower, and Triumphant Arch of London* (1623), were theological treatises that highlight the intensely religious framework of Purchas's interest in the history of travel. His magnum opus appeared only one year before his death and was entitled *Hakluytus Posthumus, or Purchas his Pilgrimes, Contayining a History of the World, in Sea Voyages & lande Lande Travells, by Englishmen and others* (1625). Gargantuan in size – it was initially published in four volumes but filled twenty when republished by the Hakluyt Society in 1905–7 – *Hakluytus Posthumus* was more comprehensive in scope than *Purchas his Pilgrimage*, beginning with the navigations of the ancient Jews, Ancients, and Christians, moving on to the Renaissance explorations of the Portuguese and Spanish in the New World, and culminating with the early modern travels of the English in the Americas and East India.

As the title suggests, *Hakluytus Poshumus* was specifically intended to stand in the tradition of the now deceased Hakluyt, to whose manuscript collection Purchas owed 121 of the narratives included in *Hakluytus Posthumus*. However, Purchas's editorial style and rhetoric were markedly different from his Elizabethan predecessor's. Thus, Hakluyt had declared at the outset of his *Principal Navigations* that "I have referred every voyage to his Author, which both in person hath performed, and in writing hath left the same" (1927: I, 6; see also Quinn 1968). The Stuart historian Purchas, by contrast, prided himself on his role as an editor – who had "forme[d] and frame[d] those Materials to their due place and order in the Aedifice, the whole Artifice (such as it is) being mine owne" (1905–7: I, xli) – extracting information from his sources that he deemed valuable, cutting out parts that he did not, and paraphrasing entire passages rather than reproducing them in the original. Although modern historians have often lamented Purchas's editorial style vis-à-vis that of Hakluyt, I have argued elsewhere that the formal differences between the works of the two collectors resulting from their different editorial styles manifest important transformations in the idea of history itself and the status of the text as a "source" – a transformation that responded to the new geopolitical demands of transoceanic empire, and that held important implications for the formal evolution of literatures emerging on the geographic peripheries of the British Empire, such as colonial American literature (see Bauer 2003: esp. 81–9). It must suffice here to consider the literary content of a few exemplary narratives included by Purchas in his collections. In general, however, we can say that whereas Hakluyt had extolled the individualistic ambitions of unruly English buccaneers, such as Hawkins, Gilbert, and Drake, as well as the private commercial initiatives conducted within the context of the great trading companies, such as the East and West India Companies as well as the Levant Company (which sponsored many of his works), the narratives published by Purchas frequently highlighted the important role that the monarchy and a strong central government had to play in the imperial project, while emphasizing the virtue of subordination on the part of imperial functionaries. The narratives hereby add up to an overall picture of the Elizabethans' overseas activities that could frequently be unflattering to the trading companies and the aristocratic leadership under whose auspices they had been conducted. Thus, whereas even Ralegh's Natives of Guiana had venerated Elizabeth, Purchas compared her reign unfavorably, as one of aristocratic incoherence, to that of James, who stood "[b]eyond our victorious Debora not in sex alone, but as Peace is more excellent then War, and Salomon then David" (1905–7: XX, 131). Ralegh himself, to whom de Bry's Frankfurt edition of Harriot's *Brief and True Report* had been dedicated, as the person by whom Virginia "hath ben descouuerd" (1972: 3) and who was invariably credited by the official accounts patronized by the Virginia Company, was now demoted in Purchas's collections. Thus, in the 1613 edition of *Purchas his Pilgrimage*, Purchas chastised Ralegh for having "perforrmed nothing, but returned with friuolous allegations" (p. 632) and, in *Hakluytus Posthumus*, Purchas asserted that Virginia was "discovered by Sir Seb. Cabot," not by Ralegh (1905–7: XIX, 226).

The ideological work performed by Purchas's collections is also manifest in his thoroughly negative portrayal of the liberal commercial empire of the Dutch in the East Indies, which now competes with that of Hakluyt's Spaniards as the main alter ego in the articulation of a distinctly British imperial identity. In the famous account of John Davis about his East Indian voyages, for example, the author records a Dutchman's experience with a native king, who

> did often demand of him, if he were not of England, which he did strongly denie, using some unfit speeches of our Nation [Purchas's marginal note: "Englishmen abused by Hollander"] ... he was not of England but of Flanders, and at the King's service. I have heard of England [Purchas's marginal note: "England famous"], said the King, but not of Flanders; what Land is that? He further enquired of the King, State, and Government; whereof our man made large report, refusing the Authoritie of a King, relating the government of Aristocratie ... Again [the King] required to show if there were no Englishmen in the ships: he answered, there be some English [Purchas's marginal note: "Diverse Englishmen in this Voyage"] in the ships, but they have been bred up in Flanders. I understand, said the King, that there be some that differ both in apparell, language, and fashion: what are those? he answered, English, of which my chiefe Pilot is one. Well, said the King, I must see those men. (1905–7: II, 313)

When the natives were informed by the English that the Dutch "had no King, but [that] their Land was ruled by Governors," they immediately discern that "the English men are good, [and that] the Hollanders are naught" (II, 486, 457).

Purchas's anti-aristocratic bias is finally manifest also in his decision to publish William Strachey's (1572–1621) "A True Repertory," an account written in 1610 that has been described by one modern historian as "probably the finest piece of writing we have from an Englishman of his time on the Americas" (Quinn 1997a: 320). The account circulated in several manuscript copies in London after its delivery to the Virginia Company by Sir Thomas Gates, one of which came into the possession of Richard Hakluyt and another into that of William Shakespeare, who is generally assumed to have based *The Tempest* on Strachey's account (see Orgel 1987: 42). However, it was never published by Hakluyt or the Virginia Company, probably due to the unflattering portrayal of the state of affairs in Virginia. Although the original is now lost – surviving only in fragments published as late as 1849 as *The History of Travaile into Virginia Britannia* – it was edited and included (against Strachey's wish) by Purchas in his *Hakluytus Posthumus*. It relates the shipwreck of the *Sea Venture* in the Bermudas in 1609 en route to Virginia, the survival of the shipwrecked men on the island, the building of pinnaces, and the passing to Jamestown. There, the survivors found the colonists so destitute and desperate that they were convinced of the hopelessness of the situation and resolved to abandon the colony and return to England. Just as they were sailing down the James River for the Atlantic Ocean, however, they encountered the fleet of Sir Thomas West, lord de la Warre, who had been sent as the new governor vested with the strong powers established by the second charter of 1609. The ships returned to Jamestown, de la Warre assumed official authority over the colony, and soon the situation was restored.

Although Strachey had originally written this account in order to vindicate the Virginia Company and the reformation of its regime under the second charter, in the context of Purchas's *Hakluytus Posthumus*, published the year after the revocation of the Company's charter in 1624, the narrative appeared to rationalize the crown's appropriation of the colony by allegorizing the importance of a strong central hand on the part of government and of the subordination on the part of colonial functionaries within the imperial chain of command. For example, soon after the wreck of the vessel in the Bermudas, a certain Stephen Hopkins "began to shake the foundations of our quiet safety."

> And sure it was happy for us who had now runne this fortune, and were fallen into the bottom of this misery, that we both had our Governour with us, and one so solicitous and carefull, whose both example (as I said) and authority, could lay shame, and command upon our people: else, I am perswaded, we had most of us finished our dayes there, so willing were the major part of the common sort (especially when they found such a plenty of victuals) to settle a foundation of ever inhabiting there; as well appeared by many practises of theirs (and perhaps of some of the better sort? Loe, what are our affections and passions, if not rightly squared? how irrelegious, and irregular they express us? (1905–7: XIX, 28)

While these "dangerous and secret discontents [that] nourished amongst us" first begin with the mariners, they soon affect also the "land-men," who, contemplating the "wretchedness and labour" to be expected once they arrive in Virginia, find that the shipwreck was not so disagreeable after all and therefore decide to "repose and seate" themselves on the island, where "pleasure might be injoyed" (XIX, 29). Thus, Strachey's narrative about tempests and shipwrecks on uninhabited islands illustrated that the "ground of all those miseries" haunting the English imperial enterprise to date was that in the New World "the head" had become separated "from the bodie." Whereas the party had survived the shipwreck on the Bermudas, the survivors found "a greater shipwracke in the Continent of Virginia, by the tempest of Dissension: every man over-valuing his owne worth, would be a Commander: every man underprizing anothers value, denied to be commanded (XIX, 67). Strachey's eyewitness testimony thus lent support to the absolutist political philosophy later articulated in Thomas Hobbes's *The Elements of Law, Natural and Politic* (1650), which was circulating in England as early as the 1640s and made ample use of the texts of empire, such as Purchas's *Hakluytus Posthumus*, as evidence for his political theory of absolutist power.

In conclusion, we can say that the English literature of travel and exploration during the period under consideration here was primarily inspired by the quest for empire, in which most Western European nations had been engaged by the end of the sixteenth century. The English literature hereby began on a note of anxiety about England's lagging behind its Iberian rivals for hegemony in Europe in the general grab for imperial possessions overseas. In that context, the literature of travel and exploration published during the last two decades of the sixteenth century was mainly engaged in the promotion and encouragement of English initiatives, on the part of aristocratic individuals and private investors, to emulate Spanish and Portuguese successes, while, at the same time, aiming to define and legitimate a distinctly "English" imperial project and national identity through a critique of the Iberian model. The literature published under the Stuarts during the first two decades of the seventeenth century, by contrast, manifests the attempt to redefine this imperial project for the context of a "British" empire by rationalizing the consolidation of the newly acquired colonial possessions under the auspices of a composite monarchy. Although in 1620, the budding English efforts at colonization were still in a feeble stage, they had been planted in fertile soil in a hemisphere that had, by a papal bull, been divided between two empires whose geopolitical power was all but disintegrating in the course of the seventeenth century. From this point of view, it could be argued that the literature of travel and exploration written during the period under consideration here had laid the foundation of the empire on which the sun would never set.

Ralph Bauer

Acknowledgment

I would like to thank William Sherman for his insightful readings and helpful comments on an earlier version of this chapter.

References and Further Reading

Alexander, Michael, ed. 1976. *Discovering the New World: Based on the Works of Theodore de Bry*. New York: Harper and Row.

Andrews, Kenneth R. 1964. *Elizabethan Privateering: English Privateering during the Spanish War, 1585–1603*. Cambridge: Cambridge University Press.

Andrews, Kenneth R. 1967. *Drake's Voyages: A Re-assessment of their Place in Elizabethan Maritime Expansion*. New York: Scribner.

Andrews, Kenneth R. 1984. *Plunder and Settlement*. Cambridge: Cambridge University Press.

Andrews, Kenneth, Nicholas Canny, and Paul Hair, eds. 1979. *The Westward Enterprise*. Detroit: Wayne State University Press.

Anghiera, Pietro Martire. 1555. *The Decades of the Newe Worlde or West Indía*. Trans. Richard Eden. Londini: [s.n.].

Armitage, David. 2000. *The Ideological Origins of the British Empire*. Cambridge: Cambridge University Press.

Bacon, Francis. 1987. *The Advancement of Learning* [1605]. A Reproduction of the Copy in the British Library, owned by Charles I. Alburgh: Archical Facsimiles.

Bauer, Ralph. 2003. *The Cultural Geography of Colonial American Literatures: Empire, Travel, Modernity*. Cambridge: Cambridge University Press.

Bucher, Bernadette. 1977. *La sauvage aux seins pendants*. Paris: Herman.

Campbell, Mary. 1988. *The Witness and the Other World: Exotic European Travel Writing, 400–1600*. Ithaca, NY: Cornell University Press.

Campbell, Mary. 1999. *Wonder and Science: Imagining Worlds in Early Modern Europe*. Ithaca, NY: Cornell University Press.

Canny, Nicholas. 1979. "The Permissive Frontier: Social Control in English Settlements in Ireland and Virginia, 1550–1650," in Kenneth Andrews, Nicholas Canny, and Paul Hair, eds., *The Westward Enterprise*. Detroit: Wayne State University Press, pp. 17–44.

Cassirer, Ernst. 1963. *The Individual and the Cosmos in Renaissance Philosophy*. Trans. Mario Damandi. Oxford: Blackwell.

Cawley, Robert. 1940. *Unpathed Waters: Studies in the Influence of Voyagers on Elizabethan Literature*. Princeton: Princeton University Press.

Certeau, Michel de. 1986. *Heterologies: Discourse on the Other*. Trans. Brian Massumi. Foreword Wlad Godzich. Minneapolis: University of Minnesota Press.

Certeau, Michel de. 1988. *The Writing of History*. Trans. Tom Conley. New York: Columbia University Press.

Cumming, William Patterson, Raleigh A. Skelton, and David Beers Quinn. 1972. *The Discovery of North America*. New York: American Heritage Press.

Eden, Richard. 1577. *The History of Trauayle in the West and East Indies*. London: Printed by Richard Iugge.

Elliot, John Huxtable. 1970. *The Old World and the New, 1492–1650*. Cambridge: Cambridge University Press.

Elsner, Jas and Joan-Pau Rubies, eds. 1999a. *Voyages and Visions: Toward a Cultural History of Travel*. London: Reaktion Books.

Elsner, Jas and Joan-Pau Rubies. 1999a. "Introduction," in Jas Elsner and Joan-Pau Rubies, eds., *Voyages and Visions: Toward a Cultural History of Travel*. London: Reaktion Books.

Fabian, Johannes. 1983. *Time and Other: How Anthropology Makes its Object*. New York: Columbia University Press.

Foss, Michael. 1974. *Undreamed Shores: England's Wasted Empire in America*. New York: Scribner.

Franklin, Wayne. 1979. *Discoverers, Explorers, Settlers: The Diligent Writers of Early America*. Chicago: University of Chicago Press.

Fuller, Mary. 1995. *Voyages in Print: English Travel to America, 1576–1624*. New York: Cambridge University Press.

Gibson, Charles. 1971. *The Black Legend: Anti-Spanish Attitudes in the Old World and the New*. New York: Knopf.

Grafton, Anthony. 1992. *New Worlds, Ancient Texts: The Power of Tradition and the Shock of Discovery*. Cambridge, MA: Harvard University Press.

Greenblatt, Stephen. 1973. *Sir Walter Ralegh: The Renaissance Man and his Roles*. New Haven and London: Yale University Press.

Greenblatt, Stephen. 1980. *Renaissance Self-Fashioning: From More to Shakespeare*. Chicago: University of Chicago Press.

Greenblatt, Stephen. 1981. "Invisible Bullets: Renaissance Authority and Its Subversion," *Glyph* 8: 40–61.

Greenblatt, Stephen. 1991. *Marvelous Possessions: The Wonder of the New World*. Chicago: University of Chicago Press.

Greenblatt, Stephen, ed. 1993. *New World Encounters*. Berkeley: University of California Press.

Hadfield, Andrew. 1998. *Literature, Travel, and Colonial Writing in the English Renaissance, 1545–1625*. Oxford: Clarendon Press.

Hakluyt, Richard. 1582. *Divers Voyages Touching the Discoverie of America, and the Islands Adjacent*. London: for Thomas Woodcocke.

Hakluyt, Richard. 1609. *Virginia Richly Valued, by the Description of the Maine Land of Florida, her Next Neighbour ... Written by a Portugall Gentlman of Elvas, Employed in All the Action, and Translated out of Portugese by Richard Hakluyt*. London: Felix Kynston for Matthew Lownes.

Hakluyt, Richard. 1927. *The Principal Navigations, Voyages, Traffiques & Discoveries of the English Nation. Made by Sea or Overland to the Remote and Farthest Distant Quarters of the Earth at any Time within the Compass of these 1600 Years*, 8 vols. Intro. John Masefield. London and Toronto: J. M. Dent and Sons.

Hakluyt, Richard. 1993. *A Particuler Discourse Concerninge the Greate Necessitie and Manifolde Commodyties that are Like to Growe to this Realme of Englande by the Westerne Discoueries Lately Attempted: Written in the Yere 1584: known as Discourse of Western Planting*. Eds. David B. Quinn and Alison M. Quinn. London : Hakluyt Society.

Hall, Donald J. 1965. *English Mediaeval Pilgrimage*. London: Routledge and Kegan Paul.

Harriot, Thomas. 1972. *A Briefe and True Report of the New Found Land of Virginia. The Complete 1590 Edition with the 28 Engravings by Theodor de Bry after the Drawings of John White*. New York: Dover Publications.

Hartog, François. 1988. *The Mirror of Herodotus: The Representation of the Other in the Writing of History*. Berkeley: University of California Press.

Helgerson, Richard. 1992. *Forms of Nationhood: The Elizabethan Writing of England*. Chicago: University of Chicago Press.

Howard, Donald R. 1980. *Writers and Pilgrims: Medieval Pilgrimage Narratives and their Posterity*. Berkeley: University of California Press.

Hulme, Peter. 1986. *Colonial Encounters: Europe and the Native Caribbean*. New York: Methuen.

Hulme, Peter and Tim Youngs, eds. 2002a. *The Cambridge Companion to Travel Writing*. Cambridge and New York: Cambridge University Press.

Hulme, Peter and Tim Youngs. 2002b. "Introduction," in Peter Hulme and Tim Youngs, eds., *The Cambridge Companion to Travel Writing*. Cambridge and New York: Cambridge University Press, pp. 1–16.

Jardine, Nicholas, James A. Secord, and Emma C. Spary, eds. 1996. *Cultures of Natural History*. Cambridge: Cambridge University Press.

Jennings, Francis. 1975. *The Invasion of America: Indians, Colonialism, and the Cant of Conquest*. Chapel Hill: University of North Carolina Press.

Johns, Adrian. 1998. *The Nature of the Book: Print and Knowledge in the Making*. Chicago: University of Chicago Press.

Jung, Carl. 1967. *Alchemical Studies*. Trans. R. F. C Hull London: Routledge and Kegan Paul.

Knapp, Jeffrey. 1992. *An Empire Nowhere: England, America, and Literature from Utopia to The Tempest*. Berkeley: University of California Press.

Lynam, Edward, ed. 1946. *Richard Hakluyt and his Successors*. London: Hakluyt Society.

McAlister, Lyle N. 1984. *Spain and Portugal in the New World 1492–1700*. Minneapolis: University of Minnesota Press.

Morison, Samuel Eliot. 1971–4. *The European Discovery of America. Vol. I: The Northern Voyages AD 500–1600. Vol. II: The Southern Voyages 1492–1616*. New York: Oxford University Press.

Nerlich, Michael. 1987. *Ideology of Adventure: Studies in Modern Consciousness, 1100–1750*, 2 vols. Minneapolis: University of Minnesota Press.

Orgel, Stephen. 1987. "Introduction," in William Shakespeare, *The Tempest*, ed. Stephen Orgel. Oxford: Clarendon Press, pp. 1–92.

Pagden, Anthony. 1982. *The Fall of Natural Man: The American Indian and the Origins of Comparative Ethnology*. Cambridge: Cambridge University Press.

Pagden, Anthony. 1993. *European Encounters with the New World: From Renaissance to Romanticism*. New Haven: Yale University Press.

Palmer, Sir Thomas. 1606. *An Essay of the Meanes How to Make our Trauailes, into Forraine Countries, the More Profitable and Honourable*. London: by H. L. for Mathew Lownes.

Parry, John Horace. 1963. *The Age of Reconnaissance: Discovery, Exploration and Settlement, 1450–1650*. Cleveland: World, and London: Weidenfeld and Nicolson.

Parry, John. 1964. *The Age of Reconnaissance*. New York: Mentor Books.

Pennington, Loren E., ed. 1997. *The Purchas Handbook: Studies in the Life, Times, and Writings of Samuel Purchas, 1577–1626*, 2 vols. London: Hakluyt Society.

Prager, Carolyn. 1993. "Early English Transfer and Invention of the Black in New Spain," in Jerry M. Williams and Robert E. Lewis, eds., *Early Images of the Americas: Transfer and Invention*. Tucson: University of Arizona Press, pp. 93–110.

Pratt, Mary Louise. 1992. *Imperial Eyes: Travel Writing and Transculturation*. New York: Routledge.

Purchas, Samuel. 1613. *Purchas his Pilgrimage; or Relations of the World. And the Religions observed in all Ages and Places. Discovered, from the Creation unto this Present. Contayning a Theological and Geographical Historie of Asia, Africa, and America*. London: William Stansby.

Purchas, Samuel. 1617. *Purchas his Pilgrimage, Or Relations of the World. And the Religions Observed in Al Ages and Places Discovered, from the Creation unto this Present*, 4 parts. London: William Stansby for Henry Fetherstone.

Purchas, Samuel. 1905–7. *Hakluytus Posthumus or Purchas his Pilgrimes* [1625], 20 vols. Glasgow: James MacLehose and Sons.

Quinn, David Beers, ed. 1940. *The Voyages and Colonising Enterprises of Sir Humphrey Gilbert*, 2 vols. London: Hakluyt Society.

Quinn, David Beers. 1955. *The Roanoke Voyages 1584–1590*, 2 vols. Cambridge: Hakluyt Society.

Quinn, David Beers. 1965. *The New Found Land: The English Contribution to the Discovery of North America*. Providence: John Carter Brown Library.

Quinn, David Beers. 1968. *Richard Hakluyt, Editor: A Study Introductory of the Facsimile Edition of Richard Hakluyt's Divers Voyages*. Amsterdam: Theatrum Orbis Terrarum.

Quinn, David Beers. 1971. *North American Discovery Circa 1000–1612*. Columbia: University of South Carolina Press.

Quinn, David Beers. 1974a. *England and the Discovery of America, 1481–1620.* New York: Knopf.

Quinn, David Beers, ed. 1974b. *The Hakluyt Handbook,* 2 vols. London: Hakluyt Society.

Quinn, David Beers. 1997a. "North America," in L. E. Pennington, ed., *The Purchas Handbook: Studies in the Life, Times, and Writings of Samuel Purchas, 1577–1626,* 2 vols. London: Hakluyt Society, I, 312–28.

Quinn, David Beers. 1977b. *North America from Earliest Discovery to First Settlements: The Norse Voyages to 1612.* New York: Harper and Row.

Quinn, David Beers. 1985. *Set Fair for Roanoke: Voyages and Colonies 1584–1606.* Chapel Hill: University of North Carolina Press.

Ralegh, Sir Walter. 1997. *The Discoverie of the Large, Rich, and Bewtiful Empyre of Guiana.* Transc., notes, and intro. Neil L. Whitehead. Norman: University of Oklahoma Press.

Ramusio, Giovanni Battista. 1550–6. *Delle Navigationi et viaggi.* 3 Vols. Venice: Nella stamperia de Giunti.

Rowse, Alfred L. 1959. *Elizabethans and America.* New York: Harper and Row.

Rowse, Alfred L. 1965. *The Expansion of Elizabethan England.* New York: Harper and Row.

Shapin, Stephen. 1994. *A Social History of Truth: Civility and Science in Seventeenth-Century England.* Chicago: University of Chicago Press.

Sherman, William. 1995. *John Dee: The Politics of Reading and Writing in the English Renaissance.* Amherst: University of Massachusetts Press.

Sherman, William. 2002. "Stirrings and Searchings (1500–1720)," in Peter Hulme and Tim Youngs, eds., *The Cambridge Companion to Travel Writing.* Cambridge and New York: Cambridge University Press, pp. 17–36.

Solomon, Julie Robin. 1991. " 'To Know, to Fly, to Conjure': Situating Baconian Science at the Juncture of Early Modern Modes of Reading," *Renaissance Quarterly* 44: 513–58.

Solomon, Julie Robin. 1998. *Objectivity in the Making: Francis Bacon and the Politics of Inquiry.* Baltimore: Johns Hopkins University Press.

Strachey, William. 1953. *The Historie of Travell into Virginia Britania* [1612]. Ed. Louis B. Wright. London: Hakluyt Society.

Taylor, E. G. R., ed. 1935. *The Original Writings and Correspondence of the Two Richard Hakluyts.* London: Hakluyt Society.

Turler, Jerome. 1951. *The Traveiler* [1575]. Intro. Denver Ewing Baughan. Gainesville, FL: Scholars' Facsimiles and Reprints.

Vickers, Brian, ed. 1984. *Occult and Scientific Mentalities in the Renaissance.* Cambridge: Cambridge University Press.

Whitehead, Neil L. 1997. "Introduction," in Sir Walter Ralegh, *The Discoverie of the Large, Rich, and Bewtiful Empyre of Guiana.* Transc., notes, and intro. Neil L. Whitehead. Norman: University of Oklahoma Press, pp. 1–116.

Williams, Jerry M. and Robert E. Lewis, eds. 1993. *Early Images of the Americas: Transfer and Invention.* Tucson: University of Arizona Press.

Williamson, James A. 1935. *The Cabot Voyages*. Cambridge: Hakluyt Society.

Wolf, Eric. 1982. *Europe and the People without History*. Berkeley: University of California Press.

Wright, Louis B. 1943. *Religion and Empire: The Alliance between Piety and Commerce in English Expansion 1558–1625*. Chapel Hill: University of North Carolina Press.

Wright, Louis B. 1958. *Middle Class Culture in Elizabethan England*. Ithaca, NY: Cornell University Press.

Zacher, Christian. 1976. *Curiosity and Pilgrimage: The Literature of Discovery in Fourteenth-Century England*. Baltimore: Johns Hopkins University Press.

Chapter 8

Private Life and Domesticity

Lena Cowen Orlin

With titles like *A Brief and Pleasant Discourse of Duties in Marriage* (by Edmund Tilney, 1568), *A Godly Form of Household Government* (by John Dod and Robert Cleaver, 1598), and *Of Domestical Duties* (by William Gouge, 1622), the early modern printing industry produced a sizable canon of guidebooks to the conduct of private life. These popular treatises advised Elizabethans and Jacobeans about ideal gender roles, courtship practices, marital relations, child rearing, servant supervision, and domestic organization. It would be tempting to think that the manuals might tell us everything we would want to know about these important contexts for English Renaissance literature. In fact, however, personal histories were far more complex and diverse than any pre-scriptive text acknowledged. The history of private life developed in a wide variety of genres, including the diaries and memoirs that made their first English appearances in this period. These are not often thought of as highly fictionalized, but, like more canonical poems and plays, they, too, show the influence of cultural myths about private practices. This chapter seeks to develop alternative perspectives on the literatures of private life, concentrating on works for which history and biography provide evidence of how partial their truths were.

In important ways, books like *A Godly Form of Household Government* were products of the Reformation (which is also discussed in chapter 2, "Religion"). Henry VIII's 1533 break with Rome had long conse-quences in terms of theology and the relationship of church and state, royal authority and the nationalization of rule, and the seizure and redistribution of church properties. The larger religious, political, and economic consequences of ecclesiastical upheaval were also to have profound repercussions for private life: a mandate for spiritual self-examination and for personal experience of the vernacular scrip-tures, a reconceptualization of the household as the crucible of public

160

order, and, through the new systems of government offices and rewards, an opening of opportunity to merit and ambition as well as inherited privilege. The popular legend of the Reformation did not acknowledge the king's aggregation of wealth and power; instead, it promulgated a story of the imperial conscience exercised upon matters domestic (for this, see also chapter 3, "Royal Marriage and the Royal Succession"). Henry's protracted quest for male heirs made his personal life a public preoccupation, and the results of this notorious conjugal drama played themselves out over the better part of a century, as each of his three children succeeded to the throne. Edward VI took the Reformation further than his father had done (1547–53), Mary I restored Roman Catholicism (1553–8), and then Elizabeth I instated the form of Protestantism that was to become known as Anglican (1558–1603). The switchback mandates of official religion had profound resonance in the private sphere. For the middle years of the sixteenth century, all people of faith were necessarily heretics during one reign or another. There were Henrician martyrs and Marian exiles, Elizabethan recusants and radical sectarians. Thus a volatile ecclesiastical history created the space for many besides Henry VIII to acknowledge and act on their private consciences. Newly enfranchised habits of personal choice and self-determination were to prove formative for western conceptions of individuality, interiority, and family.

From this point of view, the principal text of Tudor private life was a massive compendium of Protestant propaganda, John Foxe's *Actes and Monuments* (1563). Familiarly known as Foxe's *Book of Martyrs*, the collection of biographies and anecdotes created a pantheon of heroes for the new religion. Elizabeth I was herself included among them for the imprisonment she suffered during her elder sister's rule. When, in 1571, copies of the *Book of Martyrs* were placed in all cathedrals and collegiate churches, it became nearly as foundational a text for early modern society as the English-language Bible, *The Book of Common Prayer* (1549, 1552, and 1559), Erasmus' *Paraphrases* from the Gospels (1547), and the *Homilies* that were ordered read in parish churches. In the first, 1547 book of *Homilies*, Thomas Cranmer assembled a collection of twelve sermons intended for delivery seriatim, on sequential Sundays. These replaced the old, Catholic liturgy with elucidations of the new doctrine ("A Fruitful Exhortation to the Reading of Holy Scriptures," "Of the True and Lively Faith") and descriptions of Protestant practice ("Of Good Works," "An Exhortation to Obedience," "Against Whoredom and Adultery"). If a principal aim was propagandistic, to direct public belief and behavior, the *Homilies* had an equally important intended audience among the clergy, to establish the parameters for their conformity. While less educated clerics were enjoined simply to read from the authorized texts, members of the preaching ministry were expected to say nothing that diverged from them. Elizabeth I recognized the multiple uses and audiences of the *Homilies* and oversaw their expansion in 1563 with twenty new sermons ("Of the Place and Time of Prayer," "Against Gluttony and Drunkenness"). Some she edited herself. In 1570, following the Northern Rebellion, there was a last addition, "A Homily against Disobedience and Willful Rebellion," which was so extended that its oral presentation occupied six successive Sundays (Bond 1987).

More importantly for this discussion of the way the Reformation impacted private life, the 1563 *Homilies* included a sermon "Of the State of Matrimony," which, like all these texts, adduced to the social order. Marriage was described as a duty "ordained" by God for three reasons: so "that man and woman should live lawfully in a perpetual friendship," so that they would "bring forth fruit" to "enlarge" the Christian kingdom, and so that they would "avoid fornication" (Rickey and Stroup 1968: 239). The sermon went on to acknowledge "how few matrimonies there be without chidings, brawlings, tauntings, repentings, bitter cursings, and fightings" (p. 240), and it forcefully preached ways to avoid discord at home. The husband was expected "to be the leader and author of love" (p. 241), the "head of the woman, as Christ is the head of the church" (p. 242). Because the wife was known to lack his "strength and constancy of mind" by her very nature, he should be willing to "wink" at some of her "weak affections and dispositions" (p. 241). He was also advised not to be overly rigorous: "thou dost much derogate and decay the excellency and virtue of thine own authority" (p. 246). But if the wife found herself married to a man who did not "wink," and even if he beat her, she should nonetheless suffer her treatment with patience and humility: "if thou lovest him only because he is gentle and courteous, what reward will God give thee therefore?" (p. 244). The wife was required to be "subject" to her husband, to "relinquish the liberty of [her] own rule," and fully to "feel the grief and pains of their matrimony" (p. 243). In its emphasis on the inevitability of mutual incompatibility, its insistence that marriage was punitive for the daughters of Eve, and its preoccupation with the duties required of both husbands and wives, the homily on matrimony refused to romanticize the married state. It presented itself as if with no illusions that love would last, that pleasure would prevail, or that harmony would unfold naturally.

Despite its affect of practicality, however, the homily was nonetheless full of fictions, especially about hierarchy and authority. Just as the microcosm of the family was held to be analogous to the macrocosm of the state, so the preachings of the homily on matrimony were perfectly congruent with those of the "Homily against Disobedience and Willful Rebellion." In such turbulent times, when the rapid turnovers in Tudor rule were succeeded by many Elizabethan revolts and attempted usurpations (as discussed in chapter 9, "Treason and Rebellion"), the queen's government was unwilling to acknowledge that there could be group structures that were not monarchical, or that the rule of any authority figure was not absolute. Thus John Dod and Robert Cleaver, like many others, wrote that "the household is as it were a little commonwealth," with the husband as "not only a ruler, but a King, and Lord of all" (Dod and Cleaver 1598: sigs. A8^r, N1^r–^{v}). A frequently repeated construct was that love traveled downward – that is, the "lord of all" should endeavor to be benevolent – while obedience traveled upward – in other words, all those in his "kingdom" should enact their subjection to him. The political cast of domestic writing was only to be expected, because most of these authors were clergymen for whom the *Homilies* established a conceptual framework. How artificial their prescriptions could be, however, may also be suggested by the fact that two of the earliest and most influential writers on marriage, Edmund Tilney and Henry Smith (*A Preparative to Marriage*, 1591), were themselves single men when they published on the subject.

Writings that were more explicitly religious and political were robustly contested. Even Foxe did not escape unscathed; he was specifically engaged by Thomas Harding (*Confutation*, 1565) and Nicholas Harpsfield (*Dialogi Sex*, 1566). The literature of conscience also included Marian resistance tracts published on the Continent by John Ponet (*Short Treatise of Politike Power*, 1556) and Christopher Goodman (*How Superior Powers Ought to Be Obeyed*, 1558); Catholic hagiographies like William Roper's *Life of Sir Thomas More* and the autobiographies of persecuted Elizabethan Jesuits William Weston and John Gerard (these circulated without publication, as described in chapter 6, "Manuscripts in Early Modern England"); and the Puritan polemic *An Admonition to the Parliament* (1572), which cost authors John Field and Thomas Wilcox a year in prison. By contrast, however, there was no oppositional literature for private life. William Gouge was a Puritan, and so had theological differences with the established church, but on the subject of "domestical duties" he, too, insisted that wives were required to honor their husbands, to fear them, to obey them, to speak reverently to them, to admit correction by them, and to avoid sullenness, scornfulness, vanity, and willfulness. In the literature of the private sphere, the only area of real conflict had to do with the nature of women – not their roles – a controversy that was conducted in a heated pamphlet war (Henderson and McManus 1985). Neither the hyperbolic, market-driven attacks on women nor angry defenses of them entertained any notion that the basic structure of the household might be something other than that propounded by the homily "Of the State of Matrimony." Tilney's *Brief and Pleasant Discourse* synchronically entertained what Valerie Wayne has worked to identify as residual, dominant, and emergent ideologies (Wayne 1992: 3–4), and Gouge himself admitted in a preface to his readers that among his original parishioners, first auditors for the sermons collected under the title *Of Domestical Duties*, "much exception was taken against the application of a wife's subjection to the restraining of her from disposing the common goods of the family without or against her husband's consent" (Gouge 1622: sig. ¶3v). But these thin hints of controversy near the beginning and end of our period posed no substantive challenge to the larger political understandings from which all these writings proceeded. Domestic authors were unwilling to imagine a social structure different from that consisting in monogamous heterosexual couplings in nuclear households, with orderly rankings of children, servants, wives, and, at the pinnacles of power and authority, the patriarchs.

Recent research has established that there are many ways of deconstructing these premises. Queer theorists have documented the prevalence of alternative sexual practices; social historians have directed our attention to the life experiences of those who were not heads of household but were themselves in service or displaced; and demographers have demonstrated how many variations there were in early modern living arrangements. Recently, for example, Amy Froide has calculated that at any given moment as many as 40 or 50 percent of the adult female population were single, whether maids or widows (Froide 1999: 237). It was surely the case that all women were expected to wed, but that does not mean that all did so. The fact that men were far quicker to remarry when widowed is some indication of how dependent they were upon their partners for running their households, rearing children, supervising servants, and contributing to family incomes. For husbands and wives at subsistence level, for those who were ambitious to prosper in the new economy of opportunity, and for those who saw earlier achievements eroded by dearth and debt, shared economic purpose could be far more urgent than any abstract political structure. The two aspects of private life were not mutually exclusive, for hierarchy was understood to be necessary to order, and order to productivity, but it is clear that, for most, the first cause was their livelihood and advancement (as is also discussed in chapter 1, "Economics"). Political argument existed in a realm of relative abstraction, often far removed from insistent material concerns. Fundamentally, and despite public rhetoric to the contrary, the private household was an economic institution. It is no accident that when Gouge's parishioners protested his teachings, it was on the subject of the wife's rights with respect to the family's worldly possessions.

The gender hierarchy was thoroughly institutionalized in property law, and women's labor was rarely organized (they generally could not join trade guilds or be represented in government bodies). While men were identified in early modern records by their craft (as, for example, "John Shakespeare, glover"), women were identified by their status with respect to men (as singlewoman, "wife of John Shakespeare," or widow). Women were, further, even more likely than men to pursue multiple skills, shifting to their husbands' occupations with marriage and remarriage, adopting less strenuous tasks during pregnancy, or changing work products with the seasons. But if contemporary labeling habits and job flexibility have made it more difficult for us to recognize their labor histories, it did not diminish women's power in their own time not just as consumers but also as producers. Whether they were supporting themselves or contributing to families, women had vital roles and responsibilities that the domestic manuals did not fully address. Early modern political theorists borrowed from classical and Continental writings, like Aristotle's *Politics* (translated into English, 1598) and Jean Bodin's fiercely monarchical *Six Bookes of a Commonweal* (1576; translated into English, 1606). Elizabethan and Jacobean authors suppressed the fact that Aristotle had written about democracy and aristocratic, or shared, rule as well as monarchy. For households, the aristocratic model was better suited to the practical matters of daily life, with husbands and wives working as teams. This was as true for those struggling to survive as for those with aspirations to rise (Orlin 2000).

The personal genres that had their first flourishing in the Renaissance – diaries, journals, family memoirs, letters – show their authors striving to conform themselves to domestic ideals that in these and

165

other ways made unrealistic templates for private life. The impractical Nehemiah Wallington (1598–1658) was a London shopkeeper and prolific Puritan diarist who, according to biographer Paul S. Seaver, was so "vague" about the sales of his small wooden household objects that he did not realize his own journeyman had pilfered as much as £100 over the course of two years. Wallington was instead preoccupied with self-examination and salvation. He compiled fifty volumes of autobiography, spiritual exercises, meditations, and lessons learned from sermons he had heard (six of the fifty manuscript compilations have survived). In 1622 he recorded that, "having a wife, a child, a manservant, and a maidservant, and thus having the charge of so many souls, I then bought Master Gouge's book *Of Domestical Duties*." Wallington intended that with the help of Gouge, "every one of us may learn and know our duties and honor God every one in his place where God had set them." In 1632 he copied into a writing book a letter he may also have authored, which offered advice on making matches for daughters. This seems to have borrowed heavily from Dod and Cleaver's *Godly Form of Household Government*. But if Wallington represents the active constituency for such publications, he was in many ways an eccentric. As a Puritan he was a religious nonconformist; as a depressive, he had repeatedly contemplated suicide. It may be because of his troubled emotional history that he was indulged by his parents and then his wife in his daily hours of prayer, his other spiritual disciplines, his obsessive self-chronicling, his book buying, and even his own vanity "publication," an appendix to a tract on *The Loathsomeness of Long Hair* (1654). He also, in 1617, invested in a "book called *The Bearbaiting of Women*," but he did so as a form of aversion therapy, "to make me to dislike women" despite his adolescent sexual desires. In a further mark of how varied the responses to these anti-feminist diatribes could be, he finally disposed of the book "because it was contrary to God's word." Wallington's difficulties reconciling his experiences to his beliefs are best witnessed in his dogged lists of "God's mercies" when only one of his children, a daughter, survived to adulthood. Four others had died before the age of three, and, Lawrence Stone to the contrary, Wallington clearly grieved heavily for them. His journal acknowledges that in these tragedies his wife Grace proved herself anything but the weaker vessel of the two. She would have lost a husband as well as a daughter had she not resisted his despair so vigorously: "No, truly, husband, if you will believe me, I do as freely give [the child] again unto God, as I did receive it of him" (Seaver 1985: 118–19, 199, 79, 230, 175, 88–9).

Nehemiah Wallington's compulsion for self-recordation was more common in the godly community than elsewhere. Lady Margaret Hoby (1571–1633), who kept a diary for the years 1599–1605, also demonstrated a deep religiosity. Her journal may well have been an exercise practiced for her chaplain Richard Rhodes, documenting that through strenuous piety and domesticity she had made good use of her days: "After private prayer," most entries would begin, "I went about the house" to see to its ordering. Like Wallington, Hoby attended as much to the spiritual health of her servants as to their physical well-being. She took care not only to lead them in what she called "public prayers" but also, as occasion warranted, to "sit a while with my women talking of some principles with them." She was in the early years of an enforced marriage (her third, as she had been twice widowed before she turned 25) and a childless one. Like Henry VIII, she would have believed that her failure to produce children betrayed one of the "duties" of marriage and represented the withholding of divine blessings (Moody 1998: xxxvi–xxxvii, xliv–xlv). But if these traumas were motivations for her discipline, Hoby makes no reference to them. Nor is there any explanation for why, in 1605, she abandoned her journal, leaving nearly thirty more unchronicled years. It may be that, unlike the persistently melancholic Wallington, she had passed her period of personal crises or had adopted other strategies for reconciling herself to them. Wallington's notebooks were far from autobiographical, making no mention of obvious family milestones, and, as Seaver points out, so "didactic" in purpose that he seemed oblivious to "personal or political events for their own interest" (Seaver 1985: 9). Nonetheless, the level of opacity in Hoby's journal is even higher than in Wallington's. The gap between what we would want to understand about her and what she chose to tell us is an unbridgeable one, for, as was true of most early diarists, her purposes were not self-revelatory.

If this is one problem with personal documents as sources for private life, another is how often they proceeded from that small minority of the population that was leisured and learned; Wallington is a remarkable exception. Lady Grace Mildmay (1552–1620), a moderate Puritan, was nearly as prolific an author as he, but far more elevated socially. Like Hoby she was an heiress, and so had little choice in an early marriage arranged more for family alliances and property settlements than personal inclinations. Like a real-life Bertram (the reluctant husband in Shakespeare's *All's Well that Ends Well*), Anthony Mildmay fled the enforced match. Over the course of the next twenty years he spent at least half his time on diplomatic and military travels, leaving his wife behind in his parents' home (Pollock 1993b: 8–10). In a devotional meditation, Mildmay summarized others of her travails: "I was childless almost ten years" (and finally she had just one daughter), "a great part of [my] inheritance ... was given away" (to her own sister), and "no jointure was assured me by my husband or by his father" (Pollock 1993a: 86). As was true of others, her most urgent grievances were focused on economic matters. Her "adversaries," she said, were those who "should have been my chiefest friends, even fathers, sisters, and brothers" (p. 86), what Frances Dolan has termed "dangerous familiars" (Dolan 1994). Despite this, Mildmay's autobiography is thoroughly conventional. In it she honors the parents who had partially disinherited her, describing her father's careful governance of his household and declaring that "All my mother's counsels have I laid up in my mind" (Pollock 1993a: 29). Although she spent twenty of her adult years as a subordinate in the home of her in-laws, she nonetheless quoted that "a private household of family ... may resemble a whole commonwealth" (p. 47), much as had Dod and Cleaver. And even as she lived a fairly "solitary" life, she repeated familiar injunctions on the order of matrimony: "let wives be subject to their husbands" (p. 44), "let the wife see that she fear her husband" (p. 45), and "likewise the husbands dwell with them as men of knowledge, giving honor unto the wife, as unto the weaker vessel" (p. 44). In Anthony's absence, Mildmay read in unexceptional texts (particularly recommending Foxe's *Book of Martyrs*), drew and embroidered, played her lute and sang, and also produced a vast collection of scientific papers. These demonstrate how great a medical proficiency could be achieved by gentlewomen who were self-taught but who sought and shared pharmacological and therapeutic knowledge. We must know her life story (a field of research that is also discussed in chapter 12, "Life-Writing"), in order to appreciate in full the deliberate fictions and willful denials of her life-writings.

Most personal narratives of the sixteenth and early seventeenth centuries thus engaged the conformist or godly communities of discourse that also informed the domestic manuals. There were, however, alternative perspectives in other genres. One unlikely example appears in the verse collection of imaginary love letters titled *England's Heroicall Epistles* (1597). The topics of private life and domesticity are often given taxonomic shape by their presumed distinction from the high culture and state politics that inform most canonical literatures, but this ambitious gallery of poems by Michael Drayton, who took Ovid's *Heroides* as his model and new national histories for his sources, nonetheless focused on private emotion. There are twelve romantic pairs in all, presented in chronological order beginning with Rosamond's "letter" to Henry II and his response, and ending with a suppositious exchange between the nine-days'-queen Jane Grey and her husband Guildford Dudley. In his preface, Drayton explained that these could be called "England's" epistles because "the most and greatest persons herein were English, or else that their loves were obtained in England," and they were "heroical" in an Ovidian sense, referring not to "demigods" like Hercules (half-human and half-divine), but "to them, who for the greatness of mind come near to gods" (Hebel 1961: 130)). In nearly 4,300 lines of rhyming couplets, Drayton displayed a dazzling technical virtuosity. By adding long prose endnotes on classical mythology, world geography, natural science, royal genealogy, and English annals, he also demonstrated his wide learning. To avoid the accusation that "nothing but amorous humor were handled herein," he added, his annotations contained "matters historical" (p. 130). For instance, in the fictional letter from Henry VI's Queen Margaret to William de la Pole, Drayton invents a reference to "my daisy flower," and his notes explain that the French version of Margaret is Marguerite, in that language also meaning "daisy." Although this elucidation of a cross-cultural pun is not what we might term "historical," it serves Drayton's attempt to elevate a collection of love letters out of the realm of the merely private, to represent personal relations as a new national history.

For the letter from King John to Matilda, Drayton admits that this is "much more poetical than historical, making no mention at all of the occurrences of the time, or state, touching only his love to her, and the extremity of his passions forced by his desires, rightly fashioning the humor of this king" (Hebel 1961: 152). John and Matilda are one of just four legitimate royal pairs (a number that includes Jane Grey and Guildford Dudley, even though they were illegitimate monarchs). For the remaining eight couples, there are letters not between Edward II and his queen, but between her and Mortimer; not between Henry V and Katherine Valois, but between Katherine and her partner in widowhood, Owen Tudor; not between Henry VIII and any of his wives, but between his sister Mary and her second husband Charles Brandon, duke of Suffolk. The emphasis on romantic liaisons rather than political alliances is most striking in the case of Edward IV and Jane Shore, the city wife whom the already-married king took as his mistress. This fifteenth-century story remained popular through many sixteenth- and seventeenth-century retellings, but not out of any interest in Jane's "greatness of mind." In his annotations to Edward's love letter, Drayton again emphasized that he had avoided "the many battles betwixt the Lancastrian faction and" the king "or other warlike dangers," and had concentrated instead on "unlawful affection" (p. 252). His valorization of extra-marital romantic relations participated in a dialogue that was at least as influential in early modern England as were those that followed the homily "Of the State of Matrimony" and that ordered the private sphere in terms of marriage, monogamy, and duty.

With a literary corpus that also includes the Spenserian collection of nine pastoral eclogues he titled *Idea, the Shepherd's Garland* (1593), love sonnets grouped under the collective name *Idea's Mirrour* (1594), and a reworking of these poems into the sonnet sequence *Idea* (1619), Drayton was, in the words of Bernard Capp, "temperamentally drawn to the Ideal unsullied by experience" (Capp 1995: 35). And yet, as with Wallington, Hoby, and Mildmay, we have evidence of the dystopic aspects of his lived life. In 1627 (years after publishing these works), Drayton was called before the Consistory Court of London, having been accused of fornication. The incident was alleged to have taken place in the house of Elizabeth Welsh; Drayton testified that he went there to meet with her lodger John Peters. Welsh's servant Elizabeth Hobcock believed that instead Drayton rendezvoused with Peters's wife Mary, who "did hold up her clothes unto her navel," and "clapt her hand on her privy part and said it was a sound and a good one."[1] According to Hobcock's report, "Master Drayton did then also lay his hand upon it and stroked it and said that it was a good one." One questioner sought to trip Hobcock up by asking her the color of Mary Peters's "tail," but Hobcock was unflappable. "White and black," she replied. Although Drayton denied all, he found himself in the middle of a very complicated controversy: Mary Peters accused Welsh and Hobcock of having slandered her, Welsh lodged a counter-complaint that she had herself been slandered by Peters, and finally, a third case was opened at the court's initiative to determine if Drayton and Peters had committed adultery as alleged (Capp 1995).

Elizabeth Welsh portrayed herself as an honest businesswoman who, to protect the reputation of her house, had among other things concerned herself with the financial standing of her lodgers. The implication was that Mary Peters supplemented the family income through prostitution. Drayton deposed to the contrary that John Peters had prospered as a reputable attorney. Welsh's own character was damaged by association, when it came out that one of her witnesses had once been accused of running a bawdy house. The court also learned that Hobcock had been excommunicated. The most forceful witness on Welsh's behalf was another lodger, Helen True, who recalled that Mary Peters had spoken to Welsh in a "most rude and disgraceful" way: "hang the bawd, thou toothless bawd, thou impudent whore, thou rotten bawd, thou pocky bawd, thou wearest a truss for the pox." But according to True's own sister Margaret Hamblin, Welsh had credited True and her husband with half-a-year's rent for this testimony; the implication was that it was fabricated collusively. Joan Stephens, Welsh's erstwhile maidservant, contributed that the Trues were motivated by poverty so extreme that they borrowed clothes, begged for kindling, were in debt for bread and beer, and thus were desperately in need of remission for their lodging expenses. Stephens then gave the closest thing we have to a coherent explanation for the real grounds of the case. When she tried to collect her wages and possessions from Welsh, she said, Welsh and True had locked her in a room of the house. They would not release her until she agreed to falsely accuse three men of fornication and of infecting her with the pox. She secured her escape by pretending to join the plot to demand the cost of a "cure" from each. But Mary Peters warned one of the potential blackmail victims, thus arousing ire that Welsh expressed in slanderous invective. By Stephens's account, Drayton would seem simply to have been in the wrong place at the wrong time, an innocent selected to advance the retributive plot against Peters (Capp 1995).

As in so many of the church-court cases for which such tantalizing information survives, it is not possible to know the truth of the matter. Even after escaping, for example, Stephens mysteriously returned to the Welsh house again (she said she was "as it were amazed, not well knowing what she did," though it may be she still sought goods and funds due her). Undoubtedly, however, Stephens cherished her own grudges against Welsh, dating back to her term of service in the troubled lodging house. But if many events and motivations remain obscure, real meanings are nonetheless apparent. The witness depositions transcribed at such length in the church courts give us access to the interests and worldviews of small traders, craftspersons, laborers, and servants. Drayton was a conspicuous anomaly in this court, not only for his gentility but also because he left other textual traces that most such deponents did not. While the ecclesiastical courts shared with the homily on matrimony a concern for sexual behavior, it is apparent in cases like those of *Peters contra Welsh* and *Welsh contra Peters*

that accusations of adultery were the pretexts onto which other dis-
agreements, conspiracies, and profit-making schemes were mapped.
As Laura Gowing has shown, all sorts of interpersonal quarrels were
expressed in the sexualized language that the church courts trafficked
in; because those who had been accused of unchastity could claim
material damage to their reputation in this venue, accusations of
unchastity were what they alleged (Gowing 1996). If chastity was
not the real issue for Welsh, True, and Peters, then, neither were
romantic love nor the patriarchy, prescribed obedience, and social
order that feature so largely in the didactic literatures. The women
had richly textured social and economic lives independent of any
political relationship with their husbands – as is especially evident
from Joan Stephens's testimony that, before she was imprisoned in
the room in which she agreed under duress to conspire in extortion,
Welsh and True first locked their own husbands into another chamber.
Thus they conducted their campaign of terrorization uninterrupted by
men who in the domestic manuals were nominally "lords of all."

Obviously, the admonitions of authorized and conventional writings
would not have been necessary had they been universally observed.
The insistence of these messages could have been occasioned only by a
fair amount of resistance to them. For representations of the frequent
disorders of the domestic sphere, the most immediate literature may be
the stageplay. Especially symptomatic of popular concern for private
responsibility and social order was a subgenre that developed, not
coincidentally, in the 1590s. Modern critics have given it the name of
"domestic" tragedy for its emphasis on spouse killing, adultery, and
other household misadventures (Adams 1943; Dolan 1994; Orlin
1994). One of the earliest of these plays (published anonymously in
1599) was based upon a true local crime but was given a generalizing,
didactic title, *A Warning for Fair Women*. The notorious events dated back
to 1573, when London merchant George Saunders was murdered by his
wife's lover George Browne, allegedly with her collaboration. The two
were executed publicly in Smithfield along with a neighbor, Anne
Drury, and Drury's manservant, Roger Clement. The play depicts
Anne Saunders as a chaste wife who would have resisted Browne's
attempted seduction had she not been corrupted and manipulated by
his go-between, Drury. In one of the play's moralizing dumb shows, for
example, the allegorical figure of "Chastity" tries to pull Anne Saunders
away from "Lust," but Anne Drury intervenes to "thrust" Chastity
away so that Lust can safely embrace the fair wife (Cannon 1975:
120). In another, a "great tree" rises on stage. Anne Saunders refuses

the axe that Lust offers her, but Browne employs it "roughly and suddenly." Chastity then points from a portrait of George Saunders to the fallen tree in order to show Anne Saunders that it symbolizes the murder of her husband (p. 134). The last dumb show has Chastity awakening a sleeping "Justice" to ensure that all four conspirators are charged with the crime. Many long scenes detail the aftermath in trials, confessions, and executions, with Anne Sanders hoping till the end that Drury will exonerate her. A repentant Drury refuses: "We have been both notorious vile transgressors," she declares (p. 173). Finally Anne Saunders admits that she "consented" to homicide and, in a sentimental closing scene, advises her children to "learn by your mother's fall / To follow virtue, and beware of sin." Her chosen legacy to them is not "gold or silver" – "you are left / Sufficiently provided in that point" (p. 176) – but instead the collected works of Protestant martyr John Bradford, *Godly Meditations upon the Lord's Prayer, the Belief, and Ten Commandments* (this was published in 1562, seven years after he was burned at the stake in Smithfield).

Long known as an exclusively "homiletic" tragedy (Adams 1943), *A Warning for Fair Women* was in fact an example of what Jonathan Dollimore influentially termed "radical" tragedy. As Dollimore recognized, the meanings generated by any text are always larger and more complicated than the author intended, as is especially true for this play, in which the moralistic ending cannot undo the effects of the morally ambiguous actions that lead up to it (Dollimore 1984). Anne Drury's first opportunity to influence Anne Saunders comes when the good wife is prevented by her husband from settling a tradesman's account (George Saunders has taken the household funds to repay a business debt). "My breach of credit, in the while / Is not regarded" (Cannon 1975: 115), Anne Saunders bridles. She might have been one of William Gouge's parishioners, protesting her entitlement to "[dispose] the common goods of the family without or against her husband's consent." Drury remarks in an excited aside that, "thus incensed against her husband, / I shall the better break with her for Browne" (p. 114). But Anne Saunders composes herself: "I am a woman, and in that respect, / Am well content my husband shall control me" (p. 115). Drury turns this scrupulous observance of marital hierarchy on its head. Pretending to be a palm reader and prognosticator, she predicts that Anne Saunders is fated soon to have another husband, Browne. It follows that Anne Saunders should "use [Browne] courteously, as one for whom, / You were created in your birth a wife" (p. 118). Propelled into this undiscovered political landscape, Anne Saunders loses her way: "If it be so,

I must submit my self / To that which God and destiny sets down" (p. 118). In this fashion Drury uses the very logic of the homily "Of the State of Matrimony" to convince Anne Saunders that she is in political crisis, suffering a conflict of authorities and owing as much obedience to her extra-marital suitor as to her legitimate husband. Drury's easy manipulation of doctrine exposes its limitations and inflexibilities (Orlin 1994: 108–12).

The Saunders murder had an afterlife not only on stage but also in the administrative accounts (or Repertories) of the Court of Aldermen, the executive branch of London government.[2] The Aldermen had long taken a custodial role with respect to the estates of "orphans of the city," those whose fathers had been freemen, and, as the character Anne Saunders observed, Walter, Thomas, Elizabeth, and George Saunders were not left unprovided of the "gold or silver" that the Aldermen were interested to protect. However, the wealthy merchant George Saunders died intestate – his was, after all, an unexpected death – so in this case it also fell to city agents to sort out the "thirds." London custom was that a widow received one-third, children shared one-third, and the testator allocated the remaining third. Only George Saunders's brother Francis survived to represent the murdered man's interests regarding the discretionary third. More unusually, the Sheriff of London was inspired to claim the widow's third for city coffers, "by reason of the felony committed by her." When Francis Saunders protested, the issue was placed in arbitration with the Aldermen. Concerned as they were with the fiscal wellbeing of the city, the Aldermen held their professional loyalties in higher priority, and they ruled for the family of a fellow merchant. There were additional proceedings, such as the determination of child support until the heirs reached their majorities, and further complications, including a problematic attempt to recover some Saunders assets still held by his factor in Spain. As all the records accumulated, the Aldermanic vocabulary remained exclusively economic. Beginning with the Sheriff's recognition that capital might be made "by reason of the felony committed" by Anne Saunders, theirs was a focus on finance. If the murder disrupted hierarchies that were believed to order the universe, if Anne Saunders and Anne Drury embodied powerful fears about the nature of women, and if the crime had larger social, political, and moral meanings, we would not know that from the Aldermen's Repertories.

Another domestic crime that achieved widespread notoriety in early modern England involved a dissolute husband wasting his estate and then turning his self-hatred on his family, successfully murdering two of his three sons and seriously wounding his wife. The events made for a short, violent, and bitter stageplay under the title *A Yorkshire Tragedy* (published as authored by William Shakespeare in 1608, though few today accept this attribution). Far more radical was a loose adaptation of the story that purported to recuperate a comic ending from these tragic ingredients, George Wilkins's *The Miseries of Enforced Marriage* (1607). The first marriage of the play is made freely, when young William Scarborrow and Clare Harcop promise themselves to each other in a way that was as morally binding in early modern England as a church wedding. The betrothal includes a declaration of conditions that ventriloquize the domestic manuals. Scarborrow requires Clare to be obedient, chaste, and mindful that "Maids being once made wives can nothing call / Rightly their own; they are their husbands' all" (Blayney 1964: ll. 263–4). Clare asks conformably that Scarborrow should provide for her, cohabit with her peaceably, and be gentle when rebuking her. Their youthful idealism is, however, punctuated by the running commentary of Sir Francis Ilford, who abhors marriage as "the cuckold's order" (l. 71) and who himself prefers to quote from misogynistic literature: "Women are the purgatory of men's purses, the paradise of their bodies, and the hell of their minds" (ll. 148–50). Ilford's cynicism becomes the dominant tone of the play when Scarborrow's life changes in a way that no domestic guidebook could have prepared him for: his guardian forces him to wed another woman. Thus made a bigamist, he dedicates himself to despair and financial ruin: "All riot now, since that my soul's so black" (l. 999). Clare attempts to "cleanse" (l. 872) him by sacrificing herself in a bloody suicide.

Scarborrow nonetheless abandons his pregnant second wife in the country and embarks on a course of depravity in the city. He consumes his estate and also the patrimonies of his two younger brothers and sister. "Credit must be maintained, which will not be without money," one brother observes, "good clothes must be had, which will not be without money; company must be kept, which will not be without money" (Blayney 1964: ll. 1232–4). The play seems to find small fault with the siblings' subsequent, desperate strategies of stealing £300 from the grieving father of Clare Harcop, buying clothing and jewels to portray the sister as an heiress, pimping her to Ilford, and deceiving Ilford into marriage. As the circle of corruption widens, the only character to demonstrate any nobility of spirit is a subordinate, a Scarborrow family butler – though he, too, is finally contaminated by dishonorable actions undertaken in the name of family "honor." After having stabbed his brothers, questioned the paternity of his children, and accused the aged retainer of cuckolding him, Scarborrow makes an unlikely repentance when news arrives that his guardian has died. Even his moral awakening is depicted with ideological irregularity, however, as he threatens the Oxford doctor of divinity who has tried unsuccessfully to intercede with him. The play requires contrition from the doctor for having performed the bigamous marriage, as also from the guardian whose apologetic deathbed bequest to Scarborrow restores "double of the wealth [he] had" (l. 2837). Mentioning Clare shortly before this rapid reconciliation scene, Scarborrow also reminds his audience that the cost of his "happy" ending has been her blameless life. Finally, Wilkins is so cavalier with the rules and tones of genre that, were *The Miseries of Enforced Marriage* as well known as *Measure for Measure* or *All's Well that Ends Well*, it would surely be called a "problem" comedy. For this chapter, importantly, Wilkins is equally disrespectful of the rules by which early moderns were encouraged to govern their lives. As with other texts discussed here, the play has important economic subtexts that the guidebooks neglected, and it offers compelling evidence that their prescriptions could be brutally irrelevant to personal doubts and dilemmas.

George Wilkins is best remembered today as Shakespeare's collaborator on *Pericles* (1607), which dramatized a story Wilkins also told in prose form as *The Painful Adventures of Pericles, Prince of Tyre* (1608). The relationship of the two men dated back at least to 1604, when both had been lodgers in the London house of Christopher and Marie Mountjoy. In 1612 Wilkins and Shakespeare appeared together in the Court of Requests, testifying in a disputed betrothal case involving the Mountjoys' daughter and their former apprentice (Schoenbaum 1981). Wilkins was in fact frequently in court, though generally not as a witness. According to Roger Prior, he appeared before the judges of the Middlesex Quarter Sessions twelve times between 1610 and 1618, variously charged with stealing from customers and harboring thieves, antagonizing constables, brawling, savagely stomping one woman and kicking another in the belly (she was pregnant), and standing bail for a man who had committed assault with a meat hook. Wilkins also came forward three times to accuse others of battery, felony, and riot; he once alleged that a group of men had "pulled down a great part" of his house (Prior 1972). The intersection of his socially marginal life with William Shakespeare's culturally dominant one confirms, if we ever doubted it, that no early modern life could have been lived "unsullied" by experiences that often diverged from orthodox depictions of the hierarchy of the genders, the political structure of families, and the demands of duty. All English Renaissance writings were "about" private life, in the sense that they addressed issues that impinged upon persons, families, relationships, beliefs, and behaviors. For this reason, it is impossible to delimit a canon that could be termed the literature of private life. Emotional verities, cultural preoccupations, and material detail about the early modern private sphere are to be found not only in domestic polemics but also in personal narratives, imaginative literature, biographies, and archival records. All tell it true – though none tells it whole.

Acknowledgments

For opportunities to consult Nehemiah Wallington's diaries, London Consistory Court depositions, and London Aldermen's Repertories, the author is grateful to the British Library, the London Guildhall Library, the London Metropolitan Archives, the Corporation of London Record Office, and the Folger Shakespeare Library, and to the John Simon Guggenheim Memorial Foundation, the English-Speaking Union of Washington, DC, and the University of Maryland, Baltimore County.

Notes

1   London Guildhall Library MS 9189/2, Consistory Court Examination Book, fols. 2^r–3^v, 11^r–22^r, 95^r–96^v, 101^r–103^r, 132^r–^{v}, 146^v–147^r. Quotations are from fols. 3^v, 13^v, 2^r, 103^r.
2   Corporation of London Record Office, Aldermen's Repertory 18, fol. 33^r; see also Repertory 18, fols. 94^r, 108^r,123^r, 134^r–135^r, 144^r, 144^v, 160^r, 217^v; Repertory 19, fols. 35^v–36^r, 92^v, 104^r, 177^v, 186^v, 189^v.

References and Further Reading

Adams, Henry Hitch. 1943. *English Domestic or, Homiletic Tragedy 1575 to 1642.* New York: Columbia University Press.
Blayney, Glenn H. 1964. *The Miseries of Enforced Marriage by George Wilkins, 1607.* n.p.: Malone Society Reprints.
Bond, Ronald B. 1987. "Introduction," in Ronald B. Bond, ed., *Certain Sermons or Homilies (1547) and A Homily against Disobedience and Wilful Rebellion (1570): A Critical Edition.* Toronto: University of Toronto Press, pp. 3–45.

Cannon, Charles Dale, ed. 1975. *A Warning for Fair Women: A Critical Edition.* The Hague: Mouton.

Capp, Bernard. 1995. "The Poet and the Bawdy Court: Michael Drayton and the Lodging-House World in Early Stuart London," *Seventeenth Century* 10: 27–37.

Cressy, David. 1997. *Birth, Marriage, and Death: Ritual, Religion, and the Life-Cycle in Tudor and Stuart England.* Oxford: Oxford University Press.

Dod, John and Robert Cleaver. 1598. *A Godlie Forme of Householde Government: For the Ordering of Private Families According to the Direction of God's Word.* London.

Dolan, Frances E. 1994. *Dangerous Familiars: Representations of Domestic Crime in England, 1550–1700.* Ithaca, NY: Cornell University Press.

Dollimore, Jonathan. 1984. *Radical Tragedy: Identity and Power in the Drama of Shakespeare and his Contemporaries.* Brighton: Harvester Press.

Erickson, Amy Louise. 1993. *Women and Property in Early Modern England.* London: Routledge.

Froide, Amy F. 1999. "Marital Status as a Category of Difference: Single-women and Widows in Early Modern England," in Judith M. Bennett and Amy M. Froide, eds., *Singlewomen in the European Past, 1250–1800.* Philadelphia: University of Pennsylvania Press, pp. 236–69.

Gouge, William. 1622. *Of Domestical Duties.* London.

Gowing, Laura. 1996. *Domestic Dangers: Women, Words, and Sex in Early Modern London.* Oxford: Clarendon Press.

Hebel, J. William, ed. 1961. *The Works of Michael Drayton,* vol. 2. Oxford: Shakespeare Head.

Helgerson, Richard. 1992. *Forms of Nationhood: The Elizabethan Writing of England.* Chicago: University of Chicago Press.

Helgerson, Richard. 2004. *Adulterous Alliances: Home, State, and History in Early Modern European Drama and Painting.* Chicago: University of Chicago Press.

Henderson, Diana E. 1997. "The Theater and Domestic Culture," in John D. Cox and David Scott Kastan, eds., *A New History of Early English Drama.* New York: Columbia University Press, pp. 173–94.

Henderson, Katherine Usher and Barbara F. McManus. 1985. "The Contexts," in Katherine Usher Henderson and Barbara F. McManus, eds., *Half Humankind: Contexts and Texts of the Controversy about Women in England, 1540–1640.* Urbana: University of Illinois Press, pp. 1–130.

Houlbrooke, Ralph A. 1984. *The English Family, 1450–1700.* London: Longman.

Korda, Natasha. 2002. *Shakespeare's Domestic Economies: Gender and Property in Early Modern England.* Philadelphia: University of Pennsylvania Press.

Maus, Katharine Eisaman. 1995. *Inwardness and Theater in the English Renaissance.* Chicago: University of Chicago Press.

Moody, Joanna. 1998. "Introduction," in Joanna Moody, ed., *The Private Life of an Elizabethan Lady: The Diary of Lady Margaret Hoby, 1599–1605.* Stroud: Sutton, pp. xv–lii.

Orlin, Lena Cowen. 1994. *Private Matters and Public Culture in Post-Reformation England*. Ithaca, NY: Cornell University Press.

Orlin, Lena Cowen. 2000. "Chronicles of Private Life," in Arthur F. Kinney, ed., *The Cambridge Companion to English Literature, 1500–1600*. Cambridge: Cambridge University Press, pp. 241–64.

Pollock, Linda, ed. 1993a. *With Faith and Physic: The Life of a Tudor Gentlewoman, Lady Grace Mildmay, 1552–1620*. New York: St Martin's Press.

Pollock, Linda. 1993b. "Introduction," "Family Affairs," "Religious Devotions," "Medical Matters," and "Epilogue," in Linda Pollock, ed., *With Faith and Physic: The Life of a Tudor Gentlewoman, Lady Grace Mildmay, 1552–1620*. New York: St Martin's Press, pp. 1–3, 4–22, 48–69, 92–109, and 143–50.

Prior, Roger. 1972. "The Life of George Wilkins," *Shakespeare Survey* 25: 137–52.

Prior, Roger. 1976. "George Wilkins and the Young Heir," *Shakespeare Survey* 29: 33–9.

Rickey, Mary Ellen and Thomas B. Stroup, eds. 1968. *Certaine Sermons or Homilies Appointed to be Read in Churches in the Time of Queen Elizabeth I (1547–1571): A Facsimile Reproduction of the Edition of 1623*. Gainesville, FL: Scholars Facsimiles and Reprints.

Schoenbaum, S. 1981. *William Shakespeare: Records and Images*. New York: Oxford University Press.

Seaver, Paul S. 1985. *Wallington's World: A Puritan Artisan in Seventeenth-Century London*. Stanford: Stanford University Press.

Smith, Bruce. 1991. *Homosexual Desire in Shakespeare's England*. Chicago: University of Chicago Press.

Stone, Lawrence. 1977. *The Family, Sex and Marriage in England, 1500–1800*. New York: Harper and Row.

Wall, Wendy. 2002. *Staging Domesticity: Household Work and English Identity in Early Modern Drama*. Cambridge: Cambridge University Press.

Wayne, Valerie. 1992. "Introduction," in Valerie Wayne, ed., *The Flower of Friendship: A Renaissance Dialogue Contesting Marriage*. Ithaca, NY: Cornell University Press, pp. 1–93.

Wrightson, Keith. 1982. *English Society, 1580–1680*. London: Hutchinson.

Chapter 9

Treason and Rebellion

Andrew Hadfield

Treason and rebellion were closely linked, often interrelated concepts in Renaissance England. The reason for this is not hard to explain. After the Reformation, Christian Europe divided into two hostile camps. Hence any conflict or disobedience to the ruling powers resulting from religion – which, in effect, covered most forms of resistance to authority – was generally classified as treason. Secular authorities were generally reluctant to label any threat to their right to rule as heresy, as it appeared to dignify opposition as principled, even intellectual, rather than aggressive and violent. Hence the treason statutes expanded rapidly and extensively throughout the sixteenth century. The treason act, 26 Hen. VIII c. 13, which became law on November 3, 1534, made it a crime even to "compass" (i.e., imagine) the bodily harm of the monarch, a statute that was to cause numerous legal problems because either it was hard to prove that the accused had really planned to harm the monarch, or the statute allowed the crown to define treason pretty much as it wished (Bellamy 1979: 31, 35). Until this point English common law had distinguished England from the rest of Europe: now, the powers of the crown bore a much closer resemblance to those of more absolutist states such as France. Threatening the crown was rebellion and could be classified as treason. The king could use the new treason laws against his wives, Anne Boleyn and Katherine Howard, defining their adultery – real or imagined – as acts that threatened the person of the monarch. As John Bellamy has commented, Henry VIII's usage was "without respectable precedent and based on no principle save that anything which annoyed the king was to his peril and thereby traitorous" (Bellamy 1979: 43–4). Even the use of a royal pardon served to emphasize the power the monarch had over his or her subjects (Kesselring 2003).

180

Throughout the sixteenth and early seventeenth centuries, the crown published a number of treatises warning the public of the dangers of rebellion and the savage punishments that awaited those who transgressed God's law dictating obedience to the monarch as the sacred ruler anointed by God. Such works were, hardly surprisingly, invariably a response to rebellion. A number of treatises were commissioned in the wake of the outbreak of the Pilgrimage of Grace (1536–7), a northern "crusade" led by a former soldier, Robert Aske, that tried to force Henry to reverse his break with Rome and return England to the Catholic church (Dodds and Dodds 1915). Richard Morison wrote *A Lamentation in which is Shewed what Ruyne and Destruction Cometh of Seditious Rebellyon* (1536a) and *A Remedy for Sedition, wherein are Conteyned Many Thynges, Concernyng the True and Loyall Obeysance that Comes unto their Prince and Soveraygne Lorde the Kynge* (1536b). Thomas Starkey, another Protestant intellectual promoted by Thomas Cromwell, wrote *An Exhortation to the People, Instructynge theym to Unitie and Obedience* (1540). These treatises argued similar cases. It was the duty of the subject to obey their sovereign unconditionally as this was not only what God and the natural order of the universe demanded, but what would result in the best way of life for everyone. Laws were made for the safety of man and must be obeyed. If they were ignored then chaos would result.

Both Morison and Starkey, in line with Henry's radical new political and religious departure, tried to persuade readers who until recently had been loyal to the pope that he was now the figure who was most likely to harm them. Morison argued that the pope was the puppet of sedition and that Catholics were spiritual traitors. He equated political and religious rebellion as forms of treason, arguing that if friars and monks were religious men then so were rebels such as Jack Cade, Wat Tyler, and Jack Straw. He further denigrated the rebels by comparing them to Turks and beasts, concluding that they should learn from events in Lincolnshire, where Henry had brutally suppressed the rebellion, that nothing was "more odious to god and man, than treason" (Morison 1536a: sig. C3^v). In the *Remedy*, Morison argued that the duty of ordinary citizens was to serve their king as Christ demanded that his disciples served him:

He is none of myne sayth Christ, nor worthy to be my servant that can not, if just cause require hym so to do, forsake his father and mother to doo me servyce. He is none of mine saythe Englande, that canne not hate his father and mother, that canne not kyll them bothe, sooner than ones consente to my destruction. (Morison 1536b: sig. C2^r)

Morison used a gardening metaphor, frequently found in political rhetoric, to explain Henry's position. The branches of sedition had to be cut
away before it was too late. Henry's desire was to pull out the roots to
remove the evil before his people were affected. Treason was made to
seem external to the body politic (Morison writes of curing a sore), an
illness that could eventually be cured after a hard course of medicine.
The rebels were represented as an invasive, hostile disease alien to the
true English way of life, a neat reversal of the arguments of the pilgrims
that they were the guardians of England's traditions, ones that the king
had forgotten because of his evil advisers. Starkey's treatise contains an
elaborate defense of the Protestant insistence that the Bible be made
available to all who wish to read it. He acknowledges that differences of
interpretation will exist, but argues that the gospel, if read correctly, is
not only easy to understand, but yields a more or less consistently
understood message. Only the perverse machinations of the seditious
Catholic priests, eager to preserve the power that has rightly been taken
away from them, mangle the sense with subtle, perverse interpretations
that encourage people to rebel and commit treason.

Sometimes such assertive arguments are read as if they were simply
expressions of a commonly understood ideology. However, the authors
were acutely aware that they were reacting to dangerous circumstances, and their texts are fraught with ambiguity and admissions of
anxiety. Starkey makes the familiar Protestant case that the monarch
was simply advising his subjects to return to the true faith that had
become obscured by years of the false traditions added to the purity of
scripture by the usurping church of Rome. He acknowledges that losing
old customs is difficult for any community, and suggests that the effect is
as pernicious as superstition. What is required is the spread of the gospel
and extensive preaching in order to return England to its former state of
grace: "There is amonge us as true christen simplicitie and good religion,
as there is in any other christien nation" (Starkey 1540: 36). Starkey's
tactic is a subtle one, designed to offset the understandable fear that
many of his readers would have had that they were entering a brave
new world by breaking away from the certainties and tradition provided
by the late medieval church (Duffy 1992). But would many have been
convinced that they were experiencing a return to an older and more
authentic state of affairs and that their opposition to the king was really
treason? After all, Henry VIII had been a staunch defender of the papacy
in the wake of Luther's rebellion, earning himself the title of "defender
of the faith" from Pope Leo X (Scarisbrick 1968: 115–17). Morison and
Starkey's writings constantly reveal that they are all too aware of the

cataclysmic change that England has experienced, making it hard to distinguish between obedience and rebellion, conformity and treason.

It should also be pointed out that just because writers produced harsh condemnations of rebellion, this did not make them straightforwardly conformist subjects. Political choices in the early modern period could never simply be reduced to the alternatives of rebellion or loyalty to a divinely ordained monarch, whatever the desires of the king or queen in question. Political discourses derived from native traditions, classical texts (notably those written in republican Rome and democratic Athens), and other European countries, as well as complicated and compromising political circumstances, resulted in a much wider tradition of political thought and action. The actions of Henry VIII clearly disturbed many of his courtiers, notably those who wrote poetry and translated sections of the Bible, as such interventions were often construed as treason. The nuances of the text could lead to words being interpreted as treasonable, especially under a regime where the principal source of religious conflict was the question of access to scripture, which the crown wished to control while more radical Protestants wished to make it available to everyone. Given the ubiquitous concept of treason as "compassing harm to the king's person," the stage was set for extremely bloody conflict.

Starkey is much better known for his manuscript work, *A Dialogue Between Pole and Lupset*, which suggested a number of reforms to the commonwealth and shows that he was far from being a sycophantic flatterer of the king (Starkey 1989). Starkey's protagonists argued that a number of reforms would transform England into a far better country: better education for the nobility, land reform, legal reform, and resistance to papal influence. His most audacious step was to stage a discussion of the relative merits of elective and hereditary monarchy, which could be read as a reaction to Henry's assumption of excessive powers for himself. More dangerous still were the translations of the psalms produced by Sir Thomas Wyatt. Wyatt's work demands to be read in terms of the ferocious debates over the translation of the Bible between Sir Thomas More and William Tyndale. Each accused the other – in aggressive and vitriolic polemics, especially that of More – of betraying Christianity and acting no better than heathen Turks. Eventually, both were executed, More in 1535 and Tyndale in 1536. As Brian Cummings has pointed out, "Wyatt's *Penitentiall Psalms* ... represent a new kind of literature," one in which "Religion ... is a discourse without limits," as lines such as the following demonstrate:

> In slepe, in wach, in fretyng styll within,
> That neuer soffer rest vnto mynd;
> Filld with offence, that new and new begyn
> With thowsand feris the hert to strayne and bynd.
>
> (lines 283–6)

Wyatt's psalms can be read as an attempt to escape from the constraints and danger of official religion into a world of freedom from the risk of treason, however illusory that might be (Cummings 2003: 228–31; Lerer 2003). Any attempt to explore religion in the sixteenth century unfortunately exposed the writer to the accusation of treason.

Probably the most widely read official condemnation of rebellion as treason was "An Homily against Disobedience and Wilful Rebellion," first published in 1574, in the revised edition of the book of Elizabethan homilies (*Certain Sermons Appointed by the Queen's Majesty*) designed to be read in all churches on key Sundays throughout the year. This long tract was produced as a response to a crisis that was as serious as the Pilgrimage of Grace had been earlier in the century, one that threatened to overthrow Elizabeth's government. The arrival of Mary Queen of Scots in England, when she fled south of the border to escape the religious civil wars that were tearing the fabric of Scottish society apart, threatened to have the same effect in England. Mary had a claim to the English throne that was just as strong as – if not stronger than –that of Elizabeth, and Mary had been recognized as the legitimate sovereign by most of Catholic Europe when Mary Tudor died in 1558. The presence of Mary Queen of Scots inspired a series of rebellions throughout Elizabeth's reign, starting with the Northern Rebellion of 1569–70, led by the Catholic lords under the duke of Northumberland. The rebellion failed and the power of the Catholic aristocracy in the north was effectively crushed (Fletcher 1968: ch. 8). However, their actions helped to persuade Pope Pius V to issue his bull *Regnas in Excelsis*, which excommunicated Elizabeth and called on her true subjects to overthrow her as a heretic. The bull was a disaster for many English Catholics who had existed relatively happily with their Protestant neighbors, practicing mass in secret. Now their attendance at church was more carefully monitored; many more fell under suspicion; and many more priests were executed for treason. Soon after the rebellion, the Ridolfi Plot was exposed. This conspiracy sought to depose Elizabeth and replace her with Mary, who was to marry Thomas Howard, fourth duke of Norfolk. Norfolk, England's premier Catholic nobleman (although he denied his faith), had fallen under suspicion during the Northern Rebellion, and it was his failure to raise his followers that fatally weakened the enterprise. He was executed for treason in 1572.

It is necessary to read the "Homily" as a response to a crisis rather than an expression of official Tudor ideology. The subtext of the title of the collection in which it appears, *Certain Sermons Appointed by the Queen's Majesty*, concludes with the words "And by her grace's advice perused and overseen for the better understanding of the *simple people*" (my emphasis). It is clear that "An Homily against Disobedience and Wilful Rebellion" is designed to reach a mass audience – as, to a lesser extent, were the treatises of Morison and Starkey – not the sophisticated and the literate. The homily argues that all rebellion stems from the first rebellion against God by Lucifer, which in turn led to the rebellion of Adam and Eve and their banishment from the Garden of Eden, mankind being redeemed only by the intervention of Christ to save them from the consequences of their inherited sin. All human society should be characterized by obedience, from the humblest to the most exalted levels:

> Thus do you see, that neither heaven nor paradise could suffer any rebellion in them, neither be places for any rebels to remain in. Thus became rebellion, as you see, both the first and greatest, and the very root of all other sins; and the first and principal cause both of all worldly and bodily miseries, sorrows, diseases, sicknesses, and deaths; and, which is infinitely worse than all these, as is said, the very cause of death and damnation also ... God forthwith, by laws given unto mankind, repaired again the rule and order of obedience thus by rebellion overthrown; and, besides the obedience due unto his majesty, he not only ordained, that in families and households the wife should be obedient unto her husband, the children unto their parents, the servants unto their masters; but also, when mankind increased and spread itself more largely over the world, he by his holy word did constitute and ordain in cities and countries several and special governors and rulers, unto whom the residue of his people should be obedient ... kings and princes, as well the evil as the good, do reign by God's ordinance, and subjects are bounden to obey them. ("An Homily" 1850: 552–3)

This is a neat, easily remembered thumbnail sketch of a society that is rigorously hierarchical and patriarchal. But it should not be read as though every Elizabethan writer accepted this version of the society in which they lived. Certainly mainstream Elizabethan political thought countenanced a number of lively and contentious visions, and argument over the social order was common enough, even if there were also many points of agreement (Sommerville 1986). Moreover, the country was ruled by a queen, a stubborn political fact that undermined the neat vision of hierarchical order asserted in the homily (McLaren 1999). And her claim to the throne was based on that of a rebel who had deposed the king.

The other significant aspect of this passage is its insistence that princes cannot be overthrown whatever their behavior (logic that, had it been applied, would certainly have invalidated the Tudor claim to the throne). The author argues that princes exist in accordance with the behavior of the people because "God placeth as well evil princes as good." If people obey their prince they will continue to have good ones. If they disobey, then evil monarchs will take their place. It was the wickedness of the English that led to the death of "our good Josias, king Edward [VI], in his young and good years" ("An Homily" 1850: 558).

It is intriguing to note that exactly the same sort of arguments were produced by James VI of Scotland in his major political works, *Basilicon Doron*, written to advise his son Prince Henry, and *The Trew Law of Free Monarchies*, which claimed that unconditional obedience to the monarch liberated the subject from the cares of political life that should be entrusted to the king (Patterson 1997). James's attempts to ride roughshod over Parliament's traditional independence were greeted with horror in many influential circles. But it is clear that his political ideas were formed in the dangerous arena of Scottish political life, in which kings were often treated as servants of the people who could be disposed of when they failed to serve the people adequately, leading to a succession of short-lived kings and endless civil wars, as any reader of Scottish history would have observed. James was taught by the terrifying George Buchanan, a tutor imposed on him by his Protestant nobles, whose lessons endlessly reminded the king of his duties to his people and the bloody consequences of failing to please them. It is hardly surprising that James should formulate his ideas in opposition to those of his republican tutor (Mason 1994: pt. 2). While many Scottish Protestants, following Buchanan and John Knox, justified rebellion against a tyrant who was not sanctioned by God or who acted against the word of God, James argued, like the author of the homily, that rebellion could never be justified and that the king and the laws he determined had to be obeyed whether they were right or wrong. Even the most wicked of tyrants had been ordained by God for a purpose.

It is important that we do not reduce the whole of early modern political thought in Britain to this belief in the unassailable right of the anointed monarch. Many did, indeed, argue that the monarch was beyond ordinary mortals, especially during and after the civil war of the mid-seventeenth century, when it became the key component of royalist belief. But we should never lose sight of the other varied traditions of political thought existing within the British Isles. The most widely read political tract in Elizabethan England was Sir Thomas Smith's posthumously published 1583 *De Republica Anglorum*, which argued for a "mixed" constitution whereby all elements of society participated in establishing the body politic, even the lowest laborers, who were not to be altogether neglected. Smith also made comparisons between England and republican Rome, hoping, understandably enough, that some form of stability could be found in a form of government that kept everyone happy. Smith placed great emphasis on the role of Parliament as an elected body and argued that the monarch had to function as he or she existed within that institution (Smith 1906). Many adhered to beliefs similar to those of Smith, having faith in the ancient institutions of England – particularly its laws – as a means of preventing rebellion and civil war (Pocock 1987). Indeed, it can plausibly be argued that the predominant political line taken by most English writers who expressed an opinion on the subject was that there should be a monarch, but that he – sometimes she – needed to be controlled by the political nation, however that amorphous class was classified. Others, principally Catholics and Puritans (Protestants who felt that church reform had not gone far enough and that they had the right to instigate further change), were more attracted to resistance theories of government that sanctioned principled opposition to the crown.

Other factors should also be considered when trying to reconstruct the political climate in which questions of treason were determined. First, few people could forget that they were ruled by a queen, a stubborn fact that undermined any easy faith in a divinely sanctioned hierarchy, as expressed in the homily. Second, what people said and did was often at odds. James may have presented himself as an absolutist ruler, and it does seem that not only were many English men and women extremely nervous of him before he came south to inherit the throne, but many were appalled by what they felt was his arrogant, cavalier treatment of Parliament. However, he was far less autocratic in practice. Even after the Gunpowder Plot he refused to sanction a witch-hunt against Catholics and continued with his policy of attempting to reconcile religious factions rather than rooting out traitors (Patterson 1997). Elizabeth was in many ways a much less tolerant ruler. Third, as any reader of Shakespeare's history plays would have known, no English monarch ruled with an uncontested claim to the throne after the deposition of Richard II in 1399. Henry IV's claim was weak, as was that of his son, Henry V, and grandson, Henry VI. Edward IV's claim was a little better, as he was descended from the second rather than the third son of Edward III, and had Henry VI died childless his claim might have been unassailable. Edward IV's younger brother, Richard III, was reputed to have murdered his brother's son, Edward V, in order to claim the throne for himself. The triumph of the Tudors, when Richard was killed at the battle of Bosworth in 1485, brought stability to the realm. Nevertheless, their claim was contestable - through Henry's mother, Margaret Beaufort, another descendant of Edward III – and the Stuarts at least arguably had a much better right to rule England. Hence, professions of the need for absolute loyalty to the divinely ordained monarch were an unspoken fiction. Monarchs were often rebels and traitors themselves. Many clearly supported the monarchy because they believed that it brought order and stability, and was the only feasible – rather than ideal – form of government, a case most familiar in Aristotle's *Politics* (Erskine-Hill 1996).

One of the defining political events in late sixteenth-century England was the execution of Mary Queen of Scots on February 8, 1587, for treason in plotting to overthrow Elizabeth in the Babington Plot. Elizabeth had long been reluctant to have a fellow monarch executed for treason because such action threatened to undermine the basis of the monarchy and reduce kings and queens to the status of their subjects. There was, however, a groundswell of Protestant opinion against Mary, culminating in the establishment of a Bond of Association (October, 1584) designed by two of Elizabeth's chief ministers, William Cecil, Lord Burghley, and Sir Thomas Walsingham. This bond required subscribers to swear to defend the life of the queen and to punish anyone who tried to harm her. It was clearly directed at Mary, who claimed that she was the legitimate queen of England. She was either right, in which case Elizabeth was a usurper and a traitor; or deluded, which meant that Mary was a rebel, as well as a traitor.

Mary was frequently vilified in contemporary literature (Phillips 1964). Edmund Spenser attacked Mary directly as a traitor, representing her trial in book V, canto 9, of *The Faerie Queene*. Mary appears as Duessa, the female villain of the poem, who challenges the rule of Mercilla (Elizabeth). The case against Mary accuses her of having "trayterous

desynes" (V.9.42, line 2) in desiring to be queen and replacing Elizabeth, a perfectly logical case for the prosecution if Elizabeth's claim to
the throne is seen as just. Spenser outlines the case against Duessa/Mary
in painstaking detail so that there can be no question that she deserves
to die for her crimes. An array of figures attacks her. Authority accuses
Mary of violating the law of nations; Religion accuses her of defiling
God's holy laws; and Justice charges her "with breach of lawes"
(V.9.44, line 9). The defense for Mary is based on the case for pity,
who appears as an allegorical figure: "First there came *Pittie*, with full
tender hart, / And with her ioyn'd *Regard* of womanhead" (45, lines 3–
4). In the end, however, the case for the prosecution is simply too
strong, as the wealth of allegorical personae demonstrates. The chief
prosecutor, *Zele*, assembles them before the queen:

> Then brought he forth, with griesly grim aspect,
> Abhorred *Murder*, who with bloudie knyfe
> Yet dropping fresh in hand did her detect,
> And there with guiltie bloudshed charged ryfe:
> Then brought he forth *Sedition*, breeding stryfe
> In troublous wits, and mutinous vproare:
> Then brought he forth *Incontinence* of lyfe,
> Euen foule *Adulterie* her face before,
> And lewd *Impietie*, that her accursed sore.
>
> (V.9.48)

These verses were not published until 1596, although they may have
been written nearer the event. It is easy to see why they caused such
great offense. James felt that Spenser's words threatened his chances of
succeeding Elizabeth as England's monarch, and he demanded that
Elizabeth punish Spenser (McCabe 1987). When a subject was executed for treason their property was usually forfeit to the crown unless
special dispensation was made by the monarch, so James's fears are
understandable (Bellamy 1979: ch. 5). Mary is represented in *The
Faerie Queene* as guilty of a wealth of crimes that add up to a particularly
heinous form of treason, many of which, such as murder and sedition,
would have sufficed to justify her execution.

Furthermore, the defense offered for Mary reflects badly on Elizabeth, who is represented throughout *The Faerie Queene* as a monarch
who does not deal forcefully enough with rebellion and threats to her
rule and her subjects' wellbeing. The defense appeals to Elizabeth's
feelings for another woman, and it clearly works, with Elizabeth
agreeing only reluctantly to Duessa's execution, which we never

actually witness in the poem. Elizabeth has to be coerced by her male courtiers to act in all their interests and deal severely with a treacherous false monarch whose actions threaten to undermine the fabric of the state. It is these male courtiers who force her hand, and the last verse of the canto sees her shedding tears for her evil fellow queen. Spenser's representation of Elizabeth can be read as a critical assessment of the queen's ability to rule effectively in the 1590s, and perhaps as implying that women could never rule as effectively as men, words that could easily have been construed as treason. The problem that writers faced was that the scope of the treason statutes was potentially boundless. If they uttered any words that were critical of the king or queen's performance, these could be cited as compassing harm to the monarch. If they remained silent, then they risked watching the monarch commit what they believed were serious blunders that could have devastating effects. The usual tactic was to place blame on the monarch's advisers and claim that the recommended plan was the one that the monarch really wanted to adopt. In the civil war, the parliamentary forces usually claimed that they were acting to save the institution of the monarchy from the foolish actions of the incumbent monarch, Charles I.

In the same canto that contains the trial of Duessa, Spenser represents the brutal punishment of the poet Bonfont, who has his tongue nailed to a post and his name changed to Malfont, the source of evil rather than good. It is adjudged by the law

> that therewith he falsely did reuyle,
> And foule blaspheme that Queen for forged guyle,
> Both with bold speaches, which he blazed had,
> And with lewd poems, which he did comyle.
>
> (V.9.25, lines 4–7)

We never learn what these words were. The description of the fate of Bon/Malfont links him to the crimes committed by Duessa, and also those committed by Malengin, another deceiver, whose name is glossed as "Guyle" in the head note to the canto. This suggests that the scope of treason is far too wide, and that loyal subjects like Spenser, who are critical of the crown but are not rebels, are classified as similar to the most dangerous enemies of the state, like Mary Queen of Scots and the Jesuits (Skulsky 1990). Spenser's book V, the book of Justice, has as its hero Artegall. Artegall is a savage knight, brought up in remote forests, who is successful only to the extent that he is able to

use his fierce instincts and severe training to deal with serious problems. Spenser's point is that justice always risks resembling the crime it
seeks to combat, a danger that it is impossible to avoid (Mercilla's pity
for Duessa is another, more dangerous form of the same issue). But to
prevent anyone from uttering this truth only compounds the problem
and allows evil to flourish more confidently. Artegall, unlike Mercilla,
has to deal with rebellion and treason without any trace of mercy, and
it is no coincidence that the landscape of book V is littered with
dismembered body parts (Fowler 1995). Traitors endured a spectacular
and gruesome execution that was a spectacle in itself before their
bodies were displayed to remind others of their fate. The execution
was highly ritualized (Bellamy 1979: 191–210). Victims were first
hanged and then cut down before they were dead. Then they had
their innards pulled out in front of them, before they were quartered
and their body parts placed on the city walls.

Spenser shows that only spectacular violence serves to rid the
commonwealth of violent rebels and traitors. Artegall works in tandem
with Talus, the Iron Man, who carries out the most gruesome aspects
of his duties. Talus, with his iron flail, is represented as the sower of
death as he destroys the enemies of the crown:

> *Talus* sternly did vpon them set,
> And brusht, and battred them without remorse,
> That on the ground he left full many a corse;
> Ne any able was him to withstand,
> But he them ouerthrew both man and horse,
> That they lay scattered ouer all the land,
> As thicke as doth the seede after the sowers hand.
>
> (V.12.7)

Artegall is able to restrain Talus, an image of justice that allows Spenser
to distance the ideal from the full impact of the violent reality. Nevertheless, the point is clear enough: justice is an empty concept if it lacks
the requisite force to support it. Rebellion and treason are not simply
crimes, but actions that threaten the very possibility of civil society. The
book ends with Artegall and Talus well on the way to completing their
quest by reforming Irena's land by working in tandem:

> During which time, that he [Artegall] did there remaine,
> His studie was true Iustice how to deale,
> And day and night employ'd his busie paine

> How to reforme that ragged common-weale:
> And that same yron man which could reueale
> All hidden crimes, through all that realme he sent,
> To search out those, that vsd to rob and steale,
> Or did rebell gainst lawfull gouernment;
> On whom he did inflict most grieuous punishment.
>
> (V.12.26)

Talus's violence is justified, as society cannot be reformed and built anew if traitors and rebels are tolerated. However, Gloriana, the Faerie Queene, recalls Artegall to the fairy court before he has completed his task, exposing him to the slanders and lies of those who think that he is going too far. Gloriana's actions are a thinly veiled critique of Elizabeth's refusal to take the problem of rebellion and treason seriously enough. In failing to allow proper justice to be implemented, she undermines her ability to rule. Just as Artegall is uncomfortably close to the rebels and traitors he has to suppress, so is Elizabeth/Gloriana rather uncannily like her rival queen Mary/Duessa. Not only is Gloriana much too sympathetic to Duessa's plight at her trial, but Gloriana is also responsible for putting vast numbers of her subjects in danger by fostering violence. The slander produced by the figures Envy and Detraction, who eventually call up the monstrous Blatant Beast with his multiple tongues, each uttering terrible falsehoods, is undoubtedly worse than that uttered by the poet, Bon/Malfont. However, he is the one who is punished for his "crime," while their words are allowed to reach a wide audience. The apparent power of the monarch to define the scope and range of treason puts Spenser himself at risk, as he acknowledges in the final lines of *The Faerie Queene*: "Ne may this homely verse, of many meanest, / Hope to escape his [a "mighty peer," probably Lord Burghley] venemous despite" (VI.12.41, lines 1–2). Yet it should not be forgotten that the most dangerous traitor was in fact a queen.

The fear of treachery and rebellion haunts numerous other works written in England in the 1590s. It is at least arguable that Shakespeare had the example of Mary in mind when he wrote *The Rape of Lucrece* (1594). The evil king Tarquin commits a serious misdemeanor because he cannot control his lust, one of the accusations most frequently leveled at Mary. In raping Lucrece and attempting to silence her, he commits treason against the laws of Rome, as Shakespeare makes absolutely clear, abusing his position as a king. The result is that the very form of government in Rome changes and a republic replaces the

monarchy, Mary's penalty was to forfeit her life, eventually, but many
were aware of the constitutional implications of her behavior (not
least, her son). A similar situation exists in *Hamlet*, where the incumbent monarch has displaced his brother and married the brother's
widow. The play has often been linked to the events of Mary's reign,
especially in the similarities between the poisoning of the older Hamlet
and the murder of Mary's second husband, Lord Darnley (Erskine-Hill
1996: 99–108). Hamlet is placed in an impossible position through the
demands of his father's ghost: either he avenges his murder and risks
death, or he tolerates an appalling crime. Hamlet's most famous soliloquy, usually analyzed in terms of its existential philosophizing and
thoughts on suicide, may also be related to the most direct form of
rebellion, the attempted assassination of the monarch:

> To be, or not to be – that is the question:
> Whether 'tis nobler in the mind to suffer
> The slings and arrows of outrageous fortune,
> Or to take arms against a sea of troubles,
> And by opposing end them? . . .
> For who would bear the whips and scorns of time,
> The oppressor's wrong, the proud man's contumely,
> The pangs of disprized love, the law's delay,
> The insolence of office, and the spurns
> That patient merit of the unworthy takes,
> When he himself might his quietus make
> With a bare bodkin? . . .
> Thus conscience does make cowards of us all;
> And thus the native hue of resolution
> Is sicklied o'er with the pale cast of thought,
> And enterprises of great pith and moment
> With this regard their currents turn away
> And lose the name of action.
>   (Shakespeare 1987: 3.1.57–61, 71–7, 84–9)

The question of existence and non-existence is related throughout these
lines to murder as well as suicide, a point that is clear enough if we bear
in mind not just the fate of Hamlet senior, but also the fact that Hamlet
later is actually poised behind Claudius with a dagger ready to strike.
Taking arms against a sea of troubles by making use of a "bare bodkin"
(dagger) is something Hamlet fails to carry out, but he does not try to kill
himself. The references to the unfairness of having to wait patiently and
tolerate injustice are also commonly found throughout the extensive

literature of Huguenot resistance theory, which justified the assassination of evil tyrants (Brutus 1994). Hamlet's logic points him toward
immediate action, but the fear of death prevents him. He has, of course,
his own death in mind. But we should consider that one of the consequences of assassination was invariably the death of the perpetrator.
Hamlet is hardly a play that justifies immediate action and offers simple
solutions to complex problems by urging people to rebel. But it is a work
that acknowledges that treason and rebellion were key issues of the day
and had probably been considered by many people as possible solutions
to seemingly intractable political problems.

Sixteenth- and seventeenth-century writers who were absorbed by
these issues did not have to turn just to Scotland for food for thought,
as English history also supplied extensive examples of treason and
rebellion to consider. Probably the most important work produced at
the court of Edward VI, *The Mirror for Magistrates*, edited by William
Baldwin in its first version, sought to teach those who were to govern
the country how to behave. The work was a conscious adaptation of
the familiar genre of "mirrors for princes" literature, making the tools
of government available for the wider class of people who, it was
assumed, would now help rule the country. *The Mirror* consisted of a
series of complaints uttered by the ghosts of dead figures from English
history, connected by a number of prose passages in which the assembled authors discuss what lessons can be learned from the laments they
have just witnessed. Later versions of *The Mirror* expanded the book
until it became a treasure trove of versifications of famous incidents
from British and English history, diluting the original focus of the
experimental work. Baldwin's *Mirror* had a clear line of argument,
expressing a political vision at odds with that of works such as the
"Homily against Disobedience and Wilful Rebellion."

The Mirror tries to tread the fine line between properly condemning
rebellion and not giving monarchs the power to behave as they please,
so that a considered middle way is made both possible and attractive
for the reader. The authors of *The Mirror* place considerable emphasis
on the magistrate, a term that describes those actively involved in
politics and government administration, from the humblest village
official to the most powerful counselor of the monarch (Goldie
2001). They are able to criticize the monarch and advise him or her
how to govern: they are also, *The Mirror* implies but does not state, able
to resist an overmighty monarch and so control rebellion fueled by
legitimate grievances. Rebellion by the public is never permitted and it
is the magistrates' duty to punish it severely. Magistrates who fail in

their duties through greed and self-interest are guilty of serious crimes. One of the chief forms of lament in *The Mirror* is that of the justly condemned magistrate warning others not to risk his fate by lining their own pockets and neglecting the people they are duty-bound to govern. English history can teach its readers all these lessons.

Tragedies ten, eleven, and twelve are representative of the range and coherence of *The Mirror*'s political discussion. Tragedy ten shows how King James I of Scotland was murdered by his own subjects because he broke his oaths to his loyal followers and allies:

> See Baldwin Baldwin, the vnhappy endes,
> Of suche as passe not for theyr lawfull oth:
> Of those that causles leaue theyr fayth or frendes,
> And murdre kynsfolke through their foes vntroth,
> Warne, warne all princes, all lyke sinns to loth,
> And chiefely suche as in my Realme be borne,
> For God hates hyghly suche as are foresworne.
> (Campbell 1938: 10, lines 148–54)

The reader learns from James's impassioned words that kings who break their contract with the people – like Tarquin – will inevitably come to a bad end. Tragedy eleven has William de la Pole, duke of Suffolk (1396–1450), explain how he met his unhappy end at the hands of the people after he was banished for treason for the murder of Humphrey, duke of Gloucester. Tragedy twelve is the story of the most famous rebel of fifteenth-century England, Iack Cade, and bears the title, "How Iack Cade traiterously rebelling agaynst his Kyng, was for his treasons and cruell doings wurthely punyshed." Cade concludes his story with two verses that conceive the universe in terms that would later be repeated in the official homilies:

> God hath ordayned the power, all princes be
> His Lieutenants, or debities in realmes,
> Against their foes still therefore fighteth he,
> And as his enmies drives them to extremes,
> Their wise deuises prove but doltish dreames.
> No subiect ought for any kind of cause,
> To force the lord, but yeeld him to the lawes.
>
> And therefore Baldwin warne men folow reason
> Subdue theyr wylles, and be not Fortunes slaues,
> A troublous ende doth ever folowe treason,
> There is no trust in rebelles, raskall knaues,

> In Fortune lesse, which wurketh as the waves:
> From whose assautes who lyst to stande at large,
> Must folowe skyll, and flye all worldly charge.
> (Campbell 1938: 12, lines 155–68)

It is easy to assume that Cade's words express an incontrovertible orthodoxy and, in an important way, they do. Rebellion for the sake of personal gain is always wrong (Cade considers why he chose to be a traitor in the opening stanzas, concluding that he allowed forces he could not control to overrule his reason and allow his base instincts to take over.) But Cade's message is designed to explain the mentality of ordinary subjects so that magistrates will be able to deal with his like if they ever have to face treasonable rebellion. It is not intended to explain every political situation, or to make the case that all power should reside with the monarch, as the tragedy of James I of Scotland demonstrates. Kings are judged in the same way as their magistrates and subjects. Henry VI is represented as a saintly victim of evil forces. But Edward IV shows that he was a slave to his lusts and desires – rather like Jack Cade – and so caused his own death at the height of his prosperity. The case of Richard II tells an even bleaker story, as the title indicates: "Howe kyng Richarde the seconde was for his euyll gouernaunce deposed from his seat, and miserably murdred in prison." Richard is misled by his minions, whose tragedies are told in the adjacent narratives, although there can be no doubt that he richly deserved his fate for tolerating, even encouraging, traitors.

Shakespeare's extensive chronicles of English history deal with the same subject matter as *The Mirror*. Shakespeare has often been cast as a reactionary writer, celebrating the "Tudor Myth" and the dynasty's divinely inspired triumph. This reading, I would suggest, often relies on an understanding of Elizabethan and Jacobean society that disguises a more complex reality, assuming that Shakespeare, being a playwright patronized by the monarchy, was an "orthodox" thinker. This reading, I would suggest, is mistaken in two ways. It misrepresents Tudor and Stuart thought – as well as assuming that only those who blindly obeyed the monarch could live at or near court – and it misrepresents Shakespeare's writing. Shakespeare's early history plays chronicle the vicious series of civil wars in the fifteenth century that transformed England into a charnel house (the battle of Towton, March, 29, 1461, represented in the extraordinarily violent *Henry VI, part 3*, is still the bloodiest battle ever fought on English soil). *Richard III* is famous for depicting a tyrant who deserves to be overthrown. The play does, of course, function as Tudor propaganda in one sense. It also, however, makes the powerful case that monarchs cannot exceed the bounds of the law and that they are liable to be justly deposed if they do. Richard's brief, catastrophic reign ends with his famous cry, "A horse! A horse! My kingdom for a horse!" (Shakespeare 1981: 5.4.7), showing that his kingdom, which he has seen all along as a prize that the king can dispose of as he wishes, has shrunk to nothing.

The action of *Richard III* does not exist in a vacuum and has been carefully prepared for by the events represented in the trilogy of Henry VI plays. Shakespeare shows government and authority being destroyed by the actions of the self-interested aristocrats who wish to rule England for their own advantage: Richard is merely the most ruthless and successful example of this class, who are incapable of governing and destroy the country in the attempt until it is worth no more than a horse. *Henry VI, part 2* shows the rebellion of Jack Cade, who is spurred on by Richard, duke of York, for his own purposes, a relationship that has no basis in historical fact or tradition. Cade is eventually killed by Alexander Iden, a Kentish knight, and left on a dunghill. Cade is a traitor, as Iden accuses him, inventing a past to claim the throne for himself, making him part of the forces that drag the country down (although he often reminds his betters that the dispossessed are the ones who actually do useful work). Henry VI recognizes the truth: "Thus stands my state, 'twixt Cade and York distressed, / Like to a ship that having scaped a tempest / Is straightway calmed and boarded with a pirate" (4.9. 31–3) and he vows to "learn to govern better" (line 47) to prevent future rebellion. For all his insight, Henry fails. Nevertheless, his words are an accurate expression of the complex politics of treason and rebellion in Renaissance England. Rebellion was usually wrong, whether perpetrated by the upper or lower classes. But it did happen and was sometimes successful, as the Wars of the Roses, which led to the foundation of the Tudor dynasty, demonstrated. Then it had to be explained or disguised.

References and Further Reading

"An Homily." 1850. "An Homily against Disobedience and Wilful Rebellion," in *Certain Sermons Appointed by the Queen's Majesty to be Declared and Read by All Parsons, Vicars, and Curates, Every Sunday and Holiday in their Churches* [1574]. Cambridge: Parker Society.

Bellamy, John. 1979. *The Tudor Law of Treason: An Introduction*. London: Routledge.

Brutus, Stephanus Junius, the Celt. 1994. *Vindiciae, Contra Tyrannos, or, Concerning the Legitimate Power of aPrince Over the People, and of the People Over a Prince* [1579]. Ed. George Garnett. Cambridge: Cambridge University Press.

Campbell, Lily B., ed. 1938. *The Mirror for Magistrates, edited from the Original Texts in the Huntington Library*. Cambridge: Cambridge University Press.

Cummings, Brian 2003. *The Literary Culture of the Reformation: Grammar and Grace*. Oxford: Oxford University Press.

Dodds, R. and M. H. Dodds. 1915. *The Pilgrimage of Grace, 1536–7, and the Exeter Conspiracy, 1538*, 2 vols. Cambridge: Cambridge University Press.

Duffy, Eamon. 1992. *The Stripping of the Altars: Traditional Religion in England, 1400–1580*. New Haven: Yale University Press.

Erskine-Hill, Howard. 1996. *Poetry and the Realm of Politics: Shakespeare to Dryden*. Oxford: Clarendon Press.

Fletcher, Anthony. 1968. *Tudor Rebellions*. London: Longman.

Fowler, Elizabeth. 1995. "The Failure of Moral Philosophy in the Work of Edmund Spenser," *Representations* 51: 47–76.

Goldie, Mark. 2001. "The Unacknowledged Republic: Officeholding in Early Modern England," in Tim Harris, ed., *The Politics of the Excluded, c.1500–1800*. Basingstoke: Palgrave, 2001, pp. 153–94.

King James VI and I. 1994. *Political Writings*. Ed. Johann P. Sommerville. Cambridge: Cambridge University Press.

Kesselring, K. J. 2003. *Mercy and Authority in the Tudor State*. Cambridge: Cambridge University Press.

Lerer, Seth. 2003. "Errata: Print, Politics and Poetry in Early Modern England," in Kevin Sharpe and Steven N. Zwicker, eds., *Reading, Society and Politics in Early Modern England*. Cambridge: Cambridge University Press, pp. 41–71.

McCabe, Richard A. 1987. "The Masks of Duessa: Spenser, Mary Queen of Scots, and James VI," *English Literary Renaissance* 17: 224–42.

McLaren, Anne N. 1999. *Political Culture in the Reign of Elizabeth I: Queen and Commonwealth, 1558–1585*. Cambridge: Cambridge University Press.

Mason, Roger, ed. 1994. *Scots and Britons: Scottish Political Thought and the Union of 1603*. Cambridge: Cambridge University Press.

Morison, Richard. 1536a. *A Lamentation in which is Shewed what Ruyne and Destruction Cometh of Seditious Rebellyon*. London.

Morison, Richard. 1536b. *A Remedy for Sedition, wherein are Conteyned Many Thynges, Concernyng the True and Loyall Obeysance that Comes unto their Prince and Soveraygne Lorde the Kynge*. London.

Patterson, W. B. 1997. *King James VI and I and the Reunion of Christendom*. Cambridge: Cambridge University Press.

Phillips, James Emerson. 1964. *Images of a Queen: Mary Stuart in Sixteenth-Century Literature*. Berkeley: University of California Press.

Pocock, J. G. A. 1987. *The Ancient Constitution and the Feudal Law: A Study of English Historical Thought in the Seventeenth Century*, rev. edn. Cambridge: Cambridge University Press.

Scarisbrick, J. J. 1968. *Henry VIII*. London: Methuen.

Shakespeare, William. 1981. *King Richard III*. Ed. Antony Hammond. London: Methuen.

Shakespeare, William. 1987. *Hamlet*. Ed. G. R. Hibbard. Oxford: Oxford University Press.

Shakespeare, William. 1999. *King Henry VI, Part Two*. Ed. Ronald Knowles. London: Thomson.

Skulsky, Harold. 1990. "Malengin," in A. C. Hamilton, ed., *The Spenser Encyclopaedia*. London and Toronto: Routledge and Toronto University Press, p. 450.

Smith, Sir Thomas. 1906. *De Republica Anglorum: A Discourse on the Commonwealth of England*. Ed. L. Alston. Cambridge: Cambridge University Press.

Sommerville, J. P. 1986. *Politics and Ideology in England, 1603–1640*. Harlow: Longman.

Spenser, Edmund. 2001. *The Faerie Queene*. Ed. A. C. Hamilton. London: Longman.

Starkey, Thomas. 1540. *An Exhortation to the People, Instructynge theym to Unitie and Obedience*. London.

Starkey, Thomas. 1989. *A Dialogue between Pole and Lupset*, Camden Society Publications, fourth series, vol. 37. Ed. Thomas F. Mayer. London: Royal Historical Society.

Chapter 10

Shakespeare and the Marginalized "Others"

Carole Levin

When we think of the London and England of Shakespeare and Elizabeth I, traditionally we have assumed a fairly homogeneous society. But more recently scholars have recognized that England, and especially the London of early modern England, was instead a truly heterogeneous place, as was the Edinburgh of early modern Scotland. In early modern British cities, there was a wide range of peoples of different statuses and backgrounds. This chapter discusses the actual lives of those somehow perceived as different, attitudes about them, and how these attitudes were reflected in the drama of the time, especially in the works of Shakespeare. One issue I examine is representations of parents and children among those perceived as deeply different. I also look at one of the ways those who were "other" were viewed as less human by the English: in their ability to make and appreciate music.

There were many foreigners who had come to England for a variety of reasons, often economic or religious. For centuries, the French had been the classic, most prominent enemy of the English, though in the latter part of the sixteenth century that role shifted to the Spanish. Some French Huguenots came to England as religious refugees; other French people came as foreign traders and merchants, and as part of the entourage of the French ambassadors to the court. Some of the Spanish people came as spies or were there underground to reconvert England to the Catholic faith.

The French were most familiar to the English because for centuries they had been England's closest enemies, and this is depicted throughout Shakespeare's history plays, especially those set during the Hundred Years War. In *Henry V*, the night before the battle of Agincourt, which occurred in 1415, Shakespeare depicted the French dauphin and his nobility as self-satisfied and pompous. The Duke of Orleans says of Henry V: "What a wretched and peevish fellow is this King of England, to mope with his fat-brain'd followers so far out of his knowledge!" (3.7.132–4) In *1 Henry VI*, the French are not contemptuous of the English, but of one another. Joan of Arc, herself a Frenchwoman, shows her disdain for her countrymen when, after she has convinced the Duke of Burgundy to abandon the English, she says as an aside: "Done like a Frenchman – turn and turn again" (3.3.85). She recognizes that the French are not to be trusted but will go with whoever offers them the most at the moment. They "turn and turn again." At the end of the play Joan herself shows poorly; she denies her own father because he is a peasant, claiming she is nobly born. At first, assuming that being a virgin will keep the English from having her killed, she says of herself:

> Joan of Arc hath been
> A virgin from her tender infancy,
> Chaste and immaculate in very thought.
> (5.4.48–50)

Once she realizes that a claim to virginity will not save her, Joan instead states that she is with child, hoping that the English will not execute a pregnant woman. When the English mock the first man whom she names as father of her child, she keeps naming one man after another, hoping to find one that will satisfy the English, in a frenzied, unsuccessful attempt to save her life.

> O, give me leave, I have deluded you.
> 'Twas neither Charles nor yet the Duke I named,
> But Reignier, King of Naples, that prevailed.
> (5.4.76–8)

The last we see of her, she is cursing the English as she is being dragged off to be burned, the stereotype of the French woman as whore as well as witch.

But it is not only the French who are so depicted. A number of Shakespeare's villains have Spanish names, most notably Iago in *Othello*. Iago was a Spanish version of James, and the name would have resonated with Shakespeare's audiences. St James the Apostle was the patron saint of Spain. Many thought that he went to Spain to convert the infidel, and after his death back in Judea in 44 CE his body floated back to Spain in a rudderless ship. But many also believed in a later tradition that he appeared to fight for the Christians at the battle of Clavijo in 844, and he became known as St James the Moor-slayer. In the early modern period St James on horseback wearing red and trampling on the Moors on the ground was a frequent subject for paintings and statues.

While the French and Spanish appeared strange and negative to the English, others were even more different. There were people in Shakespeare's England who were neither white nor Christian. While some Jews and Africans lived relatively unmolested, others found themselves harassed, ridiculed, or even in peril of their lives. The English thought themselves the best of people and their isle the finest of living places. One foreign visitor scornfully remarked that those English who had some reason to leave their homeland complained that they were leaving the world, as if they believed England were the world. Especially at times of religious, social, economic, or cultural crisis the English would often turn on those they perceived as different, as other, though that perception of "other" could include a very wide range.

Those perceived as the most extreme "others" of the time were Africans and Jews. In both cases, although there were extremely negative portrayals, the situation was more ambiguous. Some of the Jews in England, who had to at least outwardly present themselves as Christians, lived fairly unnoticed, and not all their presentations were horrific. Black people, often called Moors though this was a term used loosely about a wide range of people, sometimes endured intense actual ill-feeling and hideous portrayals, but even some of the villains in brief moments showed a different side, and the portrayal of black people in city pageants was often more representative of the exotic than the monstrous. Yet those who were different were all too often targeted when life became difficult, which it especially was at the end of Elizabeth's reign. Poor harvests caused starvation; inflation, over 400 percent over the whole of the sixteenth century, was especially a problem at the end of the century.

Africans

The English found justification of their exploitation of Africans in the long-held popular perception that blacks were demonic, savagely behaved, unintelligent, and/or inherently lustful. In part this view was promoted by the bizarre descriptions of Africans found in many "travel books." One example comes from Johannes Boemus' *The*

Fardle of Facions Conteining the Auncients Maners, Customes and Lawes of the Peoples Enhabiting the Two Parts of the Earth called Affrike and Asie, translated into English by Willliam Waterman in 1555. He described one tribe, the Icthiophagi, as a people who went naked their entire lives. This lack of garments was an outward manifestation that they had no ethical principles. Each night the men feasted on shellfish – was it the seafood that caused their immorality? – and afterwards had sexual relations with whichever women and children were most easily available. *A Summary of the Antiquities and Wonders of the World … Out of Sixteen First Books of … Pliny*, published in 1556, was even more bizarre. The book was filled with descriptions of the various peoples of Africa as monsters in body and behavior. The book included examples of cannibalism. There were descriptions of a black race whose people had dogs' heads, and yet another who were born without heads at all – their eyes and mouth having been relocated to their breasts.

The British not only read about Africans. They saw them presented in court masques and city pageants and also had actual Africans live amongst them. The first African community was one in Edinburgh established about 1500; fifty years later there was one in London. Those in the small black community in Edinburgh in the sixteenth century were descendants of slaves seized from a Portuguese ship by order of James IV about 1500, in recompense of a Scottish ship that had been taken by the Portuguese. The Scottish king, who loved fighting, tournaments, and dressing up, held a tournament of the black knight and the black lady. While he was the black knight, the black lady was an actual African woman, gorgeously dressed at court expense, who served as the "prize" of the tournament (Fryer 1984).

The appearance of blackness, however, was negative even when not allied with the idea of "Moor," or ethnic identity. In many medieval plays the devil appeared as a black man, and this idea continued in the sixteenth century, when frequently the devil was so depicted in witch-craft trials and pamphlets. Sometimes the depiction of a black person was that of a devil or villain, but sometimes just an object of exotic strangeness. As early as 1510 the young Henry VIII had a court masque where some of the characters were portrayed as black people, by wearing black stockings, gloves, and masks. Six of the characters were female, and they were portrayed by young women of the court, including Henry's younger sister Mary. There were at least six more such masques in the next hundred years, the most famous being the 1605 *Masque of Blackness* by Ben Jonson, created for Anna of Denmark, wife of James I, who was also James VI of Scotland.

Every October 29 the Lord Mayor's Pageants were held in London to celebrate the inauguration of the new Lord Mayor. Between 1585 and 1692 in at least nineteen of the Lord Mayor's Pageants, some trade guilds presented pageants with black characters. As Anthony Gerard Barthelemy has pointed out (1987), these black characters were not villains or monsters, and their function was not to cause the crowds watching the pageants to be afraid but instead to increase the feelings of strangeness, of mystery, and extravagance. The black characters represented the feelings of success and accomplishment the English had about their explorations and world trade. In 1585 playwright George Peele organized the Pageant. In the midst of it was a black man riding a lynx, and he described himself to the crowd as "a stranger, strangely mounted." He went on to praise both the city of London and Elizabeth I, saying that both place and sovereign were famous throughout the world, known for their renown and power. To the crowd, such a statement by such as this proclaimed English supremacy. A later pageant had a Moorish king riding a leopard and happily throwing coins to the crowds: "Then commeth the King of Moores, gallantly mounted on a golden Leopard, he hurling gold and silver every way about him" (Munday 1616).

In other cases, black men themselves were equated with exotic or dangerous beasts. We can find an extreme example of this in the report of the pageant for the baptism of the Scottish king James VI's son Prince Henry in 1594. The organizers had originally planned for a lion to pull the royal carriage; but then they feared that a lion might get out of control and scare or hurt someone, particularly if it were startled by noise and the flashing of torches. So the organizers substituted a "BlackMoor," an actual black man from the Edinburgh community, who was given rich and exotic apparel and "great chaines of pure gold." The organizers even figured out a way to propel the carriage, so the man only had to pretend to haul it. London city pageants of 1613 and 1616 also had characters described as the kings of the Moors. But though kings, they were not in the pageant to demonstrate their own power. Rather, the pageants showed these kings as not only lacking in command, but also happy with that condition.

Most blacks living in England in the late sixteenth century were "employed" as household servants, entertainers, or prostitutes for wealthy men. Elizabeth herself had several black dancers and musicians in her court. The Africans, however, became an all too easy target when the economy was in a down turn. In a proclamation in 1601, Elizabeth expressed her discontent at what she claimed was a great number of black people living in her kingdom. She referred to the Africans as ''infidels,'' and argued that Africans got the help and jobs that her own liege people needed. Given the jobs open to Africans, and the relatively few there were in England, this concern might well appear more symbolic than real. The queen promised a ship to take the Africans back to their own continent whether they wished to go or not; even though some Africans in England had converted to Christianity, Elizabeth made no exceptions for them. Despite Elizabeth's decree, many stayed behind; whether this was because the ship never materialized or because their ''masters'' refused to give them up, we do not necessarily know. Further, more were brought into England throughout the seventeenth century (Cowhig 1985: 5–6).

George Peele in 1588 or 1589 wrote the play *The Battle of Alcazar* (published in 1594), which featured the first black Moor of any dramatic significance. Peele's source for the play was John Poleman's *The Second Part of the Book of Battailes, Fought in Our Age* (1587), which contained one section on the 1578 battle fought between the forces of Sebastian, king of Portugal, and Abdelmelec, the king of Morocco.

Peele portrays the villain Muly Mahamet as cruel and treacherous, and his evil is associated directly with the blackness of his skin. He is introduced as

> the barbarous Moore,
> The Negro *Muly Hamet* that with-holds
> The Kingdome from his unkle Abdimelec,
> Whom proud *Abdallas* wrongd,
> And in his throne instals his cruell sonne,
> . . . Blacke in his looke, and bloudie in his deeds,
> And in shirt stained with a cloud of gore,
> Presents himself with naked sword in hand,
> Accompanied now as you may behold,
> With devils coted in the shapes on men.
> (1.16–10, 16–20)

To secure the kingdom of Barbary for himself and his son, Muly Mahamet murders most of his own family. Eventually he battles his uncle Abdimelec, who though he clearly is also black is not referred to in the way Muly is.

After losing to his uncle, Muly Mahamet camps out in a desolate wilderness, feeding only on the raw flesh of wild animals, which suggests that Muly is something of a wild animal himself. Unrepentant to the end, he drowns in the river. His corpse is recovered, then desecrated and put on display. As a warning to potential traitors, the order is made that his body is skinned.

> That all the world may learne by him to avoide,
> To hall on princes to injurious warre,
> His skin we will be parted from his flesh,
> And being stifned out and stuft with strawe,
> So to deterre and feare the lookers on,
> From anie such foule fact or bad attempt,
> Awaie with him.
>
> (5.1.1441–7)

What does it say that Muly Mahamet's *skin* is stuffed and preserved as an exhibition? Is it a statement that he is not truly human but rather a wild animal, as the play has previously hinted, to be gawked at? Like any animal, is his value only in his hide? Will this display, in a region populated mostly by black people, be a way to keep them from acting up? Throughout the play, the other characters treat Muly Mahamet's skin color as his defining characteristic, and he is doomed to be dehumanized and reduced to mere spectacle in death as much as he was in life.

Aaron, the villain of Shakespeare's early play *Titus Andronicus*, is in certain ways in the same mode of villain as Muly. Shakespeare presents Aaron as godless and lecherous. Aaron takes great pleasure in his villainy, and he orchestrates many of the rapes, murders, and dismemberments that occur throughout the play. He too is completely unrepentant, and takes great pride in the artistry of his crimes. He makes it clear that his skin is dark: "Let fools do good, and fair men call for grace, Aaron will have his soul black like his face" (3.1.204–5). The other characters demonstrate their horror and contempt for Aaron, not necessarily for his actions, but for his blackness. They refer to him as "coal-black Moor," "wall-eyed slave," "black dog," "barbarous Moor," "accursed devil," and "inhuman dog."

Aaron, however, is not a two-dimensional monster. He does not suffer from self-hatred because of how he is perceived. Rather, he takes pride in his blackness.

> Is black so base a hue?
>
> . . .
>
> Coal-black is better than another hue,
> In that it scorns to bear another hue.
>
> (4.2.71, 100–1)

In some ways this speech prefigures the Jewish moneylender Shylock's speech in *The Merchant of Venice* about his nature as a Jew: "Hath not a Jew eyes? Hath not a Jew hands, organs, dimensions, senses, affections, passions? ... If you poison us, do we not die? And if you wrong us, shall we not revenge? If we are like you in the rest, we will resemble you in that" (3.1.55–7, 62–4). Aaron is proud of being black; Shylock proclaims his humanity as a Jew.

We finally see at least glimpses of Aaron's humanity when he receives news that his lover, the empress Tamora, has given birth to his son. The baby is detested by its nurse for its blackness, and by Tamara's two adult sons for that and also because, since the child is black, he threatens them all with discovery of Tamora's affair. The nurse describes the child as a "joyless, dismal, black, and sorrowful issue ... as loathsome as a toad," (4.2.67–8) and instructs Aaron to kill him. But it is his son's blackness that finally touches Aaron in a meaningful way and leads to the speech quoted above. His protection of his son is a defense and validation of both his blackness and his humanity. Barthelemy argues that "Though it does not effect a redemption, Aaron's uncompromising paternal devotion does soften the otherwise harsh and vile portrait of him. This chink in the allegation of blackness, however slight, separates Aaron from Muly Mohamet" (Barthelemy 1987: 97). While Muly is an uncomplicated picture of evil because of blackness, Aaron has far more complexity.

Jews

Jews were often viewed as being equally inhuman. From the early medieval period, the established Christian church had often described Jews as being responsible for the crucifixion of Jesus; in the following centuries throughout Europe, and certainly in England, Jews came to be associated with everything demonic and immoral, including sorcery, poisoning, and the ritual murder of Christian children. Often they were blamed for outbreaks of the plague because it was believed that they had poisoned the drinking water. Many Jews fled to England from France and elsewhere in Europe in the eleventh century, when the calling of the first Crusade led many to wonder why they should go all the way to the Holy Lands to slay the Infidel when they could do it so conveniently right at home. But England as more tolerant soon proved illusionary. For the coronation of Richard I in 1189, the new king called for the exclusion of all women and Jews from the ceremony. Perhaps militaristic, homosexual Richard feared that the presence of Jews and women at such a sacred ceremony would be polluting. Some Jewish leaders came anyway to profess their loyalty. Word soon spread, though untruly, that Richard in retaliation ordered the extermination of all Jews in England, leading the next year to the deaths of about one hundred and fifty Jews in York at Clifford's Tower.

A century later, Edward I, having first confiscated their wealth, ordered that all Jews who did not convert to Christianity leave England on pain of death; they could take with them only what each could carry. As a result, virtually all Jews left England in 1290, and were not legally allowed to return as Jews until the 1650s. But even if Jews converted to Christianity, the English often did not accept them as "true Christians," and feared that their mere presence in the country would weaken the Christian faith and cause people to convert to Judaism. In the centuries after the expulsion, while there were few or no actual Jews in England, the image of the Jew as dangerous monster only continued to grow.

But Jews were on occasion in England, and if they became Christian, their conversion was celebrated, and their move away from the margins toward a more English center was proclaimed with a new name. In 1532, in one of her last acts as queen, Catherine of Aragon with her daughter Mary served as godmothers to two Jewish women from southern Europe, Aysa Pudewya and Omell Faytt Isya, who converted to Catholicism, a perhaps ironic choice given that only a year later England broke from the Catholic church with Henry VIII, now married to Anne Boleyn, as the Head of the Church of England. Aysa became Katherine Whetely and Omell became Mary Cook (Adler 1939: 328–30).

In the 1530s, as part of the way to make Henry VIII's court more glamorous, Thomas Cromwell invited musicians from Italy, nineteen of whom were of Jewish background. But within a generation or two most of their descendants were practicing Christians. There was, however, in the sixteenth century a small, organized Jewish community in London that practiced the religion in secret, and a similar community in Bristol. These Jews were mostly ones who had fled the Iberian Peninsula.

When Elizabeth became queen she officially tolerated Jewish refugees as long as they outwardly conformed to the Anglican church. And again, some conversions received acclaim. On April 1, 1577, Jehuda Menda, who had lived in London for six years, publicly stated that he utterly forsook his former idolatrous ways and strange worship, leaving behind the false search for a new Messiah. He also forsook his name and asked to be called Nathaniel. Following his conversion, John Foxe preached for four hours (Adler 1939: 331–2).

Elizabeth's own physician, Roderigo Lopez, was of Jewish background, his father being forced in Portugal to convert. Lopez settled in London in 1559, was soon admitted as a fellow of the College of Physicians, and was a physician at St Bartholomew's Hospital. His reputation was excellent and he prospered, along the way marrying Sarah Anes, the English daughter of wealthy Portuguese Jewish parents. Lopez and his family outwardly practiced Anglicanism but apparently secretly continued as Jews. Lopez became the physician of Robert Dudley, earl of Leicester, and in 1581 of the queen herself, for which he was well rewarded. Lopez's success made him notable and vulnerable. He was accused of using poison and performing abortions in an anonymous tract against Leicester in 1584. A decade later, Leicester's stepson, Robert Devereux, earl of Essex, eager to gain Elizabeth's favor and prove he was keeping her safe from harm, accused Lopez of attempting to poison her. Though Lopez was most likely not guilty, Edgar Samuel suggests that he had acted "stupidly and dishonestly" (Samuel 2005), which made him an easy target. At his treason trial Attorney General Edward Coke had stressed Lopez's secret practice of Judaism. Lopez was quickly found guilty; after a few months' hesitation, Elizabeth agreed to his execution, though she returned most of his estate to his wife Sarah and their children. A decade after Lopez's death, the Spanish ambassador to England, Count Gondomar, wrote to his monarch, Philip III, that Lopez had been innocent and his conviction and execution unjust. In the late sixteenth and seventeenth centuries, the Lopez case was often an element in the creation of the idea of monstrous Jews.

Another particularly vicious attack that eventually became a popular ballad well known during the Elizabethan period occurred in Lincoln in 1255. An illegitimate 8-year-old boy named Hugh disappeared at the end of July. His body was discovered a month later in a well on the property of a Jewish man. On threat of torture and promise of pardon if he only confessed, the Jew told the authorities that the most prominent Jews of England, in Lincoln for a wedding, had participated in the murder since, he confirmed, they crucified a Christian boy every year as a ritual. Henry III had the Jew's pardon revoked and the man was brutally executed; close to one hundred Jews were taken to London and imprisoned. Eighteen or nineteen were executed, and Henry III confiscated their goods and wealth. This event was eventually portrayed in the popular ballad *Sir Hugh, or the Jew's Daughter*, where the Jew's daughter lures young Sir Hugh into her house, slaughters him, and hides his body in a gutted pig carcass. There are many versions of the ballads that developed over the centuries, and the Jew's daughter becomes more and more a monster.

> She laid him on a dressing-board,
> Where she did sometimes dine;
> She put a penknife in his heart,
> And dressed him like a swine.
>
> (Child 1965: 245)

How fascinating that the child so low in status had become a noble, the murderer a Jewish woman, and the well a gutted pig.

In the ballad the Jew's daughter is even more horrific in her actions than the depiction of the potential queen-murderer Lopez. During the time of the Lopez trial, Christopher Marlowe's play *The Jew of Malta*, written a few years earlier, was put on to standing-room crowds. *The Jew of Malta*'s main character in the play was the Jewish villain Barabas. A few years later Shakespeare wrote *The Merchant of Venice*, with his Jewish character Shylock in some ways based on Barabas, and in other ways on Lopez. Both Barabas and Shylock have a daughter, but neither Abigail nor Jessica echoes the horrific behavior of the ballad Jew's daughter; but then neither of them remains a Jew – each abandons her own Judaism and her father to convert to Christianity. Is this the only method by which a Jewish woman character can shed such a monstrous persona? Would she otherwise be a gruesome Jewish woman like the murderous Jew's daughter in the ballad?

Like Aaron, Barabas takes great pride in the artistry of his crimes, and he eventually becomes a monster and a bogeyman-figure. He brags to his Turkish slave Ithamore:

> As for myself, I walk abroad at nights
> And kill sick people groaning under walls;
> Sometimes I go about and poison wells;
> ... And [with] tricks belonging unto brokery,
> I filled the jails with bankrupts in a year,
> And with young orphans planted hospitals,
> And every moon made some or other mad.
>
> (2.3.176–8, 194–7)

Barabas is the embodiment of all the most monstrous beliefs about Jews in Elizabethan England. Similar characters appeared in non-dramatic forms of entertainment. For example, Thomas Nashe's 1594 novel, *The Unfortunate Traveler*, features two Jewish villains – one who conducts sadistic medical experiments, and another who enjoys flogging Christian women (Glassman 1975: 72).

Barabas ultimately lacks the humanity Aaron has shown in his relationship to his son; Barabas eventually murders his own daughter Abigail. At first he proclaims how much he loves his daughter, but even then she is merely a cherished possession, an object, like his wealth: "O my girl, My gold, my fortune, my felicity" (2.1.47–8). In *The Merchant of Venice*, Solanio claims Shylock makes a similar statement after his daughter Jessica has run off to her Christian lover with as much of her father's wealth as she could carry: "As the dog Jew did utter in streets: / 'My daughter! O, my ducats! O, my daughter!' " (2.8.14–15). The Christians of Venice are suggesting that Shylock does not know which disturbs him more as he cries out for "my daughter, my ducats," or if the two have coalesced in his mind. In the first act of *The Jew of Malta*, Barabas discusses his love for his daughter:

> I have no charge, nor many children,
> But one sole daughter, whom I hold as dear
> As Agamemnon did his Iphigen:
> And all I have is hers.
>
> (1.1.135–8)

But such a comparison would make the alert theatre-goer uneasy. At the bay of Aulis the Greek fleet could not have the wind to sail to Troy because Agamemnon, the military leader, had insulted the goddess Artemis. Agamemnon sacrificed his daughter Iphigenia to appease the goddess and begin his war to retrieve Helen and restore the Greeks' sense of self-honor. As for Barabas, he murdered his daughter Abigail and two hundred nuns with her, after she converted to Christianity and joined a nunnery because of her disgust at her father's actions in causing her two suitors to kill each other. While some villains of Renaissance drama commit murder and then are devastated by their acts afterwards, Barabas shows no remorse. "No, but I grieve that she lived so long; / An Hebrew born, and would becomes a Christian!"(4.1.18–19). Barabas only loved his daughter when she was dutiful; once she was not, she was completely expendable.

Music

Another area in which the English perceived Africans and Jews as inferior was their purported response to music. To the English, music was a way to connect the human on earth to God, and many talked of "the celestial music of the spheres." Many believed that listening to, or participating in, holy music was another way for humans to briefly understand the divine. For the English, the belief that they could truly compose, understand, appreciate, and make beautiful music was part of their sense of superiority. These attitudes were coupled with a belief that those who were "other," were different, could not appreciate or create beautiful music and thus were that much less truly human or able to reach toward heaven. Many of the English believed that the music of Africans was nothing more than dreadful-sounding confusion. In 1555 William Towerson returned from traveling in Africa, and told how the singing of African women "falls ill to our ears" (Barthelemy 1987: 59–60). Boemus' *The Fardle of Facions* says of the seafood-eating, sexually promiscuous Icthiophagi that they enjoy singing but it is "full untuned" (Boemus 1555: II, 39–40).

Even though the Jews who came to Henry VIII's court from Italy in the 1530s were brought to England to make music, we see the same belief system about Jews in the drama of the Elizabethan England. In *The Jew of Malta*, Barabas shows his contempt for the music that meant the most to the English audience when he proclaims, "There is no music to a Christian's knell: / How sweet the bells ring, now the nuns are dead, / That sound at other times like tinkers' pans!" (4.1.1–3) Later, he disguises himself as a French musician to more effectively eavesdrop on the traitorous Ithamore. Barabas, however, is unable to play his lute properly, and excuses his poor performance by saying the instrument is out of tune.

In *The Merchant of Venice* some of the characters call the Jewish moneylender Shylock some of the same terms that had been used about Aaron, such as "accursed devil" and "inhuman dog." But Shylock is also portrayed by Shakespeare as a man who not only cannot appreciate music, but who it actually appears to pain. In the last scene that Shylock has with his daughter Jessica, he leaves her at home to go to a feast at the home of Bassanio, the man for whom the merchant Antonio has borrowed from Shylock. As he is departing, he urges his daughter to close the windows against the music of the masquers in the street.

What, are there masques? Hear you me, Jessica
Lock up my doors, and when you hear the drum
And the vile squealing of the wry-necked fife,
Clamber not you up to the casements then,
Nor thrust your head into the public street.
To gaze on Christian fools with varnished faces;
But stop my house's ears – I mean my casements;
Let not the sound of shallow foppery enter
My sober house.

(2.5.29–37)

For Shylock, this music is not only something that could pollute his house, which has come to represent his own identity enough that he mistakes it for a moment for his ears; it could as well dangerously distract and seduce his daughter. But even more than that, however, hearing music, at least that performed by Christians, actually appears to cause him pain: "squealing of the wry-necked fife."

This is the final time Shylock gets to see his daughter, since Jessica takes advantage of his absence to elope with the Christian Lorenzo, Bassanio's friend. Lorenzo appears delighted with Jessica; whether for herself or for all the gold she has stolen from her father for him, however, is never clear. Though Jessica converts to Christianity, some of the characters still mock her as a "Jewess."

Once Jessica is in Portia's Belmont as Lorenzo's now converted wife, she herself appears ambivalent about music. While Lorenzo and Jessica are out in the gardens in the moonlight, Lorenzo calls for musicians to come and entertain them. When the music starts Jessica tells him, "I am never merry when I hear sweet music." The sadness the music calls forth from her may be a reference to the conflicted relationship Jessica had with her father, and a suggestion of how torn she may be that she had abandoned him for Lorenzo. If Jessica's wistful statement to Lorenzo, "I am never merry … " is a reference to her past, Lorenzo's response will only serve to alienate her further from her father and make her more isolated.

The man that hath no music in himself
Nor is not moved with concord of sweet sounds,
Is fit for treasons, stratagems, and spoils;
The motions of his spirit are dull as night,
And his affections dark as Erebus.
Let no such man be trusted.

(5.1.83–8)

Since Erebus is a dark place near Hell, Lorenzo seems to be telling his wife, and the audience, how the untrustworthy Shylock is so dark and dull that he is damned, an echo of Salerio, who earlier called Shylock "the devil." And one wonders how this would make Jessica feel, to be considered by her husband as the daughter of an untrustworthy, devilish Jew.

Those on the margins of Elizabethan England, especially Jews and Africans, were often feared and despised. The characterizations of members of these groups on stage both reflected and reinforced these attitudes. While in plays such as *The Battle of Alcazar* and *The Jew of Malta* the African and the Jew were unmitigated villains, in Shakespeare's *Titus Andronicus* and *The Merchant of Venice* there are more glimpses of humanity in Aaron and Shylock. One way those in Elizabeth England demonstrated their sense of superiority over those others in a frightening and changing society was their belief they could appreciate music, that *they* had music in themselves. But clearly this internal music did little to make the dominant English treat those who were different, "other," in more humane, and human, terms.

Acknowledgment

I wish to thank my colleague Professor Pamela Starr for many helpful conversations about music in English Renaissance culture and drama. Amy Gant, Cheney Luttich, and Erica Wright provided excellent research support. Teri Imus helped me think through more issues on the English and the Africans. I wish to thank them as well as the UCARE program at the University of Nebraska. My dear friends and colleagues Michele Osherow and Anya Riehl patiently listened to me talk through the points of this chapter, gave me most helpful feedback, and, in Michele's case, subsequently read a draft, and for that I am most grateful.

References and Further Reading

Adler, Michael. 1939. *Jews of Medieval England*. London: Edward Goldston.
Barthelemy, Anthony Gerard. 1987. *Black Face, Maligned Race: The Representation of Blacks in English Drama from Shakespeare to Southerne*. Baton Rouge: LSU Press.

Bevington, David, ed. 1992. *The Complete Works of Shakespeare*, 4th edn. New York: HarperCollins.

Boemus, Joannes. 1555. *The Fardle of Facions Conteining the Auncients Maners, Customes and Lawes of the Peoples Enhabiting the Two Parts of the Earth called Affrike and Asie*, trans. William Waterman, 2 vols. Amsterdam. (New York: Da Capo Press, 1970.)

Child, Frances James, ed. 1965. *The English and Scottish Popular Ballads. III*, repr. New York: Dover.

Cohen, Mark R. 1994. *Under Crescent and Cross: The Jews in the Middle Ages*. Princeton: Princeton University Press.

Cowhig, Ruth. 1985. ''Blacks in English Renaissance Drama and the Role of Shakespeare's Othello,'' in David Dabydeen, ed., *The Black Presence in English Literature*. Manchester: Manchester University Press, pp. 1–25.

Felsenstein, Frank. 1995. *Anti-Semitic Stereotypes: A Paradigm of Otherness in English Popular Culture, 1660–1830*. Baltimore: Johns Hopkins University Press.

Feuer, Lewis S. 1982–6. ''Francis Bacon and the Jews: Who was the Jew in the New Atlantis?'' *Jewish Historical Studies* 29: 1–25.

Fryer, Peter. 1984. *Staying Power: The History of Black People in Britain*. London: Pluto.

Glassman, Gerard. 1975. *Anti-Semitic Stereotypes Without Jews: Images of Jews in England, 1290–1700*. Detroit: Wayne State University Press.

Greenblatt, Stephen. 1990. *Learning to Curse: Essays in Early Modern Culture*. New York: Routledge.

Griffith, A. 1964. ''Dr Roderigo Lopez,'' *St Bartholomew's Hospital Journal, November:* 440–52.

Gross, John. 1993. *Shylock*. New York: Simon and Schuster.

Gwyer, John. 1952 for 1945–51. ''The Case of Dr Lopez,'' *Transactions, Jewish Historical Society of England* 16: 63-84.Hall, Kim F. 1995. *Things of Darkness: Economies of Race and Gender in Early Modern England*. Ithaca, NY, and London: Cornell University Press.

Hammer, Paul J. 1999. *The Polarization of Elizabethan Politics: The Political Career of Robert Devereux, 2nd Earl of Essex*. Cambridge: Cambridge University Press.

Hilton, Claire. 1987–8. ''St Bartholomew's Hospital and its Jewish Connections,'' *Jewish Historical Studies* 30: 21–50. 50.

Jones, Eldred. 1965. *Othello's Countrymen: Africans in Renaissance Drama*. Oxford: Oxford University Press.

Katz, David. 1994. *The Jews in the History of England, 1485–1850*. Oxford: Clarendon Press.

Levin, Carole. 1996. ''Backgrounds and Echoes of *Othello*: From Leo Africanus to Ignatius Sancho,'' *Lamar Journal of the Humanities* XXII(2): 45–68.

Levin, Carole. 2002. *The Reign of Elizabeth I*. New York: Palgrave.

Marlowe, Christopher. 1978. *The Jew of Malta*. Ed. N. W. Bawcutt. Baltimore: Johns Hopkins University Press.

Munday, Anthony. 1616. *Chrysanaleia: The Golden Fishing; or, Honour of Fish-mongers. Applauding the Aduancement of M. Iohn Leman to the Dignitie of Lord Maior of London. Taking his Oath on the 29. day of October. 1616. Performed at the Charges of the Worshipfull Company of Fishmongers.* London: G. Purslowe.

Mundill, Robin R. 1998. *England's Jewish Solution: Experiment and Expulsion, 1262–90.* Cambridge: Cambridge University Press.

Prouty, Charles Tyler, ed. 1952–70. *The Life and Works of George Peele,* 3 vols. New Haven: Yale University Press.

Samuel, Edgar. 2005. "Lopez, Roderigo (c. 1517–94)", in *Oxford Dictionary of National Biography,* online edition. www.oxforddnb.com.library. unl.edu:80/ view/article/17011, accessed October 19, 2005

Shapiro, James. 1995. *Shakespeare and the Jews.* New York: Columbia University Press.

Yaffe, Martin D. 1997. *Shylock and the Jewish Question.* Baltimore: Johns Hopkins University Press.

Chapter 11

Cosmology and the Body

Cynthia Marshall

Madness in literature commonly holds spiritual or political import, so physicality comes as a shock when Mavolio's supposed madness registers in terms of his urine. Urging ''Carry his water to th' wise woman'' (*Twelfth Night*, 3.4.97), Fabian refers to the practice, ubiquitous in medieval and early modern England, of inspecting urine to diagnose illness and determine its treatment. Detailed charts assisted the practitioner in judging the excreta in terms of color, clarity, and consistency. Modern medical practitioners likewise use urinalysis as a diagnostic technique, though the chemical determinations available to modern science differ markedly from the impressionistic readings of the earlier age. Given the custom of examining urine absent the patient, there was not-unreasonable concern that the examined urine might not derive from the one implicated. Yet reliance on uroscopy was then so great that the urine flask served as the iconic symbol for a physician. Behind this practice lay an assumption that maintaining internal balance was the means to mental, emotional, and physical health, and that the body's excreta would contain whatever superfluities were cast off as the system sought to achieve the correct proportion of elements.

To characterize health in the early modern period as a matter solely of the body's internal balance is somewhat misleading, however. According to prevailing Galenic ideas of physiology, the human body was porous in its constitution and gravely susceptible to external influence (atmospheric conditions, food, drink). Moreover, because the celestial forces were thought to govern all things – animal, vegetable, and mineral – interactions between environmental influences were almost certain to be complex. The second-century physician Galen had developed an elaborate system for explaining human anatomy and physiology, based on his own observations, which included dissections of animals, and his faith in Platonic notions of the cosmos.

Cynthia Marshall

That Galen's medical theories remained influential, even standard, fourteen centuries later indicates how little medical knowledge, and science in general, advanced over this period. The new science of the sixteenth century began to modify the received understanding of the heavens and of human anatomy. Literary texts of the period bear the imprint of traditional notions of the human place in the cosmos even as they register emerging ideas and, in some cases, negotiate the tension between old and new systems.

According to the traditional understanding of cosmological order, divine control over the heavens directly influenced human existence, individually as well as generally. As John Davies of Hereford framed the matter in his didactic poem *Microcosmos*,

> The *Heav'ns* and *Earth*, do make the greater *World*;
> And *Soule* and *Bodie*, make the *Lesse* (we prove:)
> The *Heav'ns* doe moue the *Earth*, & they are whirld
> By *Him*, that makes the *Soule*, the *Body* moue.
> (Davies 1603: dedication)

An elaborate set of correspondences linked the celestial and terrestrial worlds, not merely through abstract analogy but through literal intervention. In Davies's terms, "God is a sp'rite, the World a Body is, / Both which in Man are plaine Epitomiz'd" (Davies 1603: 223). The framework enunciated a conservative ordering principle that defined political, social, familial, and individual affairs in hierarchical terms. One famous visual metaphor was the great chain of being, aligning various forms of life in a vertical scale descending from God to angels to saints, from men to animals to plants. In the human realm, this model had profound implications for gender and class, naturalizing the established order in relation to both. Women, whose subordinate position was seen as divinely preordained, were defined as essentially weaker and more inconstant than men (Fletcher 1995). Likewise, class and ethnic differences were understood as essential and fixed, not as historically and culturally derived.

To the extent that this cosmology inscribed the established social order in terms of metaphysical fixity, it accorded analogically with ancient Ptolemaic astronomy, which placed the earth at the center of the universe, with the moon, planets, and stars revolving in crystalline spheres about it. That is, the earth was seen as divinely controlled, positions within the scheme were fixed, and relativism played no part in this closed conception. Even apparent challenges to the system were accommodated; for instance, the curious accident of England being ruled by a female monarch, Elizabeth I, did not alter low estimates of women's capacities: Elizabeth's exception proved the rule, her royal identity trumping her female weakness. Yet if the official picture, in terms of cosmology and social order, was traditional, hierarchical, and fixed, close examination reveals the image to be riddled with contradictions. Cosmologies hold moral implications and may therefore claim a degree of certainty that other sorts of texts are unlikely to achieve or aspire to, although the disjunction between the stable world described by moral authorities and the unfixed, variable existence acknowledged contemporaneously by astronomers, explorers, and medical writers can be astonishing. As we shall see, literary and dramatic texts draw considerable power from their negotiation of these complexities of worldview. For instance, a subtext drawing on traditional ideas may compensate for an ideologically challenging plot, or the loss of metaphysical certainty may be emphasized as a way of increasing emotional resonance.

In the area of astronomy, the Renaissance was a time of considerable intellectual ferment, with Copernicus theorizing a heliocentric model of the solar system in his *De revolutionibus orbium coelestium* in 1543. Although Copernicus retained the mistaken Ptolemaic belief that the planets move in perfect circles, his model nevertheless opened the way for Kepler's more accurate description of the laws of planetary motion in 1619. Kepler identified the path of planetary orbit as elliptical, with the sun necessarily off-center within the pattern; he specified variations in planetary speed according to distance from the sun; and he established temporal relations between planetary orbit and average distance from the sun. Kepler's model makes some degree of relativism fundamental to the solar system. "Both Copernicus and Kepler sought explanations anchored in a vertical order," writes Fernand Hallyn. With the heliocentric system, Copernicus introduced "the possibility of associating the solar center with the conception of the divine," in effect embellishing the conservative worldview. Kepler's astrophysics, however, "[gave] rise to an immense *hypercodification* of the world" (Hallyn 1990: 20, 283, 285). Superimposing the figural system of musical harmony onto that of geometrical symmetry, Kepler significantly complicated conceptual approaches to cosmology.

Widespread acceptance of these discoveries and an accompanying revolution of ideas were slow to come, however. From a modern perspective, it seems odd that astronomic discoveries of such magnitude were not immediately influential, but religion, not science, supplied the dominant discourse of the early modern period, and so religion provided the established view of universal order. Neither Copernicus nor Kepler sought directly to challenge religious authority, any more than Galileo had. We glimpse the initial stages of a transforming worldview, but not a direct confrontation between the old geocentric certainties and the emerging sense of discovery and potentiality, in John Donne's meditative remark that

> new Philosophy calls all in doubt,
> The Element of fire is quite put out;
> The Sun is lost, and th'earth, and no mans wit
> Can well direct him where to looke for it.
> (Donne 1929: lines 205–8)

Donne's skeptical comment comes in the midst of an elegy for Elizabeth Drury, and serves rhetorically to heighten the sense of loss for the young girl (she died at age 14) by suggesting a profound and general absence of certainty and potentially of meaning. By the poem's end, however, Donne affirms the comfort of a traditional arrangement: "heaven keepes Soules, / The Grave keepes bodies, Verse the Fame enroules" (Donne 1929: lines 473–4).

Perhaps more immediately relevant to most people's experience was the ongoing belief in planetary influences on human affairs. Belief in astrology introduced a principle of variability and even relativity into what seems at first glance a stable picture of physical existence. The sun, the moon, the five planets besides the earth known to exist (Mercury, Venus, Mars, Jupiter, and Saturn), and the fixed stars all exerted competing influence. But as John Maplet explains in *The Dial of Destiny*, planetary influence was secondary, hence not in conflict with divine will:

> even as by God the greatest and mightiest of all, and the first and principall cause of all things, all creatures are disposed generally to a like frame and customable order of the selfe same kind: so in lyke sorte by the second causes the Planets although inferiours yet working causes, all things here underneath are in more speciall sorte sealed and ensampled. Easy it is to see that there is no one parte in all the whole proportion and workmanship of mans body, that is not ruled or disposed by some one Planet or other, to affectate that most of all other thinges which the superior force doth frame them and enclyne them unto: so that unto me all the whole body of man, as also the bodies of all other

220

creatures here below, seeme to be possessed, busied, and as it were
incensed and set on worke by them.   (Maplet 1581: 181)

Whereas astrology today is popularly viewed as a species of fortune-
telling, in early modern England it was "a respectable science, taught
in the universities" (Beier 1987: 23). The heavenly bodies were understood to have a literal impact on people's health and activities through
multiple vectors. Since celestial forces affected everything on earth,
"medical practitioners routinely sought to assist therapy by finding out
when a favorable alignment of the heavens would occur and timing
their activities accordingly" (Sirasi 1990:149). Astrology and medicine
were to some extent coterminous; the astrological physician Simon
Forman cast horoscopes and prescribed medicinal treatments for his
patients (Traister 2001). Practitioners "consulted astronomical tables
to find out when the position or phase of the moon was best for
gathering medicinal plants, administering medicines, or performing
phlebotomy" (Sirasi 1990:149). More specifically, each celestial body
governed particular parts of the body. For instance, Thomas Vicary
(who served as surgeon to Henry VIII and his children) cites Aristotle
in describing how the brain "mooveth and followeth the mooving of
the Moone: for in the waxing of the Moone the brayne followeth
upwards, and in the wave of the Moone the brayne discendeth down-
wardes, and vanisheth in substance of vertue" (Vicary 1587: 17).
Maplet specifies that "Saturne is lord over the Lyver," while "to
Mars appertayneth and belongeth" the veins, kidney, chest, back,
buttocks, and "all that full power of the Stomacke wherein Choler is
ingendred" (Maplet 1581: 182).

The elaborate economies of humoral physiology provide the key to
understanding these bodily divisions and their cosmic correspondences. Entrenched Galenic notions identified four natural elements –
earth, water, air, and fire – that corresponded to four humors – melancholy, phlegm, blood, and choler – within the individual human
body. In their various admixtures and with their discrete characteristic
forces, the humors determined temperament and health:

> These like the Elements move in their moode:
> For bloud is hot, and humid, like the aire:
> Flegm's cold, and moist, in Waters likelyhood:
> Then Melancholy's like Earth, cold and dry'r:
> And hot, and drie is Choler, like the Fire.
>   (Davies 1603: 64)

When the humors were "in the proporcion, that nature hathe lymytted, the bodye is free from all sickenesse," writes Thomas Elyot in *The Castel of Helth*. But "by the increace or dyminucion of any of theym in quantitee or qualitee, over or under theyr naturall assignement, inequall temperature commeth into the bodie, whyche syckenesse foloweth" (Elyot 1541: 8). Since good health consisted of a state of perfect balance of the humors within the body, it was crucial to maintain internal solubility. Yet because bodily fluids were capable of transforming into one another, and because bodily function was vulnerable to multiple environmental influences, balance of humors was often elusive. A chaotic sense of internal processes resulted. Repletion, the "superfluous aboundance of humors," caused "fumes" to rise to the head, where "touching the rim wherein the braine is wrapped," they caused headache, trembling, dimness of vision, and might "pricke and annoy the sensible sinewes, whose roots are in the braine," and thus pass into the whole body (Gyer 1592: 5, 11). Humors burned within the blood, released vapors, and became "adust" and concentrated, or "depraved" and corrupted (Burton 1989: I, 167). There were concerns about "crudities," or "vicious concoctions" resulting from imperfect alteration of ingested material (Elyot 1541: 67b). "This regime imagined that bodies were perpetually in danger of poisoning themselves through their own nutritive processes," observes Michael Schoenfeldt (1999: 3). No wonder people spent considerable time and energy in the quest to achieve humoral balance, by means of diet, exercise, travel, and baths, as well as with medicinal concoctions and purges, and more radical procedures including cupping (applying pressure with heated cups to draw blood to certain areas) and phlebotomy (blood-letting), with leeches or by incision.

Whereas we tend to think of our bodies as relatively solid, contained, and autonomous, in the early modern period the body was understood to be porous and volatile. Within the bodily system, individual organs were attributed their own desires and the ability to express themselves willfully: Helkiah Crooke, physician to King James I, writes that the stomach is "delighted and refreshed" by the matter passing through it and that the spleen "from an inbred faculty of his owne, draweth unto himselfe the thicker and more earthie portion of the Chylus" (Crooke 1618: 121, 128). Organs were also thought to move about within the body. Perhaps the most famous among traveling organs was the wandering womb or uterus, whose movements were traditionally cited to account for hysterical symptoms in women (Jorden 1603: 5^v; Veith 1965). Luring the womb back to its place was one recommended treatment, and so a practitioner in Shrewsbury around 1600 directed that a patient smell bad odors while sweet substances were applied to her genitals. She was also instructed to sneeze, to force the womb down (Beier 1987: 126). Crooke denies the notion of the womb as "a gadding creature that moveth out of one place into another." Nevertheless, in his view a "wonderfull sympathy" exists between the womb and "almost all the parts of womens bodies"; the womb's "very great consent" with the brain causes "frenzies or frantick fitts," while connections with the heart lead to spells of fainting or swooning (Crooke 1618: 224, 252, 253). Thus Crooke aligns female symptoms with a particular organ, even though his knowledge of anatomy requires him to dispute the old idea of a "gadding" womb. To explain agency and the link between body and soul in general, Crooke follows classical authorities in identifying three types of "spirit" – natural, vital, and animal. He defines spirit as "*A subtle and thinne body alwayes mooveable, engendred of blood and vapour, and the vehicle or carriage of the Faculties of the soule.*" While "corporeall," it is "the finest and subtillest substance that is in this Little world." And in Crooke's view, "there is a naturall spirit, the vehicle or guide of the Naturall faculty and of the thicker sort of the blood which is from the Liver diffused into the whole body" (Crooke 1618: 174, 176).

According to Galenic economies, the digestive process converted ingested food into bodily substance through a three-step process: the stomach turned food into chyle, the liver refined chyle into blood, and the spermatic vessels transformed blood into seed. These were processes of purification, differentiating substances of increasing purity from the drossy waste. Interestingly, both male and female bodies were understood to produce seed – in this sense the difference between the sexes was effaced (see Laquer 1990) – and both were deemed necessary for conception to occur. Yet because of women's "in-bred coldness," they produce "a more imperfect seede ... more moyst, thinne and waterish," according to Crooke, who affirms that without female "imperfection ... mankinde could not have beene perfected ... The great Maister workman therefore of set purpose, made the one halfe of mankinde imperfect for the instauration of the whole kinde, making the woman as a receptacle of the seede of which a new man was to be created" (Crooke 1618: 218, 216–17). Thus Crooke affirms gender hierarchy as crucial to the divinely appointed order of creation. Significantly, men's more perfect bodies excelled at every stage of the digestive process, primarily because of their greater heat, whereas women's cooler, moister, less vigorous bodies produced an excess of blood, which was excreted as menstrual flow or converted to milk during periods of lactation. As Gail Paster has argued, "women's literal saturation by the cold clamminess of the female complexion ... philosophically undergirds the most virulent, most conservative forms of Renaissance misogyny" (Paster 1998: 430).

William Harvey demonstrated in 1628 that the amount of blood in a normal human body was not commensurate with the quantity of recently ingested food, a discovery with implications for the rigidly established caloric principle of humoralism (Whitteridge 1976: xvii). That is, Galenic theory depended on a model of blood "ebb[ing] and flow[ing] within a canalized body" (Paster 1993: 78), a model that supported a hierarchical understanding of different types of blood within the body and that explained the sluggish movement of the humors within it. The discovery of the circulatory system began to undermine humoral theory, for once the blood was understood to move continuously through the heart and lungs, it ceased to carry associations with particular parts of the body and a holistic concept became mandatory.

Although new theories understanding infectious disease to be caused by an infiltrating organism were introduced by Paracelsus in the sixteenth century, the scientific etymology of disease was slow to take hold (Porter 1997: 203–4). (To the extent that it did, the new formulation contributed to an emerging idea of the body politic threatened by foreign or external agents; Harris 1998.) Under the humoral regime, therapeutic approaches to illness focused on righting the balance of bodily humors. Phlebotomy, for instance, was standard treatment for women whose menstrual cycles were interrupted; in such cases, blood was to be drawn from the left ankle (Paster 1993: 77). Women were bled in the fourth month of pregnancy to prevent miscarriage or premature delivery (Gyer 1592: 157). John Evelyn reports being bled for a sore throat and for hemorrhoids (Beier 1987: 171). Some people believed in the prophylactic benefits of phlebotomy and had themselves bled seasonally. Phlebotomy was even advocated for grievously wounded patients who were suffering from critical blood loss (Porter 1997: 76). These therapies depended on belief in the accumulation of noxious humors in the blood and confidence in the practitioner's ability to release those humors. A skilled surgeon knew where best to make incision, how much blood to draw, and under what circumstances. Gyer specifies that account must be taken of the patient's age, sex, bodily frame and constitution, state of health, and medical history. He also provides intricate instructions for examining the expelled blood for its color, quantity, viscosity, and taste. The expelled humors would not be immediately apparent, "for when the bloud commeth forth, it appeareth simple & of one forme: but in the porrenger it loseth his colour, & every part therof congeleth severally in his own region. The watrie humor swimmeth above, not farre unlike urine … Melancholy abideth in the bottom: the red bloud & the paler flewme keepe in the middle region" (Gyer 1592: 27). To provide an accurate report, therefore, the practitioner needed to "read" the blood. Despite the proto-scientific precision of his instructions, Gyer's orderly differentiation of humors within the container of blood recalls the hierarchical arrangements of the late medieval cosmology.

Many of Gyer's patients suffered from melancholia, for which phlebotomy was a standard remedy, especially in cases of erotomania or love melancholy. Melancholy seems, in fact, to have been a widespread malady; included under the term was a host of mental, emotional, and physical complaints, ranging from manic depression to anemia and taking in moodiness and intellectual despair. Melancholia may be the most visible humoral disorder in Renaissance literature – its association with the creative temperament invited the interest of writers – and melancholic characters tend to be well developed, with Hamlet the striking example. The predominance of melancholiacs in England was in part due to climate, and not just because rainy weather induces gloom. Early modern "geohumoralism" associated good health with the temperate climate of the Mediterranean, while those from marginal zones were seen as "uncivil, slow-witted, and more bodily determined" (Floyd-Wilson 2003: 5). English gentlemen insisted on their firmness and self-control in comparison to women, but "on the world stage, they found themselves characterized as excessively pale, moist, soft-fleshed, inconstant, and permeable." Temperamentally disadvantaged because of geographical effects, the English were fascinated by melancholy because it was a humor understood as "antithetical" to their own "sanguine and phlegmatic" natures (Floyd-Wilson 2003: 13, 67).

Galenic knowledge was put to satiric use in the dramatic tradition of humors characters – personalities so strongly afflicted by choler or phlegm or bile that their behavior is flattened of complexity. A character in Ben Jonson's *Every Man Out of His Humour* explains that humor

> may by metaphor apply itself
> Unto the general disposition;
> As when some one peculiar quality

> Doth so possess a man that it doth draw
> All his affects, his spirits, and his powers
> In their confluxions all to run one way:
> This may be truly said to be a *humour*.
> (Jonson 2001: Ind. 101–7)

Jonson masterfully uses humoral knowledge "by metaphor" to delineate extreme characters. The term is also used, more generally, to mean whim or impulsive behavior, as when Shylock persists in his attempt to claim a pound of Antonio's flesh because "it is my humour" (Shakespeare, *Merchant of Venice*, 4.1.43). In these various ways, humoral theory is used to identify, develop, or extend character.

Humoral theory provided the standard way of thinking about bodily and emotional experience, not an alternative approach or embellishment. In this pre-scientific, pre-psychological era, phrases such as "when the blood burns" or "something-settled matter in [the] heart" or "like a green girl" (Shakespeare, *Hamlet*, 1.3.115, 3.1.173, 1.3.100) were not just common metaphors but were meant literally, as comprehensible expressions of shared truth. Far from a "dry recounting of Aristotle or Galen," early modern humoral theory was "a remarkable blend of textual authority and a near-poetic vocabulary of felt corporeal experience" (Schoenfeldt 1999: 3). Bodily humors were assumed to affect temperament, emotions, and mental state. Indeed, physiology determined what we consider the psychological aspects of the self; or to view the matter slightly differently, the emotions, or "passions" as they were called, effected linkage between body and soul (as suggested by Crooke's remarks on "spirit," quoted above). Nicholas Coeffeteau, for instance, explains "the diversity of passions in man" in terms of the body's emotional response to sensory data:

> So as the heart and liver beeing thus troubled in their naturall disposi-
> tions, the whole body feeles it selfe mooved, not onely inwardly, but also
> outwardly, according to the nature of the passion which doth trouble it.
> For in motions of joy and desire, the heart melts with gladnesse. In those
> of feare, it growes pale and trembling. A Lovers words are sweete and
> pleasing, and those of a cholerick man are sharpe and rough: Finally,
> there riseth no passion in the soule, which leaveth not some visible trace
> of her agitation, upon the body of man. (Coeffeteau 1621: 16–17)

Emotions were felt as bodily effects; by the same token, humoral disturbances – so difficult to avoid, as we have seen – had emotional as well as physical correlates. The theory compounded causes and effects through a circular kind of reasoning. In Robert Burton's account,

> the distraction of the minde, amongst other outward causes and perturbations, alters the temperature of the body, so the distraction and distemper of the Body will cause a distemperature of the Soule, and 'tis hard to decide which of these two doe more harme to the other ... as anger, feare, sorrow, obtreactation, emulation, etc. ... cause grievous diseases in the Body, so bodily diseases affect the Soule by consent. (Burton 1989: 1.2.5.1 [I, 372])

A person might, in other words, produce bad blood because of his melancholy, or feel sad and distracted because of bad blood. In Thomas Wright's words, "Passions ingender Humors, and Humors breede Passions" (Wright 1604: 64).

Humoral theory thus provided the language for naming and describing characters' temperaments and for identifying and describing emotional effects. For instance, it is said of Lord Angelo that "when he makes water his urine is congealed ice" (Shakespeare, *Measure for Measure*, 3.2.104–5), an extreme description of Angelo's cold nature, registering in humoral terms his physical unsoundness, emotional flaccidity, and lack of masculine vigor. Perhaps reassuringly, medical handbooks of the day insist that a defective temperament of this sort could be remedied. Falstaff observes that Hal, the future Henry V, has improved on "the cold blood he did naturally inherit of his father" by treating the blood like barren land to be "manured, husbanded, and tilled with excellent endeavor of drinking good and good store of fertile sherris, that he is become very hot and valiant" (Shakespeare, *The Second Part of King Henry the Fourth*, 4.3.115–16, 117–20). Falstaff even expounds on the physiological effects of drinking, describing "a twofold operation." First, "it ascends me into the brain, dries me there all the foolish and dull and crudy vapors which environ it, makes it apprehensive, quick, forgetive, full of nimble, fiery, and delectable shapes, which, delivered o'er to the voice, the tongue, which is the birth, becomes excellent wit" (4.3.95–100). The comedy here derives largely from Falstaff's flattering account of the effects of alcohol, his own quick wit and nimble tongue evidently attesting to his alacrity in imbibing. The second result of drinking, he says, "is the warming of the blood, which, before cold and settled, left the liver white and pale, which is the badge of pusillanimity and cowardice. But the sherris warms it and makes it course from the inwards to the parts extremes" (4.3.101–6). The liver was regarded as the seat of courage (as when Hamlet excoriates his own cowardice by saying "I am pigeon-livered and lack gall"; *Hamlet*, 2.2.516), but Falstaff is not speaking in emblematic or metaphorical terms here; he describes the effects of drinking as dually physical and, in a humoral sense, altering of temperament. Falstaff's ode to drink has a distinct ideological edge: "demure boys" who abstain from strong drink risk "male green-sickness" – a form of anemia typically associated with young girls – "and then, when they marry, they get wenches" (4.3.89, 92–3) – referring to Galenic notions of conception, whereby male vigor determines the sex of offspring. For the masculinist tutor Falstaff, the fear of being like a girl, or of begetting girls, would and should drive any man to drink.

The humoral conception of experience was not limited to mortal affairs; even when describing events outside a realistic human frame, authors employed humoral language. Michael Drayton's *Endimion and Phoebe*, an erotic mythological poem, or epyllion, recounting the love of Phoebe, goddess of the moon, for a beautiful shepherd boy, maintains a tension between natural and supernatural forces. Endimion's lover must appear to him disguised, "For had shee come adorned with her light, / No mortall eye could have endur'd the sight" (Drayton 1963: lines 107–8). Ultimately he will function more as an allegory of beauty than a beautiful mortal, yet when first smitten with the disguised, unapproachable (he thinks) Phoebe, his longing is described in standard humoral language:

> melancholy from the Spleene begun,
> By passion moov'd, into the veynes doth run;
> Which when this humor as a swelling Flood
> By vigor is infused in the blood;
> The vitall spirits doth mightely appall;
> And weakeneth so the parts organicall.
>
> (lines 459–64)

When his beloved approaches him, Endimion blushes violently, and Drayton, not content to describe the signs of passion, explains their physical causes. Although Endimion lacks a dimension of psychological interiority, the humoral understanding of experience renders causes transparent to the knowing observer.

> The minde disturbed forth-with doth convart,
> To an internall passion of the hart,
> By motion of that sodaine joy or feare,

> Which we receive either by the eye or eare,
> For by retraction of the spirit and blood,
> From those exterior parts where first they stood,
> Into the center of the body sent,
> Returnes againe more strong and vehement:
> And in the like extreamitie made cold,
> About the same, themselves doe closely hold,
> And though the cause be like, in this respect
> Works by this meanes a contrary effect.
>
> (lines 543–54)

The narrative halts for a pseudo-medical treatise on blushing, a digression that contributes nothing to an erotic theme; it can, however, be accounted for structurally as an element in Drayton's Neoplatonic vision of union between matter and idea.

An astronomy lesson climaxes the poem: the lunar goddess whisks her lover into the sky, where he views the perfect order of the Ptolemaic universe, centered on the earth "in perfect roundnes of a ball" (line 667). The "heavenly secrets" she imparts are those of harmony and degree, the planets moving in "prefixt" circles in conjunction with the stars and "extend[ing] their severall powers, / Unto this little fleshly world of ours" (lines 697–8). Certainly the astronomy is dated (although Milton would include a basically Ptolemaic scheme in *Paradise Lost*, 1667, suggesting its continued appeal to poets) and the tone more didactic than one would expect in a mythological love poem. Yet rather than registering a static belief in astrology, Drayton's astral journey, and early modern fascination with astronomy in general, carries cognitive, emotional, and ideological weight. At stake, Alastair Fowler suggests, were "discoveries imagined as blurring, or even breaking down, the immemorial division between mutable and immutable – between the corrupted and uncorrupted parts of the macrocosm" (Fowler 1996: 44). Fowler's theory explains why Drayton's science is not more *au courant* for 1595 and why the philosophical aim of *Endimion and Phoebe* outweighs its erotic texture; what initially seems a love poem on the order of *Hero and Leander* or *Venus and Adonis* turns out to be a Neoplatonic allegory about the union of spirit and matter. The point of the astronomy lesson is not to account for celestial influences on earth, but to deliver neatly the knowledge granted to the enlightened shepherd.

Galenic concepts of the body play a more complexly structural part in Shakespeare's *Twelfth Night*. The play's fiction involves a cross-dressed heroine, Viola, who appeals to both Duke Orsino and the

Lady Olivia. In the end, the problem of same-sex attraction, as well as the difficulty of Orsino and Olivia desiring the same object, is resolved by the appearance of Viola's lost twin brother, yet for most of the play's action a remarkable ambiguity describes Viola's gender identity, an effect that early modern staging would have heightened, since a male actor would play the female Viola who dons the male disguise of Cesario. Viola/Cesario's dual, or layered, gender occasions the play's demonstration of sexual desire as mercurial, unfixed, and perhaps unpredictable. An openness to experience and distinct freedom of mind characterize central figures of the play. For instance, Viola, ship-wrecked in a strange land, decides in a flash to "conceal me what I am" and to serve the Duke in the figure of "an eunuch" (1.2.53, 56). Later, when her brother Sebastian shows up and is urged to the altar by Olivia, he scarcely pauses to consider:

> Or I am mad, or else this is a dream.
> Let fancy still my sense in Lethe steep;
> If it be thus to dream, still let me sleep!
> (4.1.58–60)

These characters enjoy a flexibility enabling them to "entertain the offered fallacy" (*Comedy of Errors*, 2.2.185), a refusal to be bound by bodily strictures or the settled certainties of Renaissance cosmology and humoral theory.

Interestingly, in counter-balance to its whimsical plot and the fluid identity structures of its central characters, *Twelfth Night* is riddled with comments asserting traditional ideas, like the astrological influence evoked when Sir Toby Belch urges dancing by saying "Were we not born under Taurus?" (1.3.128–9), referring to the zodiacal sign governing legs and feet. Conservative theories of essential gender difference and of the physiological bases of emotions figure large; in Paster's terms, "a recuperative medical subtext provided by humoral physiology" works against the "social subversion" of the cross-dressing plot (Paster 1998: 434). Orsino, so fickle himself that his mind is said to be "a very opal" (2.4.75), espouses the inferiority of women's love:

> Alas, their love may be called appetite,
> No motion of the liver but the palate,
> That suffer surfeit, cloyment, and revolt;
> But mine is all as hungry as the sea,
> And can digest as much.
> (2.4.94–8)

Orsino locates his strong, masculine passion in the liver, contrasting its insatiability to women's supposedly more fleeting appetites. Not only does he draw a strictly gendered contrast, but he roots the essential differences in the body – no woman's heart is big enough, he claims, to hold the love his does. He relates female lack of emotional constancy with the humoral sense of women's moist, leaky bodies: "they lack retention" (2.4.96). In the following scene, this theme registers parodically in Malvolio's remark, when reading a letter supposedly penned by Olivia, "thus makes she her great P's" (2.5.84–5). As Paster has discussed at length, the joke registers against both Olivia, whose urinary habits are named and exposed, and Malvolio himself, whose "compulsory inferiority of rank" is revealed by his "presumptive familiarity" with her bodily waste (Paster 1993: 31).

The "medical subtext" undercuts declarations of love with physiological renditions of passion. Boasting of the plot to fool Malvolio into thinking Olivia returns his affection, Fabian cries out "This wins him, liver and all" (2.5.91). Fabian himself would be "boiled to death with melancholy" (2.5.3) before he would miss the sport. His comments, and the gulling of Malvolio in general, set into comic perspective Viola/Cesario's account of unrequited love in the preceding scene. Referring to an imaginary sister, she/he tells the Duke,

> She pined in thought;
> And with a green and yellow melancholy
> She sat like Patience on a monument,
> Smiling at grief.
>
> (2.4.112–15)

The lines are sadly evocative, for Viola describes a woman whose unacknowledged and unreturned passion turns her to stone, a fate Viola might imagine for herself, since she cannot, disguised as she is as the boy Cesario, confess her love for Orsino. The "green and yellow melancholy" suggests a pale and sallow complexion, caused by humoral imbalance. Yet the evocation of passion in such literal, and literally colorful, terms allows a note of ridicule to creep into the speech; soulful she may be, but Viola's own humors seem too balanced for melancholy to turn her green and yellow. In *Twelfth Night*, then, as so often in Shakespearean comedy, troubling issues, like the potentially fatal effects of lovesickness, are opened for consideration but held in check by a balancing cynicism. So too the play offers its basically conservative audience the titillating pleasure of imagining subversion of assigned gender roles, while providing the reassuring ballast of a subtext within which gender is an utterly predictable, essential, and hierarchical bodily truth.

If comedy makes reference to a stable cosmology as a way of holding in check its more radical impulses, tragedy heightens a sense of loss by provoking doubt in the macrocosmic order and by exacerbating the uncertainties built into the humoral view of emotions. *King Lear*, a tragedy of old age, gestures toward the natural, reassuring scheme of man's seven ages (famously articulated by Jacques in *As You Like It*) when Lear announces his intention "To shake all cares and business from our age, / Conferring them on younger strengths while we / Unburdened crawl toward death" (1.1.39–41, conflated text). Because he wishes to control even as he gives up power, and because of the malice present in his kingdom, his scheme goes wildly wrong, resulting in universal upheaval. The king finds himself ruled by his daughters; his entourage is decimated; a fool speaks the truth; servants are insolent and rise against their masters. Society's ordering principles – naturalized in this period, as we have seen, as cosmological principles – are shattered. The nobleman Edgar, taking on the role of a mad beggar, approaches the line distinguishing man from beast ("the basest and most poorest shape / That ever penury, in contempt of man, / Brought near to beast"; 2.3.7–9), or actually slips beneath that mark, abjecting himself by drinking "the green mantle of the standing pool" (3.4.132). Albany says Lear's offspring have behaved as "Tigers not daughters," and he offers a desperate prophecy:

> If that the heavens do not their visible spirits
> Send quickly down to tame these vile offenses,
> It will come,
> Humanity must perforce prey on itself,
> Like monsters of the deep.
>
> (4.2.41, 47–51)

Political and familial disorder are couched in terms of nature's destructive capacities.

In *King Lear*, those who license cosmic order and mourn its loss are generally the more gullible characters. Gloucester cites "these late eclipses in the sun and moon" (1.2.104) as portents of the mutinies and divisions troubling the kingdom. His skeptical son Edmund denounces belief in astrology as "the excellent foppery of the world"; he sends up the "admirable evasion of whoremaster man," who blames his lechery on a star (1.2.119, 127). Clever and corrupt, Edmund complicates a modern audience's response; his worldview strikes us today as accurate, yet his treachery knows no bounds – not only does he play the two married sisters Regan and Goneril against one another, but he delivers his father to Cornwall's torture. The tight moral design Edgar proclaims late in the play – "The gods are just, and of our pleasant vices / Make instruments to plague us" (5.3.172–3) – offers a tempting resolution to these issues. Ultimately, though, *King Lear* requires a more nuanced, or perhaps a more despairing, understanding of the connection between moral behavior and cosmic design. There is little evidence of just gods at work, quite a bit to suggest a world abandoned by divine oversight.

Asymmetries of rank and gender reflect the absence of order. "A peasant stand up thus?" (3.7.81), Regan challenges the servant who attempts to save Gloucester. She kills the servant, prompting another to appeal for divine intervention, declaring "women will all turn monsters" (3.7.103) if Regan is allowed to thrive. Lear represents his own internal disarray in gendered terms, vowing not to weep because tears are feminine: "let not women's weapons, waterdrops, / Stain my man's cheeks" (2.4.277–8). Even more strikingly, Lear speaks of his mounting emotion and the discomfort in his chest as an attack of "the mother," or wandering womb:

> O, how this mother swells up toward my heart!
> *Hysterica passio*, down, thou climbing sorrow;
> Thy element's below.
>
> (2.4.55–7)

Lear's appropriation of the female malady suggests his own deviation from masculine authority, or a certain feminine capacity lodged within him (Kahn 1986). Later in the scene he refers to "my rising heart" (2.4.119), so there appears to be a conflation of womb and heart as alternative sites of extreme emotion.

Attack of the mother surfaces again, more obliquely, late in the play. When Lear carries Cordelia's body on stage, he affirms "she's dead as earth" (5.3.267). Yet doubt immediately takes hold, and he calls for a looking glass, and then a feather, to test for breath. These are the tests Helkiah Crooke advocates in cases of hysterical collapse; he considers the glass more reliable than the feather. According to Crooke, the great sympathy between the womb and the brain causes women to be vulnerable to fainting fits, "desperate swoondings, the cessation of breathing and intermission of the pulse." The attacks can ape death ("such women live onely by transpiration, that is by such aer as is drawne through the pores of the skin"; Crooke 1618: 253); Thus Crooke recommends, as a precaution, postponing burial of dead women for several days. He even cites one ludicrous case of a female beggar "who had a Coffin carried with her, and oftentimes she fell into those Hystericall fits, and would lye so long in them, nothing differing from a dead carkasse, till the wonted time of her reviving" (Crooke 1618: 253).

Lear's wavering ability to acknowledge Cordelia's death is usually understood as his final heroic battle between delusion and reality, but the echo of medical lore complicates the matter. If the appearance of death in women was as unreliable as Crooke suggests, Lear might well resort to the feather and the glass. Granted, he has seen her hanged, although a hurried battlefield hanging might be botched; people some-times survive hanging, if the neck is not broken. Perhaps Lear would not be altogether deluded to suspect Cordelia has collapsed from "suf-focation of the mother" – the common name indicating the symptom of "choaking in the throat" (Jorden 1603: 5) – rather than strangling to death. The Galenic worldview regularly conflated internal condi-tions and external causes. Moreover, the question of whether Cordelia lives or not carries an added resonance in theatrical performance, since an actor's necessarily breathing body represents Cordelia's supposedly still one. The threat of *hysterica passio*, first introduced by Lear, migrates at the end to his daughter, correcting its assignment in terms of gender but introducing an unsettling element of doubt in terms of the play's plot. When Lear's own death is initially misread by Edgar, who says "He faints" (5.3.318), confusion between hysteria and mortality surfaces once more. Gender assignments are again cast into doubt; so too are the demarcations of life and death, ambiguating the firm certainties of closure and suggesting the real difficulty of knowing "when one is dead, and when one lives" (5.3.266).

King Lear officially laments the loss of political order associated with the old king and the stability of his strongly hierarchical, patriarchal rule. In this sense the play supports a conservative ideology and affirms an overarching cosmological framework. Yet complexities abound in relation to specific characters and situations. Indeed, in terms of dra-matic emotion, Shakespeare deliberately cultivates in his audience a sense of painful loss and uncertainty. Rather than defending against the sense of physical vulnerability inherent in the available concep-tions of the universe and of the body's place within it, Shakespearean tragedy, and *King Lear* in particular, promotes in its audience sensations of undoing or loss of control, following the classic logic of dramatic catharsis, in the particular terms of early modern experience (Marshall 2002). Terror of the apocalypse looms large in *King Lear*'s final scene (Kermode 1967). Political instability and shifting ideas of sovereignty, ownership, and authority are indexed as deep concerns of viewers (Barker 1993; Dollimore 1984). And as in all his plays, Shakespeare draws on early modern understandings of the body to promote and solidify thematic and structural ideas.

Whereas Shakespearean drama is today considered an intellectual or artistic achievement, attending the theatre in the early modern period was not primarily an affair of the mind and spirit. It was instead a shared group experience in which emotions were pricked and inflamed. This worried Puritans who objected to the often lust-provoking spectacles on stage. At the extreme, humoral concepts of emotion meant that theatrical responsiveness might actually alter viewers' bodies. Stephen Gosson attributes remarkable power to poetic speeches, which, entering "by the privie entries of the eare slip downe into the hart and with gunshotte of affection gaule the minde" (Gosson 1973: Sig. B7). Gosson also maintained that theatrical "spectacles effeminate, & soften the hearts of men, vice is learned in beholding, sense is tickled, desire pricked, and those impressions of mind are secretly conveyed over to the gazers, which the players do counterfeit on stage" (Gosson 1972: Sig. G4). In an era that understood emotions and bodily states as not only related but mutually constituting, what we think of as private or internal experience – indeed, we often think of our emotions as most definitive of who we are – was structured along rather different lines. For these reasons, a sense of emotion as bodily, as something that might be purged or catharted, holds particular relevance to the drama of the early modern period.

Mapping the relation between the body and the cosmos, early modern writers appeal to a rigid set of hierarchies, yet prove unable or unwilling to contain human experience within cosmological structures. This was in part the result of changing scientific understanding, in part an outcome of the instability of physical existence within a humoral regime, and in part a matter of exploding linguistic and imaginative power. When Thomas Nashe remarks that "In all points our brains are like the firmament, and exhale in everie respect the like grose mistempred vapors and meteors," we glimpse the elasticity of cosmological analogy (Nashe 1594: Sig. G^v). The brain corresponds to the heavens above, but as a breathing force, not a stable form.

Cynthia Marshall

References and Further Reading

Barker, Francis. 1993. *The Culture of Violence: Essays on Tragedy and History.* Chicago: University of Chicago Press.

Beier, Lucinda McCray. 1987. *Sufferers and Healers: The Experience of Illness in Seventeenth-Century England.* London: Routledge and Kegan Paul.

Burton, Robert. 1989. *The Anatomy of Melancholy* [1621], 6 vols. Eds. Thomas C. Faulkner, Nicolas K. Kiessling, and Rhonda L. Blair. Oxford: Clarendon.

Coeffeteau, Nicholas. 1621. *A Table of Humane Passions.* Trans. Edward Grimeston. London.

Crooke, Helkiah. 1618. *Microcosmographia: A Description of the Body of Man.* London: Jaggard.

Davies, John. 1603. *Microcosmos: The Discovery of the Little World, with the Government Thereof.* Oxford.

Dollimore, Jonathan. 1984. *Radical Tragedy.* Brighton: Harvester.

Donne, John. 1929. "An Anatomie of the World. The First Anniversary" [1611], in Herbert J.C. Grierson, ed. *The Poems of John Donne,* 2 vols. Oxford: Clarendon, pp. 206–21.

Drayton, Michael. 1963. "Endimion and Phoebe: Ideas Latmus" [1595], in Elizabeth Story Donno, ed. *Elizabethan Minor Epics.* New York: Columbia University Press, pp. 180–206.

Elyot, Thomas. 1541. *The Castel of Helth.* London.

Fletcher, Anthony. 1995. *Gender, Sex, and Subordination in England 1500–1800.* New Haven: Yale University Press.

Floyd-Wilson, Mary. 2003. *English Ethnicity and Race in Early Modern Drama.* New York: Cambridge University Press.

Fowler, Alastair. 1996. *Time's Purpled Masquers: Stars and the Afterlife in Renaissance English Literature.* Oxford: Clarendon.

Gosson, Stephen. 1972. *Plays Confuted in Five Actions* [1582]. New York: Garland.

Gosson, Stephen. 1973. *Schoole of Abuse* [1579]. New York: Johnson.

Gyer, Nicholas. 1592. *The English Phlebotomy.* London.

Hallyn, Fernand. 1990. *The Poetic Structure of the World: Copernicus and Kepler.* Trans. Donald M. Leslie. New York: Zone.

Harris, Jonathan Gil. 1998. *Foreign Bodies and the Body Politic: Discourses of Social Pathology in Early Modern England.* Cambridge: Cambridge University Press.

Jonson, Ben. 2001. *Every Man Out of His Humour* [1600] (Revels Plays). Ed. Helen Ostovich. Manchester: Manchester University Press.

Jorden, Edward. 1603. *A Briefe Discourse of a Disease called the Suffocation of the Mother.* London.

Kahn, Coppélia. 1986. "The Absent Mother in *King Lear,*" in Margaret W. Ferguson, Maureen Quilligan, and Nancy J. Vickers, eds., *Rewriting the Renaissance: The Discourses of Sexual Difference in Early Modern Europe.* Chicago: University of Chicago Press, pp. 33–49.

Kermode, Frank. 1967. *The Sense of an Ending: Studies in the Theory of Fiction*. New York: Oxford University Press.

Laquer, Thomas. 1990. *Making Sex: Body and Gender from the Greeks to Freud*. Cambridge, MA: Harvard University Press.

Maplet, John. 1581. *The Dial of Destiny*. Repr. in James Winny, ed. 1957. *The Frame of Order: An Outline of Elizabethan Belief Taken from Treatises of the Late Sixteenth Century*. New York: Macmillan, pp. 180–96.

Marshall, Cynthia. 2002. *The Shattering of the Self: Violence, Subjectivity, and Early Modern Texts*. Baltimore: Johns Hopkins University Press.

Nashe, Thomas. 1594. *The Terrors of the Night or, A Discourse of Apparitions*. London.

Paster, Gail Kern. 1993. *The Body Embarrassed: Drama and the Disciplines of Shame in Early Modern England*. Ithaca, NY: Cornell University Press.

Paster, Gail Kern. 1998. "The Unbearable Coldness of Female Being: Women's Imperfection and the Humoral Economy," *English Literary Renaissance* 28(3): 416–40.

Porter, Roy. 1997. *The Greatest Benefit to Mankind: A Medical History of Humanity*. New York: Norton.

Schoenfeldt, Michael C. 1999. *Bodies and Selves in Early Modern England: Physiology and Inwardness in Spenser, Shakespeare, Herbert, and Milton*. Cambridge: Cambridge University Press.

Shakespeare, William. 2002. *The Complete Works* (New Pelican Text). Eds. Stephen Orgel and A. R. Braunmuller. New York: Penguin.

Sirasi, Nancy G. 1990. *Medieval and Early Renaissance Medicine: An Introduction to Knowledge and Practice*. Chicago: University of Chicago Press.

Traister, Barbara Howard. 2001. *The Notorious Astrological Physician of London: Works and Days of Simon Forman*. Chicago: University of Chicago Press.

Veith, Ilza. 1965. *Hysteria: The History of a Disease*. Chicago: University of Chicago Press.

Vicary, Thomas. 1587. *The Englishe-Mans Treasure: With the True Anatomie of Mans Bodie*. London.

Whitteridge, Gweneth. 1976. "Introduction," in William Harvey. *An Anatomical Disputation Concerning the Movement of the Heart and Blood in Living Creatures*. Oxford: Blackwell, pp. xii–lxii.

Wright, Thomas. 1604. *The Passions of the Minde in Generall*. London.

Chapter 12

Life-Writing

Alan Stewart

Today, biography is one of the publishing industry's most lucrative genres, with the life stories of figures both historical and contemporary appearing weekly, and dominating the review pages of broadsheet newspapers. Within the academy, however, biography as a genre has become deeply unfashionable. Whereas once early modern historians would pin their studies on a single man or woman's life, the trend since the 1960s has been away from the individual and toward the community, class group, or geographical area. Within Renaissance literary studies, the movement has been even more marked: there is now a distinct reluctance to write academic studies that are founded on the notion that a person's life-history or personal psychology can illuminate that person's literary output. The strong influence of poststructuralist criticism has focused attention instead on the literary text, while the tenets of New Historicism, cultural materialism, the history of the book, and other methodological approaches have relocated understanding of that text in various contexts – social, economic, political, religious, and cultural, but rarely if ever narrowly biographical.

One side-effect of this marginalization of biography as a methodological tool for the study of early modern literature has been an accompanying marginalization of the study of biography as one of the genres of early modern literature. And yet this is a definite oversight. It is the contention of this chapter that biography was a vital force in the early modern period – or perhaps more usefully "life-writing," to avoid the anachronistic term *biographia* apparently first Englished by John Dryden in the late seventeenth century.[1] Life-writing from classical and more recent times, of course, served as material from which to produce new works of literature. William Shakespeare's use of "lives" as sources, especially for his Roman plays, is well known. *Julius Caesar*, for example, draws on the lives of

Caesar, Brutus, and Cicero in the English version by Sir Thomas North in 1579, entitled *Plutarch's Lives of the Noble Grecians and Romanes* (and more commonly known as North's Plutarch). *Antony and Cleopatra* plunders the same source for the lives of Antonius and Octavius Caesar; *Coriolanus* similarly uses North's Plutarch's life of Caius Martius Coriolanus (Bullough 1964). Among prominent contemporary vernacular sources for Shakespeare and his peers were the *Chronicles* and *Annals* of writers such as Edward Hall, Raphael Holinshed, John Stow, and William Camden. Unlike North's Plutarch, these were not explicitly couched as life-writings, but their groupings of chronological events within individual sovereigns' reigns gave rise to an understanding of a particular period's history through the life and character of its monarch – an extended form of national life-writing that still informs our understanding of terms such as "Elizabethan" and "Jacobean."

In recent years, a small group of scholars, including Judith Anderson, Thomas F. Mayer, and D. R. Woolf, have endeavored to advance our understanding of life-writing in the early modern period (Anderson 1984; Mayer and Woolf 1995a). Their work has shown that several models of life-writing, not necessarily compatible, were available for writers in Tudor and Stuart England. From the classical tradition were inherited the exemplary lives of individuals, focused either on their characters (as with Plutarch) or their deeds (as with Suetonius). From the humanist tradition, largely Italian and of course hugely influenced by the classical tradition, came the *vita* of a celebrated individual, such as Boccaccio's life of Dante, or Bruni's lives of Dante and Petrarch, and the collection of lives, such as Petrarch's *De viris illustribus* and Boccaccio's *De casibus virorum illustrium* and *De mulieribus claris* (Mayer and Woolf 1995b).

Of equal significance, from the medieval Roman Catholic church came the hugely popular hagiographical tradition, primarily comprising the lives of the saints, which Thomas J. Heffernan has helpfully dubbed "sacred biography." As he argues, the role of sacred biography "is to teach the truth of the faith through the principle of individual example" (Heffernan 1988: 19). Bede writes in the prologue to his *Ecclesiastical History*:

> if history relates good things of good men, the attentive reader is excited to imitate that which is good; or if it mentions evil things of wicked persons, nevertheless the religious and pious hearer or reader, shunning that which is hurtful and perverse, is the more earnestly excited to perform these things which he knows to be good and worthy of God. (Bede 1969: 2 quoted in Heffernan 1988: 28)

The goal of a sacred biography was usually to tell the life story of a saint – or a saint in the making. This led to a narrowing of subject matter to focus on the subject's often precocious piety and spiritual knowledge, her or his good deeds, suffering and good death (sometimes martyrdom), and the miracles observed during the life or after death. Typically, sacred biography took such local stories, anecdotes and legends concerning its subject, and, in Heffernan's words, "selected, adapted and retold [them] so as to conform to the dictates of the Vatican's administrative policy concerning canonization and to promote the cultus of the saint beyond its original locale" (Heffernan 1988: 22).

While England's sixteenth-century literature played a formative role in the Reformation, Protestant life-writing by no means repudiated the models provided by Catholic hagiography. Most famously, John Foxe's foundational text of English Protestantism, *Actes and Monuments of these Latter and Perillous Dayes, Touching Matters of the Church* (1563), was rightly known as the "Book of Martyrs," since its structure was to tell the story of the persecution of the "true" English church through a series of life stories about martyrs (Woolf 1995). As we shall see in a selection of major English life-writings (both biographical and autobiographical), the structuring paradigms of classical, humanist, and hagiographical models remained vital throughout the early modern period.

Theories of Life-Writing

In English vernacular writings, Leonard Coxe's 1532 handbook, *The Arte or Crafte of Rhetoryke*, led the discussion of the genre of life-writing by outlining the key points that should be covered by a narrative of a life:

> The Narracion or tale wherin persones are praysed / is the declaryng of theyr lyfe & doynges after the fasshion of an historie. The places out of the whiche it is sought are: The persones byrthe. His chyldhode. His adolescencie. His mannes state. His olde age. His dethe and what foloweth after.
>
> In his byrthe is considered of what stocke he came / what chaunced at the tyme of his natiuite or nighe vpon / as in the natiuite of Christe shepeherdes hard angelles synge.
>
> In his chyldhode are marked his bryngynge vp and tokens of wysdome commynge: As Horace in his fourthe Satire sheweth / how in his chyld-

hode his father taught hym by examples of suche as were than lyuynge
to flee from vice and to gyue hym selfe to vertue.
In adolescencie is considered where to he than gyuethe hym selfe ...
In mannes state and olde age is noted what office or rule he bare among
his citisens / or in his contrey / what actes he dyd / how he gouerned
suche as were vnder him / howe he prospered / & what fortune he had
in suche thynges as he went about ...
The dethe of the persone hathe also his praises / as of suche whiche haue
ben slayne for the defence of theyr contrey or prince. (Coxe 1532:
B.iiij.ᵛ–C.i.ᵛ)

Although Coxe's summary makes it sound as if a fairly straightforward
narrative would be at the core of a life-writing, there are hints even
here of the kind of embellishments that should be sought to make
sense of the historical facts – the angels heard singing at Christ's
nativity, for example. And indeed, it is clear from the advice of other
Renaissance scholars that what the modern world might accept as
historical verisimilitude was not of primary concern to early modern
life-writers. As F. W. Conrad has demonstrated (Conrad 1995), the
great humanist scholar Desiderius Erasmus' massively influential *De
copia verborum ac rerum* (1511), for example, explicitly addresses the
ways in which the writing of a life may be enhanced:

Particularly appropriate to character delineation is *dialogismos*, dialogue,
in which we supply each person with utterances appropriate to his age,
type, country, way of life, cast of mind, and character. Utterances of this
kind may be introduced into historical writing, hence all the speeches in
Thucydides, Sallust, and Livy. Letters and striking sayings may also be
composed, and even thoughts expressed, as of a man talking to himself,
though this is commoner in the poets. (Erasmus 1978: 586)

There were, however, limits, as Erasmus himself admitted:

The exposition of facts can be greatly enhanced by the figure which some
call *sermocinatio* "dialogue" in which we assign suitable utterances to one
or more persons ... In this the historical writers are particularly worthy
of admiration, for everyone accepts that they are allowed to put speeches
into the mouths of their characters. I refer to pagan historians. It is
doubtful whether Christian ones may do the same, except that something similar seems to be done in the story of the seven Maccabees, and,
apart from others who have written lives of the martyrs, St Ambrose
seems to have allowed himself to do so in his *Life of St Agnes*. (Erasmus
1978: 649–50)

Admitting that certain stories might strain credulity, Erasmus' guideline is not historical truth but rhetorical probability:

> If entirely fictional narratives are introduced as if they were true because they will help us get our point across, we must make them as much like the real thing as possible. There are well-known features, listed in the handbooks of rhetoric, which make a story credible. As an example of this type, we may mention the story about Memmius in Cicero, and possibly the one about Volteius in Horace. I observe that some people have been excessively fond of this sort of thing and, relying on the gullibility of the crowd, have imported into Christian literature the most stupid miraculous events as if they were absolutely true. (Erasmus 1978: 634–5)

As F. W. Conrad notes, writers in the years following the appearance of *De copia* were keen to follow Erasmus' advice. Niccolò Machiavelli published his *La Vita di Castruccio Castracani da Lucca* in 1520 and put into Castruccio's mouth *sententiae* Machiavelli had found in Diogenes Laertius' *Lives and Opinions of the Eminent Philosophers*. Antonio de Guevara invented speeches and letters to illustrate the life of Roman emperor Marcus Aurelius in his *Libro aureo de Marco Aurelio* (1529). And in England, Sir Thomas Elyot composed new speeches, dialogues, and letters for his biography of the Roman emperor Alexander Severus in *The Image of Governance* (1541) (Conrad 1995: 139).

It becomes clear, then, that while care might be taken to establish the key events of the subject's life, it was the goal of the writer to embellish and enhance this rhetorically – as long as this remained, in Erasmus' terms, "appropriate" to the subject at hand. In the remainder of this chapter, I shall examine four key life-writings of the English Renaissance, to test in practice these theories: William Roper's life of his father-in-law, Sir Thomas More; Fulke Greville's life of his friend Sir Philip Sidney; and the self-life-writings of Edmund Spenser and Francis Bacon.

The Life of a Saint: Sir Thomas More

From the opening sentence, the agenda of William Roper's *Lyfe of Sir Thomas Moore* is clear:

> Forasmuche as Sir Thomas Moore, knighte, sometyme lord Chauncelor of England, a man of singular vertue and of a cleere vnspotted consciens,

as witnessethe Erasmus, more pure <u>and</u> white then the whitest snowe, <u>and</u> of such an angelicall witt, as England, he saith, neuer had the like before, nor neuer shall againe, vnyvarsaly, as well in the Lawes of our owne realme (a study in effecte able to occupy the whole life of a man) as in all other sciences, right well studied, was in his dayes accompted a man worthy pe<u>r</u>petuall famous memory. (Roper 1935: 3)

As might be suspected, Roper's aim is to present his father-in-law very much as a man who died for his Roman Catholic faith. Thus, in line with the typical hagiographies of the late medieval period, Roper identifies moments in More's early life that prefigure his later genius: when he was being raised in the household of Cardinal Morton,

> thoughe he was younge of yeares, yeat wold he at Christmas tyde sodenly sometimes steppe in among the players, <u>and</u> neuer studying for the matter, make a pa<u>r</u>te of his owne there presently among them, w<u>h</u>ich made the lookers on more sporte then all the plaiers beside. In whose witt <u>and</u> towardnes the Cardinall muche delightynge, wold often say of him vnto the nobles that divers tymes dined with him: "This child here wayting at the table, whosoeu<u>er</u> shall liue to see it, will proue a mervailous man." (Roper 1935: 5)

Studied mention is made of his piety: after time spent at Lincoln's Inn and Furnival's Inn (which is glossed over quickly), "he gaue himselfe to devotion <u>and</u> prayer in the Charter house of London, religious lyvinge there, without vowe, about iiij^{er} yeares" (Roper 1935: 6). Although More falls in love with Master Colte's second daughter, "yeat when he considered that it wold be both greate greif <u>and</u> some shame also to the eldest to see her yonger sister in mariage preferred before her, he then of a certayne pity framed his fancy towards her, <u>and</u> soone after [maryed] her" (Roper 1935: 6). The stand against his sovereign that ultimately cost him his life is prefigured in a stand-off with Henry VII, where More argues in Parliament against a proposed heavy subsidy: the king is told that "a beardless boy had disapointed all his purpose" (Roper 1935: 7); in revenge, since More had nothing to seize, the king "devised a cawseles quarrel against [his] father, keeping him in the tower vntill he had made him pay to him an hundrethe pounds fyne" (Roper 1935: 7–8); and so on.

Throughout the *Lyfe*, much is made of More as a devoted family man, and only a reluctant success in public life. Several speeches and letters, some now known to be artfully doctored from original sources, are quoted at length to establish More's moral and ethical credentials,

Alan Stewart

so that his eventual downfall appears to be the natural outcome of his accustomed principled behavior. As is dictated by the genre of the *ars moriendi*, the art of dying well, his execution finds him cheerfully facing the next life, joking with the Lieutenant of the Tower, "I pray you, master Leieutenaunte, see me salf vppe, and for my cominge downe let me shifte for my self," and begging his executioner "Plucke vpp thy spirites, man, and be not afrayde to do thine office; my necke is very shorte; take heede therefore thow strike not awrye, for savinge of thine honestye" (Roper 1935: 103).

Roper's account has been analyzed by F. W. Conrad, who draws particular attention to its ending:

> Soone after [More's] deathe came intelligence thereof to the Emperour Charles. Whervppon he sent for Sir Thomas Elliott, our English Embassadour, and said vnto him: "My Lord Embassador, we vnderstand that the Kinge, your master, hath put his faithfull seruaunt and grave, wise Councelour, Sir Thomas Moore, to deathe." Whereunto Sir Thomas Elliott awneswered that he vnderstood nothing thereof. "Well," said the Emperour, "it is too true. And this will we say, that if we had bine maister of such a servante, of whose doings our selfe haue had these many yeares no small experience, we wold rather haue lost the best city of our dominions then haue lost such a worthy councellour." Which matter was by the same Sir Thomas Elliott to my self, to my wife, to maister Clement and his wife, to master John Haywood and his wife, and [vnto] diuers other his Friends accordingly reported." (Roper 1935: 103–4)

As Conrad points out, this might be seen as an unexpected ending to the *Lyfe*:

> Instead of engaging in an extended and passionate eulogy, or dwelling upon the details of his subject's execution ... Roper opts to transport his readers to the court of Charles V. There the emperor himself conveys a brief memorial tribute to the then resident English ambassador ... Roper's rhetorical restraint here serves to emphasize the idealized image of his father-in-law presented throughout *The Lyfe*: more than a mere series of episodes regulated by the caprice of Fortune, More's life was lived in harmony with historical patterns beyond human design. First we learn that Sir Thomas dies, in fulfilment of his hopes, on the eve of the day honoring an earlier martyred English saint named Thomas ... Immediately thereafter, Charles V's sententious judgement echoes the prescience of More's earlier assessment of Henry VIII: "If my head [could] winne him a castle in Fraunce ... it should not faile to goe." (Conrad 1995: 140 quoting Roper 1935: 21)

Roper's account of the emperor's praise gripped the imagination of other early modern writers: it is repeated and elaborated in Nicholas Harpsfield's *The Life and Death of Sir Thomas More* (1557); a Latin life by Thomas Stapleton (1588); "Ro: Ba:"'s 1599 biography; and Cresacre More's version in 1631; as well as in a life of Bishop John Fisher written in 1576 (Conrad 1995: 140–3). But as Conrad points out, the scene is historically impossible: Elyot's stint as ambassador ended in April, 1532, and at the time of More's death, Elyot was in Oxfordshire. Even if the conversation with Charles refers to the moment when More resigned his chancellorship (May, 1532), Elyot would not have been at Charles's court. So it seems that, to a lesser or greater extent, Roper has confected his final scene, to include not only the praise of a major Continental (and Roman Catholic) ruler but also the words of the man who by the time Roper came to pen his treatise had become England's most prominent humanist scholar, Sir Thomas Elyot (Conrad 1995: *passim*).

Finally, More's death is made to resonate with the death of another Thomas, St Thomas Becket, who had also opposed his king, another Henry, Henry II: "So passed Sir Thomas Moore out of this world to god, vppon the very same daye in which himself had most desired" (Roper 1935: 103). Given Roper's depiction, it comes to no surprise that Sir Thomas More would, four hundred years after his death, also become St Thomas – this is very much the life of a saint.

When Biography Becomes Autobiography: Fulke Greville and Sir Philip Sidney

The Life of the Renowned Sir Philip Sidney, written by Fulke Greville and first published in 1652, has become one of the founding texts of Sidney biography. Greville had been a friend of Sidney since they went to Shrewsbury School together in 1564 – and he made a point of letting people know this decades after Sidney's death from a battle-wound in 1586. After Greville met his own death, at the hands of a servant in 1628, the epitaph on his tomb at Warwick records "Fulke Greville, servant to Queen Elizabeth, councillor to King James, and friend to Sir Philip Sidney." Indeed, Greville even planned an elaborate joint tomb for himself and his friend in St Paul's Cathedral, which he described as follows:

> Too deynty large stones of touche delycately porlished, borne up one above an other, by 4 pillers of brass 3 foote & a halfe highe & double

guylt. The uppermost worthily his [Sidney's], the nether myne. [N]ow because I would not marr the delicacy of the stones, or embose ther lusre [lustre] with adding any thing to cover it. I have devysed a pillar of the same touche, raysed above & yet disjoyned from the tombe, and placed at the upper end of Sir Philips which shall carry skutchions for his armes, and inscriptions, to be graven upon it in guilded letters, & in lyke manner at the lower end, marry only halfe the tombe highe, a more humble one to carry myne.[2]

Several critics have now taken issue with Greville's depiction of Sidney (van Dorsten et al. 1986; Duncan-Jones 1991). In particular, critical attention has been paid to Greville's account of Sidney's final days, following his injury in battle at Zutphen. Perhaps the best-known moment in the "Dedication" comes as Sidney is being carried, mortally wounded, from the battlefield:

In which sad progress, passing along by the rest of the army where his uncle – the general – was, and being thirsty with excess of bleeding, he called for drink, which was presently brought him; but as he was putting the bottle to his mouth he saw a poor soldier carried along, who had eaten his last at the same feast, ghastly casting up his eyes at the bottle; which Sir Philip perceiving, took it from his head before he drank, and delivered it to the poor man with these words: "Thy necessity is yet greater than mine." And when he had pledged this poor soldier, he was presently carried to Arnhem where the principal chirurgeons of the camp attended for him. (Greville 1986: 77)

As John Gouws has noted (Gouws 1986: 62), this anecdote first appears in Greville's tract; Greville himself was not with Sidney, but rather in England at the time of the battle, and none of the eye-witness accounts, of which there are many, mentions such an encounter. Moreover, the episode sounds suspiciously like a passage in Plutarch's *Life of Alexander*:

In consequence of his pursuit of Dareius, which was long and arduous … most of his [Alexander's] horsemen gave out, and chiefly for lack of water. At this point some Macedonians met him who were carrying water from the river in skins upon their mules. And when they beheld Alexander, it being now midday, in a wretched plight from thirst, they quickly filled a helmet and brought it to him. To his enquiry for whom they were carrying the water, the replied: "For our own sons; but if thou livest, we can get other sons, even if we lose these." On hearing this he took the helmet into his hands, but when he looked around and saw the horsemen about him all stretching out their heads and gazing at the water, he handed it back without drinking any, but with praises for the men who had brought it. "For," said he, "if I should drink of it alone, these horsemen of mine will be out of heart." But when they beheld his self-control and loftiness of spirit, they shouted out to him to lead them forward bodily, and began to goad their horses on, declaring that they would not regard themselves as weary, or thirsty, or as mortals at all, so long as they had such a king. (Plutarch 1919: 349–51)

Although Greville's anecdote may be more a borrowing from Plutarch than a transcription of historical fact about Sidney, it nevertheless fulfils the requirements laid down by Erasmus: it is "appropriate," coming from the correct genre of battlefield anecdote, and permits the expression of Sidney's uncompromised nobility and generosity of spirit even at his darkest hour.

But there is a different issue to be addressed here. Given Greville's enduring predilection for entwining his own life story with Sidney's, we might well be suspicious that *The Life of the Renowned Sir Philip Sidney* may in fact be as much about its author as it is about its putative subject. And indeed, as recent critics have insisted (McCrea 1995), despite its printed title, the *Life* was not intended as a stand-alone life at all, but rather as the prefatory material, "A Dedication to Sir Philip Sidney," to a collection of Greville's poems, which he dubs "these exercises of my youth." The opening sentence of the tract reveals Greville's purpose:

The difference which I have found between times, and consequently the changes of life into which their natural vicissitudes do violently carry men, as they have made deep furrows of impressions into my heart, so the same heavy wheels cause me to retire my thoughts from the free traffic with the world and rather seek comfortable ease or employment in the safe memory of dead men than disquiet in a doubtful conversation among the living; which I ingenuously confess to be one chief motive of dedicating these exercises of my youth to that worthy Sir Philip Sidney, so long since departed: for had I grounded my ends upon active wisdoms of the present, or sought patronage out of hope or fear in the future, who knows not that there are noble friends of mine, and many honourable magistrates yet living, unto whom both my fortune and reputation were, and are, far more subject? (Greville 1986: 3)

His life of Sidney is best understood, as Adriana McCrea has shown, not as a simple biography but rather a negotiation of Greville's own, somewhat checkered political career. Only thirteen of the eighteen chapters

Alan Stewart

of the tract are devoted to Sidney: Sidney dies in the thirteenth but the text "maintains its momentum," with Sidney now being "invoked only for inspiration." Chapter 14 discusses why Greville composed various treatises and the tragedies *Mustapha* and *Alaham*, but suddenly embarks on a passionate apology for Greville's patron during the 1590s, Robert Devereux, second earl of Essex, who was executed for treason in 1601. This leads to a three-chapter, highly positive digression on Elizabeth's reign – Greville was writing in the Jacobean period – included to prevent readers from misjudging the queen for her "high justice" against that "brave spirit," Essex. The final chapter sees Greville once again discussing his own literary work, with an explicit comparison of his writings to Sidney's (McCrea 1995: 301–2).

There is nothing odd about a writer of the early seventeenth century wanting his or her work to be read against Philip Sidney's. In the aftermath of his death, Sidney received the literary equivalent of canonization, with multiple tributes and eulogies being written on him. His family circle – Mary Sidney Herbert, the countess of Pembroke (Sidney's sister and editor), Robert Sidney (his younger brother), and Mary Wroth (his niece) – constructed their literary careers with explicit reference to his; a whole host of writers (one might name Edmund Spenser, Michael Drayton, Nathaniel Baxter, Anthony Stafford, Gervase Markham, John Florio, Samuel Daniel, William Davison, John Harington, Henry Constable, William Alexander, Barnabe Barnes, Bartholomew Griffin, John Dickenson, James Johnstoun, and Richard Belling) either invoked Sidney as muse or modeled their work, lyric and prose alike, on his (Alexander 2006).

Here, then, Greville is positioning himself vis-à-vis Sidney – and then determining what it is that "Sidney" should stand for. McCrea demonstrates that Greville systematically argues that a firm agenda existed for Sidney's literary output. Greville insists that "his end was not in writing, even while he wrote; nor his knowledge moulded for the tables or schools, but both his wit and understanding bent upon his heart to make himself and others, not in words or opinion, but in life and action, good and great" (Greville 1986: 12). In discussing the prose romance *Arcadia*, Greville argues that Sidney's "end" or objective "was not vanishing pleasure alone, but moral images and examples, as directing threads, to guide every man through the confused labyrinth of his own desires and life" (Greville 1986: 134). Cataloguing Sidney's deeds, Greville again shows that "his chief ends" were "not friends, wife, children, or himself, but above all things the honour of his maker and service of his prince or country," as befits a "patriot," "this Briton Scipio" (Greville 1986: 25, 76). As McCrea concludes, "Greville seems intent instead on clarifying for posterity the priorities in Sidney's life as he believes (or argues) them to have been" (McCrea 1995: 304). And in shaping Sir Philip Sidney for posterity, Fulke Greville hoped to shape his own future.

Self-Fashioning Lives

Fulke Greville was not alone. Poets, playwrights, and philosophers plundered the lives of the ancients not only for material for their writings, but also – and increasingly – to provide a sense of their own lives as writers. In his important study *Self-Crowned Laureates*, Richard Helgerson describes the workings of this "laureate self-fashioning" (Helgerson 1983: 25), in which poets imagined themselves in terms of their forebears, both classical and more recent. Perhaps the most determined of these writers is the first, Edmund Spenser.

When Edmund Spenser first breaks onto the literary scene in 1579 with *The Shepheardes Calender*, for example, he does it not as Edmund Spenser but anonymously – or rather through a series of pseudonyms. The *Calender* comes complete with its own critical commentary provided by "E. K.," who identifies the poet in the guise of one of the poem's characters, Colin Clout. The poet himself ends his valediction to the *Calender* ("Goe little booke") as "Immeritô" (Spenser 1579: ¶ᵛ) As Helgerson writes, Spenser chose "publicly to abandon all social identity except that conferred by his elected vocation. He ceased to be Master Edmund Spenser of Merchant Taylors' School and Pembroke College, Cambridge, and became Immerito, Colin Clout, the New Poet. No other writer of his generation was willing to take such a step" (Helgerson 1983: 63). But his new "life" has its precedents. E. K. places the *Calender*'s author in a line of Greek, Roman, Italian, and French writers of pastoral. This serves not merely to place the anonymous Spenser among a set of literary greats, but also to point to the use made of pastoral in those writers' lives. "Our new poet," E. K. insists, is

> following the example of the best & most aunticent Poetes, which deuised this kind of wryting . . . at the first to trye theyr habilities[:] and as young birdes, that be newly crept out of the nest, by little first to proue theyr tender wyngs, before they make a greater flyght. So flew Theocritus, as you may perceiue he was all ready full fledged. So flew Virgile, as not yet well feeling his winges. So flew Mantuane, as being not full somd. So

Petrarque. So Boccace [Boccaccio]; So [Clement] Marot, Sanazarus, and also diuers other excellent both Italian and French Poetes, whose foting this Author euery where followeth … So finally flyeth this our new Poete, as a bird, whose principals be scarce growen out, but yet as that in time shall be hable to keepe wing with the best. (Spenser 1579: ¶.iij.ʳ)

E. K.'s invocation of a line of poetic models for the anonymous poet is echoed by Philip Sidney in his *A Defence of Poesie*, albeit with a caveat: "The *Shepheardes Calender* hath much poetry in his eclogues, indeed worthy the reading, if I be not deceived. (That same framing of his style to an old rustic language I dare not allow, since neither Theocritus in Greek, Virgil in Latin, nor Sannazaro in Italian did affect it)" (Sidney 1989: 242). Among those authors it is Virgil who is the most influential in determining the poetic "life" of Spenser the poet. Virgil famously moved in his career from eclogues to georgics to epic, culminating in his national epic the *Aeneid*. Spenser moves from his own eclogues, *The Shepheardes Calender*, in 1579 to the first installment of his national epic, *The Faerie Queene*, in 1590. There he self-consciously traces his progression:

Lo I the man, whose Muse whylome did maske,
As time her taught, in lowly Shephards weeds,
Am now enforst a farre vnfitter taske,
For trumpets sterne to chaune mine Oaten reeds:
And sing of Knights and Ladies gentle deeds,
Whose praises hauing slept in silence long,
Me, all too meane, the sacred Muse areeds
To blazon broade emongst her learned throng:
Fierce warres and faithfull loues shall moralize my song.
(Spenser 1590: A2ʳ)

The move is misleadingly simple, but powerful in its influence. For with his laureate self-fashioning Spenser made sure that he would be dubbed "England's Virgil" – and that his *Shepheardes Calender* would forever be seen as the first installment of a literary career that would end in the major epic that, in 1579, can only have been in the earliest stages of planning.

Francis Bacon was himself a life-writer, who produced a short life of Queen Elizabeth and, at greater length, *The Historie of the Raigne of King Henry the Seventh* (1622) (Anderson 1984: 170–203). He also wrote of the theory of life-writing in his *De augmentis scientiarum* (1623) (Anderson 1984: 157–69):

Lives, if they be well and carefully written (for I do not speak of elegies and barren commemorations of that sort), propounding to themselves a single person as their subject, in whom actions both trifling and important, great and small, public and private, must needs be united and mingled, certainly contain a more lively and faithful representation of things [than chronicles do], and one which you may safely and happily take for example in another case. (Bacon, quoted in Mayer and Woolf 1995b: 1)

It is perhaps then not surprising that Bacon, like Spenser, took the opportunity to present his life as a writer to the world in a particular light.

The picture bequeathed to posterity of Bacon's final years seems to owe much to his chaplain and editor William Rawley's version of events. "The last five years of his *Life*, being with-drawn from *Civill Affaires*, and from an *Actiue Life*," Rawley wrote, "he employed wholly, in *Contemplation*, and *Studies*. A Thing, whereof his *Lordship* would often speak, during his *Active Life*; As if he affected, to dye in the *Shadow*, and not in the *Light*; which also, may be found, in severall Passages, of his *Works*." It was during these five years, according to Rawley, that "he composed, the greatest Part, of his *Books*, and *Writings*, Both in *English* and *Latin*," which Rawley listed "(as near as I can,) in the just Order, wherein they were written" as:

The *History*, of the *Reign*, of *King Henry*, the *Seventh*: *Abecedarium Naturæ*; or A Metaphysicall Piece; which is lost [this has now been rediscovered]: *Historia Ventorum*: *Historia vitae & Mortis*: *Historia Densi, & Rari*, not yet printed: *Historia Gravis, & Levis*, which is also lost: a *Discourse*, of a *War*, with *Spain*: A *Dialogue*, touching an *Holy War*: The *Fable* of the *New Atlantis*: A *Preface*, to a *Digest*, of the *Lawes* of *England*: The *Beginning*, of the *History*, of the *Reign*, of *King Henry*, the *Eighth*: *De Augmentis Scientiarum*; Or the *Advancement* of *Learning*, put into *Latin*, with severall Enrichments, and Enlargements: *Counsells Civill*, and *Morall*; Or his *Book* of *Essayes*, likewise, Enriched, and enlarged: The *Conversion*, of certain *Psalms*, into *English Verse*. The *Translation* into *Latin*; of the *History*, of *King Henry* the *Seventh*; of the *Counsells, Civill, and Morall*; of the *Dialogue*, of the *Holy War*; of the *Fable*, of the *New Atlantis*; For the Benefit, of other *Nations*. His Revising, of his *Book, De Sapientiâ Veterum*. *Inquisitio* de *Magnete*; *Topica Inquisitionis*, de *Luce, & Lumine*; Both these, not yet Printed. Lastly, *Sylva Sylvarum*, or the *Naturall History*. These were the *Fruits*, and *Productions*, of his last five years. (Rawley 1657: $(b4)^v–(c)^r$)

When Francis Bacon was disgraced on charges of taking bribes and effectively banished from London in 1621, his published output was not the "works" we now think of when his name is mentioned. Most were what Bacon himself referred to as "the Recreations of my other Studies"; of the writings which later editors were to consider the "Philosophical Works," only the *Novum Organum* was yet available to the public. In fact, as the editorial endeavors of Graham Rees are showing, the vast majority of the works claimed by Rawley to belong to the period after April, 1621, were in progress, albeit some in extremely fragmented form, considerably before 1621 (Rees 1996).

It may seem that it was the faithful Rawley who deliberately and misleadingly separated his master's proper intellectual work from the compromising practicalities of his civic life. But in fact, as his correspondence demonstrates clearly, Bacon himself ingeniously recast his change in life by reference to the lives of classical writers (Jardine and Stewart 1998: 474–6) He seized on his forced retirement to his country estate at Gorhambury as a new strategy to serve his king, James VI and I, in a letter dated July 16, 1621 (Bacon 1874: 371-2):

> Utar, saith Seneca to his Master, magnis exemplis; nec meae fortunae, sed tuae [I may use great examples, not of my fortune but of yours]. Demosthenes was banished for bribery of the highest nature, yet was recalled with honour; Marcus Livius [Salinator] was condemned for exactions, yet afterwards made Consul and Censor. Seneca banished for divers corruptions; yet was afterwards restored, and an instrument of that memorable Quinquennium Neronis. Many more. This, if it please your Majesty, I do not say for appetite of employment, but for hope that if I do myself as is fit, your Majesty will never suffer me to die in want or dishonour. (Bacon 1874: 296–7)

The comparison with Demosthenes and Seneca – with the addition of Cicero – was amplified the following year in a letter to his old friend Lancelot Andrewes, now bishop of Winchester. These men, Bacon thought, were "the most eminent and the most resembling" he had come across "through the variety of my reading"; all three had "held chief place of authority in their countries"; all three were ruined "by justice and sentence, as delinquents and criminals"; all three were "famous writers" – the fame of their writings meaning that "the remembrance of their calamity is now as to posterity but as a little picture of night-work, remaining amongst the fair and excellent tables of their acts and works." Lastly, all three would "quench any man's ambition of rising again," since their efforts in that vein led "but to their further ruin and destruction, ending in a violent death."

His three chosen exemplars gave Bacon a chance to compare "how they did bear their fortunes, and principally how they did employ their times, being banished and disabled for public business." Each took a different path: the softened, dejected Cicero wrote "nothing but a few womanish epistles," while Demosthenes, condemned for "bribery in the nature of treason and disloyalty," took it upon himself "to counsel the state by letters," and Seneca took a middle path: "though his pen did not freeze, yet he abstained from intruding into matters of business; but spent his time in writing books of excellent argument and use for all ages; though he might have made better choice (sometimes) of his dedications." These examples persuaded Bacon to "a resolution (where-upon I was otherwise inclined) to spend my time wholly in writing; and to put forth that poor talent, or half talent, or what it is, that God hath given me, not as heretofore to particular exchanges, but to banks or mounts of perpetuity, which will not break" (Bacon 1874: 372–3). Denied the opportunity of the "particular exchanges" of an engaged political, legal, and court life, Bacon now saw it as imperative that "perpetuity" should be the forum in which his ideas would be allowed their true voice. In the recently rediscovered draft of his *Abecedarium nouum naturæ* (*A New Abecedarium of Nature*) (1622), Bacon wrote,

> From time to time I am put in mind of the *bon mot* of the man from Greece who, when somebody had finished a great speech on behalf of a rather small town, replied, My friend, your words lack only a city big enough to match. As for me, I am pretty sure that, because I have little faith in the genius of our times, my own words ... could be accused of lacking an age or era to match them. Nevertheless, in saying this I do not have the slightest intention of disparaging the talents of the present age in any way; rather I say it because, as one or other of the political writers has remarked, Certain things give satisfaction immediately, certain others bear fruit with the passage of time. That is why I am devoted to posterity and put forward nothing for the sake of my name or the taste of others, but, knowing well enough the nature of the things that I impart, I deal out work for ages to come. (Bacon 2000: 172–3)

By drawing on the life stories of the ancients, whose long-term reputations had outlived their short-term disgraces, Bacon attempted to fashion in advance a rehabilitated reputation for himself. If perhaps he wasn't wholly successful in that respect, he – and Rawley following his lead – certainly managed to peddle the myth that his greatest writings came from a time and place untainted by the corruptions of political life – a myth that historians, editors, and critics are only now beginning to unravel.

The Unwritable Life: Shakespeare

In a period when life-writing was so widely practiced, and so artfully stylized, it is bracing to realize that, despite their best efforts, the most famous Renaissance English writer has eluded life-writers to this day. When Sidney Lee wrote his entry on William Shakespeare for the *Dictionary of National Biography* in 1897, it was the longest article in the entire collection. And yet, compared to the lives of Thomas More, Philip Sidney, or Francis Bacon, the details of the life of William Shakespeare – his "byrthe ... chyldhode ... adolescencie ... mannes state .... olde age ... dethe and what foloweth after" (Coxe 1532: B.iiij.ᵛ) – are relatively undocumented. While his works are studied in minute detail, they exist in isolation from their author (only a page of a play manuscript in Shakespeare's hand survives). Documents concerned with Shakespeare are sparse and largely impersonal. This has been a godsend for Shakespeare biographers. Unhampered by empirical evidence, they can weave beautiful and bizarre stories, drawing on the literature at will, and filling the many gaps of the chronology of Shakespeare's life. Shakespeare can be a good husband, a philanderer, a career playwright, a career player, orthodox or heterodox, Protestant or Catholic, conservative or radical. Indeed, the gaps appear wide enough that in the work of some he has become Francis Bacon, Christopher Marlowe, or the earl of Oxford. Readers wishing to know what is known are referred to Samuel Schoenbaum's marvelous *Shakespeare's Lives* (Schoenbaum 1991): others are invited to fill the blanks for themselves. Ironically, thanks to the paucity of facts that might hinder, William Shakespeare can serve as the ideal life for a Renaissance life-writer, a clean slate for embellishment and elaboration.

Notes

1 For "life-writing" see Anderson (1984: 2), and its use by Mayer and Woolf (1995a: *passim*). For Dryden's *biographia*, see *Oxford English Dictionary*, s.v. "biography."

2   Fulke Greville to John Coke, autumn, 1615. British Library, London, Additional MS 64875 ff. 164–171^v, printed in Bray (2003: 43).

References and Further Reading

Alexander, Gavin. 2006. *Writing After Sidney: The Literary Response to Sir Philip Sidney, 1586–1640*. Oxford: Oxford University Press.

Anderson, Judith H. 1984. *Biographical Truth: The Representation of Historical Persons in Tudor-Stuart Writing*. New Haven: Yale University Press.

Bacon, Francis. 1874. *Letters and Life. Vol. 7*. Ed. James Spedding. London: Longman.

Bacon, Francis. 2000. *The Oxford Francis Bacon. Vol. 13*. Ed. Graham Rees. Oxford: Oxford University Press.

Bede. 1969. *Ecclesiastical History of the English People*. Ed. B. Colgrave and R .A. B. Mynors. Oxford: Clarendon Press.

Bell, Susan G. and Marilyn Yalom, eds. 1990. *Revealing Lives: Autobiography, Biography, and Gender*. Albany: SUNY Press.

Bray, Alan. 2003. *The Friend*. Chicago: University of Chicago Press.

Bullough, Geoffrey, ed. 1964. *Narrative and Dramatic Sources of Shakespeare. Vol. 5: The Roman Plays*. London and Henley: Routledge and Kegan Paul.

Conrad, F. W. 1995. "Manipulating Reputations: Sir Thomas More, Sir Thomas Elyot, and the Conclusion of William Roper's *Lyfe of Sir Thomas Moore, Knighte*," in Thomas F. Mayer and D. R. Woolf, eds., *The Rhetorics of Life-Writing in Early Modern Europe: Forms of Biography from Cassandra Fedele to Louis XIV*. Ann Arbor: University of Michigan Press, pp. 133–62.

Coxe, Leonard. 1532. *The Arte or Crafte of Rhetoryke*. London: Robert Redman.

Duncan-Jones, Katherine. 1991. *Sir Philip Sidney: Courtier Poet*. New Haven and London: Yale University Press.

Epstein, William H. 1987. *Recognizing Biography*. Philadelphia: University of Pennsylvania Press.

Erasmus, Desiderius. 1978. *De copia verborum ac rerum*. Trans. Betty I. Knott, in *Collected Works of Erasmus. Vol. 24*. Toronto: University of Toronto Press.

Gouws, John. 1986. "Fact and Anecdote in Fulke Greville's Account of Sidney's Last Days," in Jan van Dorsten, Dominic Baker-Smith, and Arthur F. Kinney, eds., *Sir Philip Sidney: 1586 and the Creation of a Legend*. Leiden: Brill and Leiden University Press, pp. 62–82.

Greville, Fulke. 1986. *The Prose Works of Fulke Greville, Lord Brooke*. Ed. John Gouws. Oxford: Clarendon Press.

Heffernan, Thomas J. 1988. *Sacred Biography: Saints and their Biographers in the Middle Ages*. New York: Oxford University Press.

Helgerson, Richard. 1983. *Self-Crowned Laureates: Spenser, Jonson, Milton and the Literary System*. Berkeley: University of California Press.

Jardine, Lisa and Alan Stewart. 1988. *Hostage to Fortune: The Troubled Life of Francis Bacon 1561–1626*. London: Victor Gollancz.

Kadar, Marlene, ed. 1992. *Essays on Life Writing: From Genre to Critical Practice*. Toronto: University of Toronto Press.

Le Goff, Jacques. 1989. "The Whys and Ways of Writing a Biography: The Case of St Louis," *Exemplaria* 1: 207–23.

McCrea, Adriana. 1995. "Whose Life Is It, Anyway? Subject and Subjection in Fulke Greville's *Life of Sidney*," in Thomas F. Mayer and D. R. Woolf, eds., *The Rhetorics of Life-Writing in Early Modern Europe: Forms of Biography from Cassandra Fedele to Louis XIV*. Ann Arbor: University of Michigan Press, pp. 299–320.

Mayer, Thomas F. and D. R. Woolf, eds. 1995a. *The Rhetorics of Life-Writing in Early Modern Europe: Forms of Biography from Cassandra Fedele to Louis XIV*. Ann Arbor: University of Michigan Press.

Mayer, Thomas F. and D. R. Woolf. 1995b. "Introduction," in Thomas F. Mayer and D. R. Woolf, eds., *The Rhetorics of Life-Writing in Early Modern Europe: Forms of Biography from Cassandra Fedele to Louis XIV*. Ann Arbor: University of Michigan Press, pp. 1–37.

Plutarch. 1919. *Plutarch's Lives. Vol. 7: Demosthenes and Cicero, Alexander and Caesar* (Loeb Classical Library). Trans. Bernadotte Perrin. Cambridge: Harvard University Press.

Rawley, William. 1657. "The Life of the Honourable Author," in Francis Bacon, *Resuscitatio*. Ed. William Rawley. London: William Lee, pp. (b2)^r–(c4)^v.

Rees, Graham. 1996. "Introduction," in Graham Rees, ed., *The Oxford Francis Bacon. Vol. 6: Philosophical Writings 1611–1618*. Oxford: Clarendon Press, pp. xvii–cx.

Roper, William. 1935. *The Lyfe of Sir Thomas Moore, Knighte*. Ed. Elsie Vaughan Hitchcock. London: Early English Text Society.

Schoenbaum, S. 1991. *Shakespeare's Lives*, rev. edn. Oxford: Clarendon Press.

Sidney, Philip. 1989. *The Oxford Authors: Sir Philip Sidney*. Ed. Katherine Duncan-Jones. Oxford: Oxford University Press.

Spenser, Edmund. 1579. *The Shepheardes Calender*. London: Hugh Singleton.

Spenser, Edmund. 1590. *The Faerie Qveene*. London: William Ponsonbie.

van Dorsten, Jan, Dominic Baker-Smith, and Arthur F. Kinney, eds. 1986. *Sir Philip Sidney: 1586 and the Creation of a Legend*. Leiden: Brill and Leiden University Press.

Woolf, D. R. 1995. "The Rhetoric of Martyrdom: Generic Contradiction and Narrative Strategy in John Foxe's *Acts and Monuments*," in Thomas F. Mayer and D. R. Woolf, eds., *The Rhetorics of Life-Writing in Early Modern Europe: Forms of Biography from Cassandra Fedele to Louis XIV*. Ann Arbor: University of Michigan Press, pp. 243–82.

Index

Jonson, Ben 2, 27, 45–6
  humoral theory 225–6
  manuscript circulation 122
  patronage relations 4, 77–80, 81,
    85
  religious-political issues 45–6
  works
    The Alchemist 78
    Catiline 78, 80
    Eastward Ho 85
    Entertainment at Highgate 79
    Epicene 80
    Epigrams 4, 77, 78, 122
    Every Man Out of His Humour
      225–6
    The Forest 4, 77, 78
    The Magnificent Entertainment 79
    The Masque of Blackness
      79, 203
    The Masque of Queens 79, 80
    The New Inn 80
    Panegyre 79
    Sejanus 45–6, 80
    "To My Muse" 78
    "To Penshurst" 78
    "To Sir Robert Wroth" 78
    Volpone 28–9
    Works 77–8, 79

Kello, Bartholomew 124, 125
Kenilworth Castle 57
Kepler, Johann 9, 219, 220
Keymis, Lawrence 146
King, Henry 121
King's Men 24, 71, 82
Kirby, Lucas 40
Knox, John 186

labor market 13, 14
Lane, Ralph 138, 141
Langley, Francis 19
Langlois, Nicholas 124
Latin composition 96–7
Latin learning 94, 96
Lee, Sir Henry 58
Leicester, Robert Dudley,
    earl of 34, 38, 57–9, 62, 63,
    64, 65, 82, 127–8, 209

Leicester's Commonwealth 6,
  45, 128
Leo X, Pope 182
Leslie, John, *Treatise of
  Treasons* 45
letter-writing manuals 101, 104
Levant Company 150
Lewkenor, Sir Lewis 47
  *The Estate of English Fugitives under
    the King of Spaine and his
    Ministers* 47
licensing and censorship 4–5, 81–2,
  83, 84–5, 86, 87, 88–91,
  114, 129, 130–1,
  131, 132
  see also Master of the Revels
licensing fees 20, 24, 25
life-writing 10, 168, 238–54
  autobiography 247–54
  Catholic 239–40
  classical model 239
  diarists 166–8
  hagiographical model 239–40,
    242–5
  humanist model 239
  laureate self-fashioning
    249–54
  Protestant 240
  sacred biography 239–40
  theories of 240–2
  verisimilitude and 241
Livy 241
Lodge, Thomas, *Reply to Gosson* 36
logic 97, 101, 102
London
  economic vitality 14–15
  Great Fire 15
  as play setting 29
Lopez, Roderigo 209
Lord Admiral's Men 2, 11,
  12, 17, 21, 24, 25, 39,
  48, 84
Lord Chamberlain's Men 2, 17,
  23, 48, 84, 87
Lord Leicester's Men 83
Lord Mayor's Pageants 204
Lord Strange's Men 39, 47,
  48